Microsoft Teams®

A Wiley Brand

Microsoft Teams®

2nd Edition

by Rosemarie Withee

Microsoft Teams® For Dummies®, 2nd Edition

Published by: **John Wiley & Sons, Inc.,** 111 River Street, Hoboken, NJ 07030-5774, www.wiley.com

Copyright © 2021 by John Wiley & Sons, Inc., Hoboken, New Jersey

Published simultaneously in Canada

Contents at a Glance

Table of Contents

Introduction

s it just me or does the pace of technology seem to be speeding up? It feels like just the other day Microsoft bought Skype and transformed its Lync product into Skype for Business. Well, hold on, because Microsoft Teams has come along and it has displaced all of them! After its release in 2017, Teams has gone on to become the fastest growing product in the history of Microsoft.

Microsoft Teams is a communications and collaboration tool that enables you to chat, call, and meet and collaborate with others in real time. It is available either as a free, stand-alone app that you can download from the Internet, or as part of a bundle of software, such as Microsoft 365. If you are ready to learn what all the hype is about with Microsoft Teams, you are in the right place.

About This Book

This book is designed to get you the information you need to use Microsoft Teams quickly and efficiently without getting bogged down in the weeds. You learn how to get up and running with Teams in just a few minutes. You then discover how to add users, create teams, and communicate and collaborate with others in real time. In addition to learning the basics of Teams, you discover many tips and tricks you need to know to get the most out of the product to facilitate remote work and learning, and even how to use Teams to stay connected to family and friends.

To make the content more accessible, the book is organized into seven parts:

>> Part 1: Getting Started with Microsoft Teams

>> Part 2: Exploring Chat, Teams, Channels, and Apps

>> Part 3: Staying in Sync with Meetings and Conferencing

>> Part 4: Taking Communications to the Next Level with Voice

>> Part 5: Becoming a Microsoft Teams Administrator

>> Part 6: Molding Teams to Fit Your Unique Organization

>> Part 7: The Part of Tens

Each part is organized based on the way you will use Teams. For example, in Part 2, you learn about the different methods of communication available in Teams. In Part 5, you learn about Teams administration. You might need to jump straight into Teams administration if you find yourself as an "accidental admin," or you might want to start at the beginning of the book and build up your knowledge bit by bit. The Part of Tens offers three top ten lists: tips for getting the most out of Teams, the best apps to install in Teams, and the best places you can go to learn more and continue your Teams journey.

The book is designed so you can read the chapters and parts in any order and jump back and forth as you explore and use Teams.

Foolish Assumptions

In this book I assume that you have at least heard of Microsoft Teams, have an interest in getting the most out of the product, and have access to a computer. In the chapter about using Teams on a mobile device, I assume you are interested in using Teams on your iOS or Android smartphone or tablet. Microsoft designed Teams from the ground up to be intuitive and easy to use, so if you have access to a computer, you should be all set.

Icons Used in This Book

Throughout this book, icons in the margins highlight certain types of valuable information that call out for your attention. Here are the icons you'll encounter and a brief description of each.

TIP

The Tip icon marks tips (duh!) and shortcuts that you can use to make learning about Teams easier.

REMEMBER

Remember icons mark the information that's especially important to know. To siphon off the most important information in each chapter, just skim through these icons.

TECHNICAL STUFF

The Technical Stuff icon marks information of a highly technical nature that you can skip over if you don't want all the technical detail.

The Warning icon tells you to watch out! It marks important information that may save you headaches when getting up to speed with Teams.

Beyond the Book

As you continue to learn and work with Microsoft Teams, you may want to find shortcuts. I maintain an online cheat sheet that you can use as a quick reference to get common tasks done in Teams in a hurry. You can find this cheat sheet online by going to www.dummies.com and searching for *Microsoft Teams For Dummies Cheat Sheet* in the search box.

Where to Go from Here

Now that you know a little about this book, it is time to get started. If you are new to Microsoft Teams, then jump right into Chapter 1 where you get up and running in just a few minutes. If you already have Teams installed, then skip ahead to areas of Teams you would like to learn more about right away. If you find yourself with Teams administration tasks on your plate, then head straight to Part 5. There is no right or wrong answer in where to start when learning Teams. The best advice I can give is to just jump in and start using it to communicate with others!

1

Getting Started with Microsoft Teams

IN THIS PART . . .

Discover what makes Teams so special and why it has surpassed SharePoint as the fastest growing product in Microsoft's history.

Find the Teams app online and take a quick spin around the Teams interface.

Learn the basic Teams terminology.

Get a feel for the Teams layout and how Teams can be used across multiple devices.

Create a new team and invite others to that team.

Discover how to manage the team you created and set personalized settings for each team.

Chapter **1**

Getting Up and Running with Microsoft Teams

admit that when I first heard about Microsoft Teams, I was not very impressed. The market was already filled with chat programs. Microsoft even purchased the most popular one, Skype! So why did Microsoft decide to create more software that was redundant? Well, that was a few years ago, and since then, I have experienced firsthand the vision Microsoft had for Teams, what it has become, and why it has surpassed SharePoint as the fastest growing product in Microsoft's history.

In this chapter, you see what makes Teams so special. First, you take a quick spin around the Teams interface and learn some of the basic Teams terminology. Then, you get up and running with the Teams app in a quick tutorial that helps you find the Teams app online. After that you find out how to sign up and sign in. Let's get *Team*-ing!

Wrapping Your Head Around Microsoft Teams

Microsoft Teams is a relative newcomer to the world of business communication software. It was first announced in 2017, and when I first heard about it, I wasn't sure what to make of it. I had been using Skype to chat with friends and family for years, and I had used Lync (later rebranded Skype for Business) for business communications. Since its announcement, Teams has been integrated with just about every product Microsoft offers and has swallowed all the features that used to make Skype for Business so great. You can make phone calls, chat, conduct meetings, share your screen, and have video calls, just to name a few of the features Teams offers.

Microsoft Teams as a communications platform, replacing Skype for Business, is nice, but that is not what has made it the fastest growing product in Microsoft history. What makes Teams so special is that Microsoft has invested heavily to make it the face and entry point to almost all other Office services. For example, I am writing this book using Microsoft Word, but I am doing so from within the Teams app, as shown in Figure 1-1.

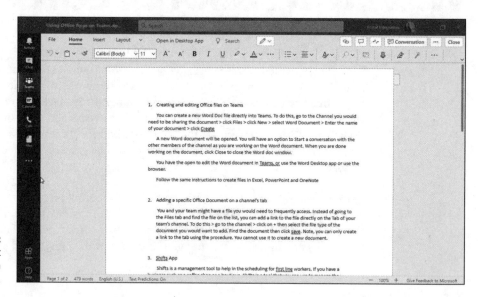

FIGURE 1-1:
Using Microsoft Word from within Teams.

In addition to integrating with Microsoft Office, Teams also integrates with many third-party applications, as shown in Figure 1-2.

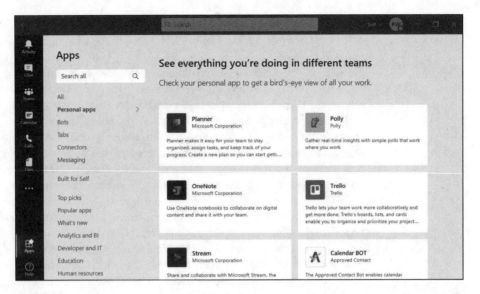

FIGURE 1-2:
Some of the apps
that integrate
with Teams.

To be fair, the big competitor to Teams called Slack (`https://slack.com`), is also racing to integrate other software and be the primary business tool you use for communications and productivity. Slack had a head start — hitting the market in 2013 — and became incredibly popular very quickly. However, Microsoft had a big advantage in that so many people already used Office products, so when Microsoft integrated Office with Teams, it was an easy move for users to start using Teams. In fact, in 2020 it was announced that there are more active users of Teams now than Slack. That is a big milestone!

Don't get me wrong; I still use Slack in my consulting business, since some of my clients only use Slack and don't use Teams. In fact, I use other apps, too, such as Google Workspace (`https://workspace.google.com`) and Zoom (`https://zoom.us`). Zoom has become extremely popular for video calling especially for groups. However, Zoom is focused on video calling and lacks the integrated capabilities needed to do effective remote work and collaboration.

Microsoft Teams is becoming the one app to rule them all in the Microsoft world. It has become the entry point for Office applications as well as other non-Microsoft software. This is the reason it has grown so quickly. If you are using Microsoft 365, you may find yourself using the integrated services through Teams instead of trying to remember how to use them independently.

TEAMS IN THE TIME OF COVID-19

In 2020, a global pandemic changed the way many people around the world work, communicate, and collaborate. Governments around the world introduced stay-at-home orders, and those workers who could work remotely were told to do so. Although working from home is not a new concept, the COVID-19 pandemic forced the arrangement on almost everyone seemingly overnight. Most organizations did not have a remote-work policy in place; pre-pandemic, managers often dealt with the issue on a case-to-case basis. However, that all changed when the pandemic hit. Any job that could be done remotely became remote-only, and workers immediately adapted to it.

Microsoft Teams and other virtual collaboration tools helped with that transition by helping to maintain resiliency in team dynamics. The pivot from working together in-person to working together in a virtual fashion was made easier. Like many others, my routine went from attending many in-person meetings to attending all virtual meetings. I found that I rarely thought about where the other person was physically located anymore. Once these tools are embraced, anyone can work from any location with the only requirement being a stable Internet connection.

Getting Familiar with Teams Terminology

Just like every other software program out there, Microsoft Teams has its own set of words. But the good news is that the list is short! Whew. Throughout this book you will explore the concepts of Teams in detail, and keeping the terminology in Teams straight can be a challenge. For example, you will eventually find yourself inviting one of your teammates to your Teams team. Or asking what Teams team your coworker is talking about. Once you get used to it, the terminology will seem normal.

To get a jump on the terms, here are some quick definitions:

>> **Teams:** Use the term *Teams* (uppercased) to refer to the product itself.

>> **Team:** A *team* (lowercased) is a group of users. You can specify settings for teams and have multiple teams within Microsoft Teams. For example, you might want to create a team for accounting, a team for legal, and another team for external contacts.

>> **Channel:** A *channel* is a group chat within a team. A team can have multiple group chats with the idea being that you can create a chat for different topics.

>> **Thread:** A *thread* is a specific topic of discussion within a channel. For example, one person might start a new thread in the channel and then others can reply to that thread. You can have multiple threads going in a channel at the same time.

>> **External/guest user:** An *external* or *guest user* is a user that is not part of your organization. For example, you might be a consultant and need to communicate with the company's accountant. You can invite that person as a guest user to your team.

There are, of course, many more terms that you will become familiar with as you continue on your Teams journey, but these are the basic terms to get you started. Once you get familiar with the relationship between Teams, a team, a channel, and a thread, you have all the knowledge you need to dive in further and get productive.

Getting Started with the Teams App

Now that you have an idea of what makes Microsoft Teams a useful tool for online collaboration and communication and got a glimpse at some of the Teams terminology, it's time to dive in and take a look at the app for yourself.

Microsoft Teams is available either as a free, stand-alone app that you can download from the Internet, or as part of a bundle of software, such as Microsoft 365. The free, no-commitment version of Teams offers such features as unlimited messages and search capabilities, 10GB of shared storage across the app, and audio and video calls between members.

TIP

The more robust version of Teams is available through a subscription to Microsoft 365 and provides all of those features as well as a whole host of others, including 1TB of storage per organization, Exchange email hosting, access to OneDrive, SharePoint, and other Microsoft 365 services, enhanced security features, and 24/7 phone and web support among other administrative tools. A snapshot of the various Teams versions is shown in Figure 1-3. More details can be found at www. microsoft.com/en-us/microsoft-teams/compare-microsoft-teams-options.

Getting Teams for free

You can sign up for Teams for free without buying the Microsoft 365 bundle. You won't get all the integrations and benefits Microsoft 365 provides, but you will get Teams.

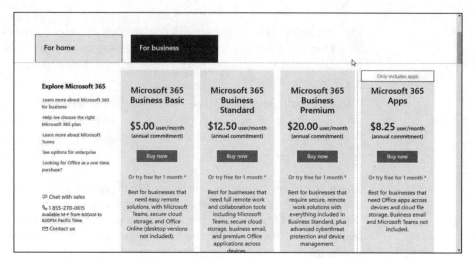

FIGURE 1-3:
Teams comes in many different flavors depending on your needs.

To sign up for the free version of Microsoft Teams, follow these steps:

1. Open your favorite web browser and go to https://products.office. com/microsoft-teams.

2. Click the Sign Up For Free button.

3. Enter your email address and either sign in with your existing Microsoft account or create a new one.

If this is the first time you are using a Microsoft service, you will be asked to verify your email address. A code will be sent to your email address and you will be asked to enter that code.

Once you verify your account (or sign in with your existing account), you will be asked to either download the Teams app to your local computer or use the web-based version as shown in Figure 1-4. For this example, I chose the web version.

4. Click the option to use the web-based version.

Your web browser will refresh and sign you in to the main Teams web application located at https://teams.microsoft.com.

A message will then display letting you know how to invite people to join your team, as shown in Figure 1-5.

5. Click Got It to then be taken to your new Teams workspace in your web browser, as shown in Figure 1-6.

Congratulations! You are now using Microsoft Teams for free.

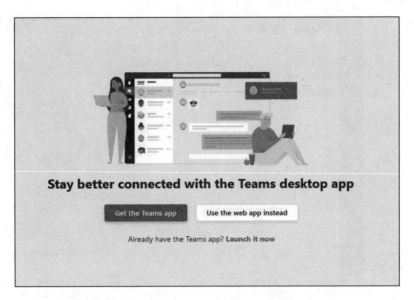

FIGURE 1-4:
Choosing the
option to use the
web-based
version of Teams.

FIGURE 1-5:
Inviting people to
join your team
after loading the
web-based
version.

When you invite guest users to your Teams channel, they will go through a very similar process as you just went through to sign in to Teams. However, instead of having to navigate to the Microsoft Teams website, they will get an email inviting them to join your Teams channel. External access is a popular topic; I cover it in depth in Chapter 7.

TIP

I have found the value of Teams comes from how it integrates and works with other Microsoft software, such as Office. For this reason, I recommend using Teams with Microsoft 365 instead of as a stand-alone free chat app. I talk about accessing Teams through these subscription-based services next.

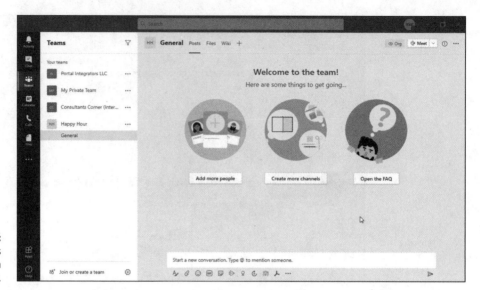

Getting Teams through Microsoft 365

Another way to sign up for Teams is by signing up for a Microsoft 365 subscription. Microsoft 365 offers a free trial, so you can get started with it without having to pay up front. Here's how:

1. **Open your favorite web browser and navigate to** www.office.com.

2. **Click the Get Office button, as shown in Figure 1-7.**

To get Teams, you will need a business plan subscription. (The personal plans do not include Teams.)

3. **Click the For Business tab to see the available business plans, as shown in Figure 1-8.**

You can choose between the Microsoft 365 Business Basic plan or the Microsoft 365 Business Standard plan, which includes the latest Microsoft clients like Word, Excel, Outlook, and PowerPoint. For this example, I chose the Microsoft 365 Business Premium plan.

4. **Scroll to the bottom of the page and click the "Try free for 1 month" link under the Microsoft 365 Business Premium plan.**

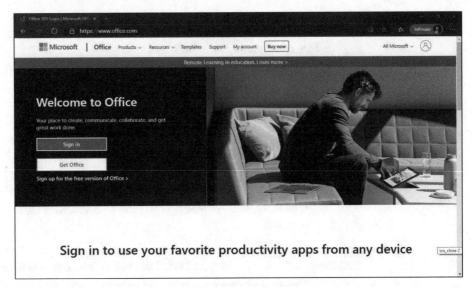

FIGURE 1-7:
The main office.
com landing
page.

FIGURE 1-8:
Choosing a
Microsoft 365
Business plan.

5. **Provides the requested information and walk through the setup wizard to get up and running with Microsoft 365.**

Note that you can use your own name as a business name and choose that your business size is 1 person. Next, you will be asked to choose a domain name that is `<your choice>.onmicrosoft.com`. This is your Microsoft 365 domain. In this example, I chose `teamsfd.onmicrosoft.com` for the domain. You can always add a custom domain later down the road if you prefer. For example, I might connect teamsfordummies.com to our Microsoft 365 account and get email there, too.

Once you have filled out the information, your free trial will be created, as shown in Figure 1-9. This can take a few minutes, so be patient.

6. **Click the Get Started button.**

A tutorial walks you through adding a domain and additional users. Once you walk through the setup, you are presented with your Microsoft 365 dashboard where you see a quick tutorial. After the tutorial you are presented with the Microsoft 365 main landing page.

Congratulations! You are now up and running with Microsoft 365 and Microsoft Teams.

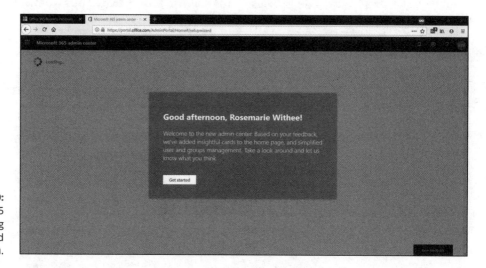

FIGURE 1-9:
The Microsoft 365
page creating
your trial and
welcoming you.

TIP

You can always get back to your Office 365 dashboard by opening your web browser and going to www.office.com and logging in with the username and password you created.

For more information on using Office 365, check out the latest edition of *Office 365 For Dummies* (Wiley).

Chapter **2**

Navigating Microsoft Teams

O pening Microsoft Teams for the first time can feel overwhelming. The reason for this is that Microsoft has added a jaw-dropping number of features to Teams over the last couple of years, bringing Teams to feature parity with Skype and Skype for Business. All this useful stuff is nice when you need it but can be overwhelming when you first start to use it.

In this chapter, you discover how to navigate the Teams app. You download, install, and open the app on your computer and then get a feel for the layout and how to navigate through the interface. You also look at how Teams can be used across multiple devices.

Downloading, Installing, and Opening Teams

You can use Teams in three primary ways: You can use the web-based app, you can install the client on your laptop or desktop computer, or you can install the Teams mobile app on your smartphone or tablet. Regardless of how you use

Teams, the concepts remain the same. Let's first log in to the web-based app and then install the client on your desktop. (I walk you through signing up for the free version of Teams in Chapter 1, and I cover installing Teams on your mobile device in Chapter 6.)

TIP

Teams is available around the world and localized in 53 different languages. People all over the world have jumped into the Teams ecosystem, especially since 2020, when the coronavirus pandemic forced many to work from and stay at home.

To log in to the web-based version of Teams, follow these steps:

1. **Open your favorite web browser and navigate to** `https://teams.microsoft.com`.

2. **Log in using the account credentials you created when you signed up for the Microsoft 365 trial in Chapter 1.**

   Refer to "Getting Started with the Teams App" in Chapter 1 if you need to sign up for the Microsoft 365 trial and a Teams account.

3. **When presented with the option to download Teams or use the web app, click the Use the Web App Instead link.**

   After logging in, you are presented with the main Teams app running inside your web browser, as shown in Figure 2-1.

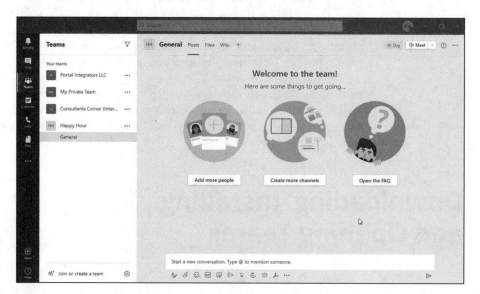

FIGURE 2-1:
Microsoft Teams running in a web browser.

TIP

Many people just use this web-based experience to use Teams. However, I prefer the client that I download and install on my local computer. I find it has much more functionality and integrates better with devices like my headset for making phone calls and my webcam for making video calls.

To install the Teams client on your Windows laptop or desktop computer, follow these steps:

1. **Open your web browser and navigate to** https://teams.microsoft.com.

If you have not yet logged in to the web app from the previous set of steps, you will be asked to log in. If you have already logged in, you will see the Teams web app displayed in your browser (shown in Figure 2-1).

2. **Log in to the Teams site by entering the credentials you set up in Chapter 1, if you aren't already logged in.**

REMEMBER

When you first log in to the Teams site (https://teams.microsoft.com), you are presented with an option of installing the Teams client or continuing to the web app. In the previous set of steps, we continued to the web app. Here, we will install the desktop client.

3. **Click your profile icon that appears in the top-right corner and choose Download the Desktop App as shown in Figure 2-2.**

FIGURE 2-2:
Your profile
drop-down menu
has options to
install the
desktop and
mobile apps.

4. **Save the file to your computer.**

TECHNICAL STUFF

You can set the location on your computer's hard drive where your web browser downloads files. By default, files are usually set to download to a Downloads folder, which is where all downloads are stored. If you can't find the file you downloaded, check the configuration for your web browser to see where it places files it has downloaded.

5. **Once the Teams setup file has downloaded, open and run the file (see Figure 2-3).**

After a few moments, a dialog box appears asking you to sign in, as shown in Figure 2-4.

6. **Enter your username and click Sign In.**

If you have already signed in to Teams using your web browser, you won't be asked for your password again.

The Teams client loads and lets you know that there is one last step to get Teams set up and connected to Office, as shown in Figure 2-5.

FIGURE 2-5:
A dialog box lets you know Teams will now be connected to Office.

One more step to set up Teams with Office

Click **Let's do it**, then click **Yes** in the next screen to get everything hooked up.

Let's do it

7. **Click Let's Do It to continue and then click Yes to allow Teams to make changes to your computer.**

Teams works in the background to connect with Office on your computer and then loads the Teams application, as shown in Figure 2-6.

Congratulations! You now have Teams running on your local computer.

FIGURE 2-6:
The Teams client running on your local computer.

Taking a Quick Spin Around Teams

If you have been following along in this chapter, you may notice that Teams running in the client on your computer (Figure 2-6) looks a lot like Teams running from within your web browser (Figure 2-1). Microsoft did this on purpose. The design thinking is best practice, and I was glad to see Microsoft adopt it. This way, if you usually use Teams on your desktop computer at work and find yourself logging in to Teams using a web browser on your computer at home, you don't have to worry about learning a different interface.

Primary navigation appears on the left side of the screen and includes the following icons: Activity, Chat, Teams, Calendar, Calls, and Files, as shown earlier in Figure 2-6. Clicking one of these main options opens that associated screen in the main part of the app.

Activity

If you click the Activity icon in the navigation pane, you will see your feed as shown in Figure 2-7. In the Activity feed you will find your notifications about things going on around Teams that you might find interesting. For example, if there is an unread message in a channel or someone sends you a chat message, you will see it appear in your Activity feed. Think of it as your one-stop-shop for everything that has happened in Teams since you were last there.

FIGURE 2-7:
The Activity feed
in Teams.

One thing you will find is that Teams can get very noisy very quickly. Just a handful of people chatting and carrying on is enough to tempt you to ignore it entirely. Using the Activity feed, you can tune-in to only the things that are important to you. I cover the Activity feed in more detail in Chapter 8.

Chat

The Chat area is where you will find all of your personal and group chats. There is a subtle difference between conversations in chats and conversations in channels. I like to think of chats as ad hoc messages to one other person or a few other people. Chats come and go and are spontaneous, whereas a channel is a dedicated area that persists and where people can communicate about a particular topic.

TIP

You can have one-on-one chats with another person or group conversations with several people at the same time in the Chat area.

Teams

The navigational area where I seem to spend all my time, and likely you will too, is the Teams area. Yes, the product is called Teams and the navigation component is also called Teams (see the left side of Figure 2-6). And within the Teams navigation component you have individual teams called a *team*. Confused yet? I don't blame you! But don't worry; it will become clear shortly.

Clicking the Teams icon in the left navigation pane opens all the Teams you are a member of. In Figure 2-6 you can see that I am only a member of one team: Portal Integrators LLC. This is the team that showed up by default when I created the Microsoft 365 subscription in Chapter 1. Within the Portal Integrators team is a channel called General, which is the default channel that is created automatically when a new Team is created. If I click the General channel, I can see all of the chats going on in the channel. Right now, it is empty because I am the only person in the team and in the channel. (I cover working with teams in Chapter 3 and working with channels in Chapter 4.)

TIP

Clicking the icon next to Join or Create a Team at the bottom of the left navigation pane allows you to join an existing team or create a new one. Teams can be by invitation only or open and discoverable to anyone in your organization.

Calendar

The Calendar area is focused on your calendar of events and meetings, as shown in Figure 2-8. If you have ever scheduled a meeting in Microsoft Outlook, then you will be familiar with working with your calendar in Teams. The calendar area is where you can have real-time meetings, and I cover how to do this in Chapters 9 and 10.

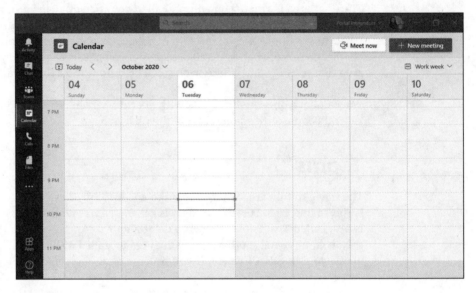

FIGURE 2-8:
The Calendar in
Teams.

WARNING

The Calendar is integrated with Microsoft Outlook. If you don't have Outlook installed on your desktop computer or laptop, then you won't see the Calendar in Teams. This type of integration empowers my view that Teams has quickly become the "face" of all of the Office products and services, which also explains why it has seen such explosive growth.

Calls

The Calls area is where you can make and receive phone calls, as shown in Figure 2-9. If you have ever used Skype, then this area will feel familiar to you. I cover the calling and voice functionality of Teams in Chapters 11 and 12.

FAST AND FASTER

Microsoft moves fast with iterating on its software these days. In the past, you could expect a new version every few years. Now, a new version of software seems to be available every month. And with more people using Teams than ever, the updates feel like they are coming on a daily basis. Most of the changes in new versions involve new features and bug fixes. But occasionally, the user interfaces change, too. For example, the Calendar section in the Teams navigation pane used to be called "Meetings."

My Teams software updated one night, and as I went back and re-read this chapter, I realized I still referred to this component as "Meetings." This all happened in one week. When I compared what I had written to the new Teams update, it turned out that the underlying functionality is the same, but the name of the button to navigate to it had changed.

So, as you are reading and learning about Teams, keep in mind that while exact names and wording of things might change, the concepts will remain the same.

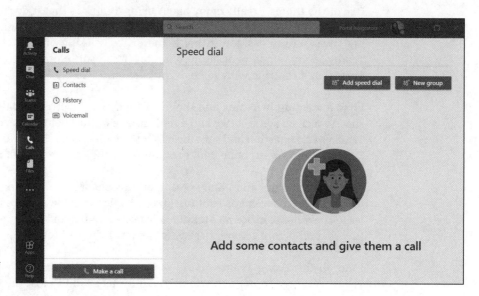

FIGURE 2-9: The Calls area of Teams.

Files

The Files area is where you can save and share digital files. If you have ever used SharePoint or OneDrive, then you will be happy to learn that you are already ahead of the game. Teams uses SharePoint and OneDrive behind the scenes of Teams, and at any point you can jump out of Teams and open the same files in the Share-Point or OneDrive applications.

In addition to SharePoint and OneDrive, you can also set up other cloud-based locations for your files and access them all from within Teams. Currently Teams supports Box, Dropbox, Egnyte, Google Drive, and ShareFile, and I am sure others will follow in the coming days.

Using Teams Across Many Devices and Platforms

One of the things I really enjoy about using Teams is that it doesn't matter what device I am using; I can instantly pick up where I left off. For example, this morning I was on my desktop in my home office working on this chapter inside of Teams on my Windows desktop computer (Microsoft Word files open right within Teams) and chatting with some of my clients.

I had a meeting in Teams and then walked down the street to my favorite coffee shop to pick up some coffee and a muffin. One of the clients I was chatting with in Teams had a question and sent me a follow-up message. The message appeared in Teams on my smartphone, and I responded while I was waiting for my coffee.

Now, it is evening, and I am working on this chapter and writing this paragraph using the Teams web app running on my Apple MacBook Air. Tomorrow, I will be back in my home office and taking some screenshots and putting some polish on this chapter before calling it ready for review by my editors.

I did all this using Teams across many different devices and places, and since Teams is synced through the cloud (the Internet), I didn't lose my train of thought and work that was in progress. Teams on all my devices are always in sync. It is one of the things I love the most about working with an app born in the cloud like Teams. Figure 2-10 illustrates the various ways I can use Teams throughout the day. I cover using devices with Teams in Chapter 6.

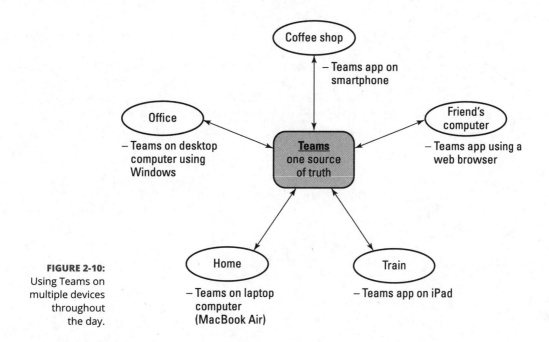

FIGURE 2-10:
Using Teams on
multiple devices
throughout
the day.

Using Teams to Organize Your Life

Toggling between several apps for work and home can sometimes be confusing. I use Teams for work and use Viber and WhatsApp to message family and friends. Both work for messaging and sending photos and videos, but not for sharing files, to-do lists, and so on. So, I find myself toggling between the messaging apps and my email. Teams recently released a new feature to keep things more organized when making plans with friends and family. The best part is, it's the same app you are already using for work. I discuss how to do this in Chapter 6.

Chapter **3**

Starting Your First Team and Managing Settings

One of the nice things about Microsoft Teams is that the name of it says it all. Teams is about communicating and collaborating with other people as part of a team. At the heart of the Teams app is a team of people. Whether you work in the same office building with your team or each team member works remotely from home, you are still the same team. A *team* in the context of Microsoft Teams, consists of a group of one or more people (though a team of one is boring). Within a team is where you create channels to chat, share files among teammates, use apps, and do all sorts of other nifty things.

In this chapter, you find out how to create new teams and invite others to them. You also discover how to manage teams you created and personalize each team's settings.

Creating a New Team

When you first log in to Microsoft Teams, you will see that a default Team is created for you automatically using the account information you provide when you first sign up for Microsoft 365, Office 365, or the stand-alone Teams app.

TO CREATE OR NOT CREATE A NEW TEAM

While setting up a new team is quick and easy, the number of teams you have in your organization can increase exponentially. If there are already existing teams, think before you create another one. Before you hit the Create button, consider the goals of the new team: What do you want the members of the new team to achieve? Is there already a team created that can accomplish this same goal? Are the members of this new team the same members of an existing team or will there be new members? Are the goals and objectives similar, or are the goals different from an existing team? Membership to teams can change over time. As much as you would consider creating a new team, also consider modifying existing ones and deleting teams that are no longer active.

My default team is called Portal Integrators LLC, because that is the company name I provided when I signed up for the Office 365 trial in Chapter 2. (For a reminder on how to log in to Teams, see "Downloading, Installing, and Opening Teams" in Chapter 2.)

I suspect many people just use the default Team and don't realize they can create more teams. (Perhaps they also didn't make the wise decision to read this book like you did.) However, creating new teams involves only a few steps.

When you create a new team, you can customize it and build it out the way you want for your specific situation. For example, you might want the team to be private instead of the default org-wide team that is created that everyone is automatically a member of. You might also want to create a team for a focus area, such as carpooling or human resources or accounting. Once you have spent a little bit of time in Teams, you will find yourself creating new teams and trimming old teams as a regular habit.

To create a new Team, follow these steps:

1. **Open Microsoft Teams.**

2. **Click the Teams icon in the left navigation pane and then click the link to "Join or create a team" that appears in the bottom-left corner of the screen, as shown in Figure 3-1.**

   Join or create a team appears in the main Teams workspace.

TIP

   If you don't see the "Join or create a team" link, as shown in Figure 3-1, two situations may be at play. The first, and most likely, is that you are a guest user to Teams, and thus have restricted access to the Office 365 — and Teams — products. If you are a licensed member of the organization but still don't see the ability to create a new team, then your administrators may have locked down the Office 365 tenant your organization is using. If that is the case, you will need to contact your administrator in order to create a new team.

FIGURE 3-1:
Clicking the link to join or create a new team.

Click to create a new team

3. **Click the Create a Team tile, as shown in Figure 3-2.**

   The Create Your Team dialog box appears, as shown in Figure 3-3. You can choose to create a team based on an existing group of users in Microsoft 365, or create a team from scratch. For this example, let's create a team from scratch.

4. **Select the Build a Team From Scratch option.**

   Next, you need to decide what type of team you want to create. You have three options, as shown in Figure 3-4:

   - *Private:* A private team requires members to have permission to join.

   - *Public:* A public team is one that anyone can join.

   - *Org-wide:* An organization-wide team is one that everyone in the organization belongs to automatically when they log in to Teams.

   For this example, let's create an org-wide team that everyone belongs to automatically so that we don't have to worry about adding people. (I cover how to add members to your teams later in this chapter.)

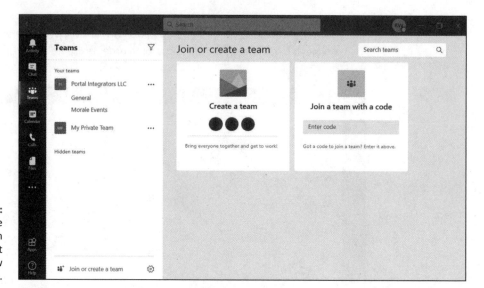

FIGURE 3-2:
Clicking the Create a Team tile to start creating a new team.

FIGURE 3-3:
Choosing to build a team from scratch.

5. **Select the Org-wide option.**

TIP

As your organization becomes larger, you probably want to start using either private teams or public teams. This is because the number of teams within an organization can grow quickly, and if everyone in your organization is automatically joined to them, Teams can become very noisy and people may start to ignore it.

FIGURE 3-4:
Choosing what
type of team to
create.

6. **Enter a name and description for your new team and then click Create, as shown in Figure 3-5.**

Teams will take a few moments and go about its work of creating a new team for you. When it is done, you will see the new team appear in your list of teams in the left navigation pane, as shown in Figure 3-6. Notice that when the new team was created, a channel called General was automatically created. In Chapter 4, I cover how to create additional channels for your team.

As a user of Teams, you can either be a *team owner*, a *team member*, or a *guest user*:

>> **Team owner:** Team owners can manage the team, which includes the ability to add members, approve or deny requests to join the team, create channels, change the team settings, view analytics, and add apps. Note that a team owner is not limited to the person who created the team. A team can have up to 100 team owners.

>> **Team member:** Team members make up a team. Team members interact and collaborate with other team members, team owners, and guest users. They can also view and make changes to documents (depending on the permissions set on the documents).

>> **Guest user:** Guest users are non-licensed users that have limited access and who must be invited to each team explicitly.

FIGURE 3-5:
Providing a team
name and
description when
creating a new
team.

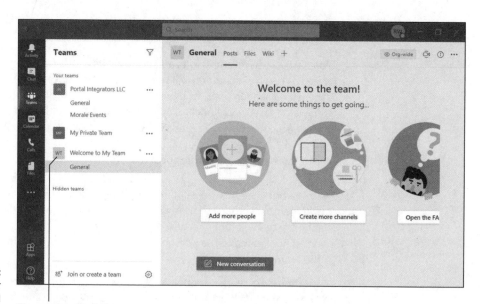

FIGURE 3-6:
Viewing your
newly created
team.

The newly added team

A user can join a team either by receiving an invite to join or request to join an existing team. If a team is set up as private, then new users will need to be invited as they won't be able to see the team and ask to join.

Inviting People to Your Team

Once you have your team set up, you can add people to the team. In the last section, "Creating a New Team," we created an org-wide team so that everyone within the organization is automatically added to the team. In this section, we go through the same process as before to create a new team, but this time we'll create a public and a private team and add members first during the creation process and then after we've already set up the team.

To invite people to your team during the initial team creation process, follow these steps:

1. **Follow Steps 1–4 in the previous example to create a new team.**

2. **When asked, "What type of team will this be?", instead of selecting the Org-wide option (shown earlier in Figure 3-4), choose Public or Private to create either a new public or private team.**

   When you create a public or private team, you are also presented with a dialog box to invite people to join it just after the team is created, as shown in Figure 3-7.

Add members to Welcome to My Team

Start typing a name, distribution list, or mail enabled security group to add to your team.

| Start typing a name or group | Add |

Close

FIGURE 3-7: The dialog box to invite people to your team during the creation process.

3. **Start typing the name of the person you want to invite to the team in the text box.**

The search functionality automatically looks for and populates the text box based on the letters you are typing. This happens in real time so that you can see the results of your search as you are typing. This is helpful if, for example, you only know the first part of someone's name, or if you only know that the name starts with a certain letter.

4. **Once you find the correct person, click that person's name and then click Add.**

5. **Continue adding people until you've invited all the team members you wish to add.**

The users will be notified of their new team membership depending on how they have notifications set up. I cover notifications in detail in Chapter 8.

You can invite people to your public or private team after it is created, too. Suppose a new person joins your organization and you want to add that person to your team. The only way people can join a private team is if you invite them, whereas anyone in the organization can join a public team. With an org-wide team, everyone in your organization is automatically included in the team.

To invite people to your public or private team after it has been created, follow these steps:

1. **Click the Teams icon in the left navigation pane to see a list of your teams.**

2. **Click the ellipsis next to the name of the team you want to invite someone to join.**

This opens a menu with more options.

3. **In the More Options drop-down menu that appears, select Add Member, as shown in Figure 3-8.**

The Add Members dialog box that was shown earlier in Figure 3-7 appears. This is the same dialog box that appears when you first create a public or private team.

4. **Start typing the name of the person you want to invite to the team in the text box.**

5. **Once you find the correct person, click that person's name and then click Add.**

The users will be notified of their new team membership depending on how they have notifications set up. I cover notifications in detail in Chapter 8.

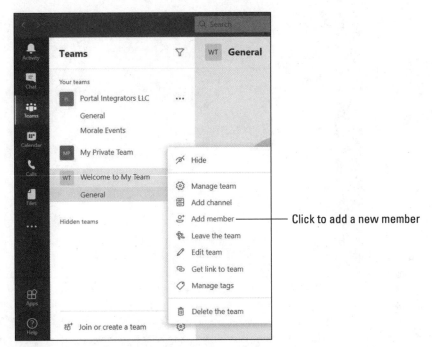

Click to add a new member

FIGURE 3-8:
Adding members to a team already created.

Managing Your Team Settings

You can control many different settings in Teams, such as adding and configuring channels, users, and chat behavior, and you will discover how to change these settings in the next section. The settings you will likely use the most frequently are for your specific teams. These include adding and removing owners, members, and guests; adding and deleting channels; and working with apps.

To open the settings for a team, click the ellipsis next to the name of the team to open the More Options drop-down menu (shown earlier in Figure 3-8) and select Manage Team.

The Manage Team settings screen contains the following tabs at the top, as shown in Figure 3-9:

>> **Members:** The Members screen is where you add new members to the team. You can add people as members of the team or as guests. A *guest user* is a user who has access to Teams and can chat with you, but does not have access to the rest of your Microsoft 365 ecosystem. I cover guest user access in detail in Chapter 7.

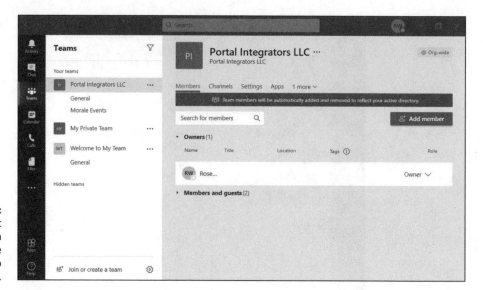

FIGURE 3-9:
The management
screen for a team
with the
Members tab
open.

>> **Channels:** The Channels screen is where you can add a channel. A *channel* is an area of a team where you can chat about a common topic. For example, you might have a channel for carpooling, a channel for accounting, and a channel for clients. I cover channels in Chapter 4.

>> **Settings:** The Settings screen is where you manage the settings for a team, as shown in Figure 3-10. On the Settings screen you can set the team picture, set the permissions of users including what permissions you want to give to guest users, set up how @mentions (pronounced "at mentions") work, get a link to the team that you can share so others can join the team, and other fun stuff such as adding virtual stickers.

TIP

An *@mention* is when someone uses the @ ("at") symbol followed by the name of a user in a message. It is essentially tagging the person so that Teams knows who the person is that is being mentioned. When your name is @ mentioned, you will get a notification that someone has mentioned your name in a message. This will help you scroll through and find messages that are pertinent to you. I cover mentions and feeds in Chapter 8.

>> **Apps:** The Apps screen is where you can add apps to the team. You can see that some apps are installed by default. You can also add more by clicking the More Apps button. I cover apps in Chapter 5.

>> **Analytics:** The Analytics tab, which appears when you select the Apps tab, is a dashboard of the activities and usage of a Teams channel. It includes information such as a summary of the number of users, apps, and data usage. It also shows metrics for engagement. Engagement is measured by the number of posts, replies, mentions, and reactions. It is a simple count on how busy the channel is based on the activity.

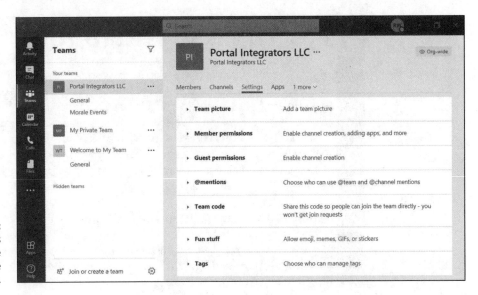

FIGURE 3-10:
The Settings
screen is where
you can configure
team settings.

You may also see the following additional tab if you have folks wishing to be part of your team:

>> **Pending Requests:** The Pending Requests tab is where you will see people asking to join your team. To accept or deny a request, select your team from the team list and then select the three ellipses next to the team name. Select manage team from the menu that appears and then select pending requests.

Other settings that appear in the More Options drop-down menu are fairly straightforward. Like many Microsoft products, there are multiple ways to achieve the same result in Teams. For example, you can add a channel using this menu or you can add a channel via the Channels tab on the Manage Team settings screen.

TIP

I also like to think of the More Options drop-down menu as a shortcut to common tasks. For example, I often use it to hide a less important team from my list, get a link to share the team, and manage tags. (I discuss more about hiding chatting teams and channels in Chapter 8.)

The additional items you will find on the More Options drop-down menu for a team include:

Hide

Add channel

Add member

Leave the team

Edit team

Get link to team

Manage tags

Delete the team

Managing User Settings

Several settings are unique to each individual Teams user. I like to think of these as your user settings; you can also think of them as your profile settings. These settings are found in the drop-down menu that appears when you click your profile image in the top-right corner of the Teams window, as shown in Figure 3-11.

You can use this menu to:

>> Set your current status such as Available, Do Not Disturb, and Away. I sometimes even set my status to Appear Away so that I can get work done without people knowing I am busy on my computer.

>> Set your status message so that others see a message and know what you are up to or what you want people to know. For example, I sometimes set this to the music I am listening to or a quote that I find particularly captures my current mood.

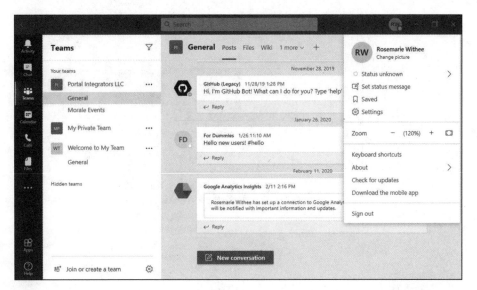

>> View chats and messages you have saved throughout Teams.

>> Open your profile settings (more on this shortly).

>> Adjust your zoom settings to zoom in and make items in your Teams window bigger or zoom out to make things smaller.

>> Change your keyboard shortcuts so you can maneuver around Teams with a few taps of your keyboard.

>> Learn more about Teams such as the version number you are currently using and legal notices.

>> Check for any updates to Teams so that you can be sure you have the latest version.

>> Download the mobile app so that you can have Teams on your smartphone and in your pocket so that you are never out of touch.

>> Sign out of Teams. I rarely do this when using Teams normally, but have used it plenty of times while writing this book when I've needed to sign in and out of various accounts. You might use this if you are a member of multiple organizations and you need to sign into one account or the other.

When you select the Settings option from your profile menu, you can change several options that are specific to your account. The settings menu, shown in Figure 3-12, includes settings for six different categories: General, Privacy, Notifications, Devices, Permissions, and Calls. I provide a brief overview of these sections here, and cover these settings in more detail throughout the book. For example, in Chapter 8, I cover setting up your notifications.

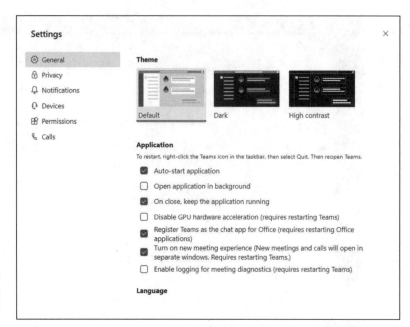

General

The General section includes settings for the appearance of Teams and how the application behaves in general. For example, you can change the way Teams looks by changing the theme you are using. You can also change the language you want to use.

In the application section, you can decide how you want Teams to behave on your computer. The options include:

>> **Auto-start application:** When selected, Microsoft Teams will open upon starting up your computer.

>> **Open application in background:** When selected, Microsoft Teams will open when you start up your computer, but it will only run in the background and not as an open window.

>> **On close, keep the application running:** When selected, Microsoft Teams will remain running even though you have closed the application.

>> **Disable GPU hardware acceleration:** This is probably a setting that most people won't need to bother with. GPU, or *graphics processing unit,* is a specialized processor designed to accelerate graphics processing. If your computer has performance issues (such as running too slowly), selecting this option may help with your computer's performance.

>> **Register Teams as the chat app for Office:** When selected, Teams becomes the default chat app for Office. This option is useful when you are part of an organization that is moving from Skype to Teams.

>> **Turn on new meeting experience:** Selecting this feature means you will get to experience a new meeting experience before it becomes available to all users. You get to preview a recent change or addition to the calling feature.

>> **Enable logging for meeting diagnostics:** Selecting this feature means Teams will log meeting diagnostics. The logs will be useful if there are any issues, as customer support usually looks at the diagnostic logs to help resolve any problems.

And one last general setting: You can change the language format and keyboard layout you are using.

Privacy

In the Privacy section, you will find settings to manage priority access, turn on or off read receipts, and turn on or off surveys.

Priority access defines who you will allow to interrupt you when your status is set to Do Not Disturb. For example, you might want your boss to be able to send you messages at any time, but everyone else must wait until you set your status to Available.

TIP

The Blocked Contacts option is where you can manage contacts you need to block or unblock. Think of it as your own "do not call" list. Select Block calls with no caller ID if you do not want to get calls from phone numbers with no caller ID. Click on Edit Blocked Contacts button to see the list of contacts you have blocked.

Read receipts is used to inform others when you read their messages. If you don't want people to know that you have read a message, you can turn this off.

The Surveys option is a tool Microsoft uses to improve Teams. If you don't mind giving feedback, you can leave this option on. If you don't want to be bothered with it, then turn it off and Microsoft won't survey you for your opinion on how to improve Teams.

Notifications

The Notifications area is where you set your preferences for how Teams should notify you about things. You can set various events to show up in your banner (a pop-up window that appears in the lower-right corner of your computer) and through email, only in your Activity feed, or turn them off completely. I cover notifications in detail in Chapter 8.

Devices

You configure the devices you are using with Teams in this settings section. A device includes things like your speaker, microphone, smartphone, headset, or camera. I cover devices in detail in Chapter 10.

Permissions

You can turn on or off permissions for Teams in this section. For example, do you want Teams to be able to use your location or be able to open external links in your web browser? You configure those permissions here.

Calls

Teams provides a full voice solution. What does this mean? It means that Teams can replace your regular telephone. In this section, you can configure how incoming calls are answered as well as setting up and configuring your voicemail and ringtones. You can also set accessibility options such as using a teletypewriter (TTY) device for people who are deaf or hearing impaired. I cover calling in detail in Chapters 11 and 12.

TIP

You can also access your Teams settings by clicking the Activity icon in the left navigation pane and clicking the gear icon. Did I mention that Microsoft is notorious for creating many different ways to achieve the same result? I guess the idea is that someone will stumble upon what they are trying to do just like stumbling around trying to find Easter eggs. Just remember that if you are in an argument with a coworker about how to do something in Teams, you might both be right!

2

Exploring Chat, Teams, Channels, and Apps

Discover how to send chat messages to others on your team via channels.

Learn how to create and configure new channels and use some of the cool features of channels including tagging others, using emojis, and tracking activity.

See how Microsoft Teams embraces integration with all types of software in the form of add-on apps.

Find, install, and use apps in Teams, both those created for Microsoft Office and those created by third-party companies for use in Teams.

Discover how to use Teams on your mobile device and smartphone and how doing so can make you a lot more productive.

Find out how to set the Activity feed to filter conversations, pin and follow channels that are of interest to you, and set up notifications for things that are important to you.

Chapter **4**

Staying Connected to Others with Channels and Chat

S ending instant communication over chat has been around since the dawn of the Internet. If you are as old as me, you may remember the days of AOL Instant Messenger and Internet Relay Chat (IRC) — which was invented in 1988, by the way. The Internet has come a long way since then, but one thing hasn't changed. Using the Internet to send communications back and forth in real time is still used by most people on a daily basis, and that capability is more valuable than ever. Have you heard of Slack? It relies on instant messaging. Have you used Skype to send chat messages? That is instant messaging, too. Microsoft Teams just wouldn't be valuable if it didn't include instant messaging.

In this chapter, you discover how to send chat messages to others on your team via channels. You learn how to create new channels and configure them. You also discover some of the cool features of channels beyond sending simple chat messages such as tagging others and using emojis. You also learn the difference between chatting within a channel and private chats, and you take a look at how assigning a team moderator can help keep your channel organized.

Instant Messaging in Teams

Before we started using Teams to chat, my team and I had been using a different chat application for which we paid a monthly fee to use. However, we also had an Office 365 subscription (which included Teams). Teams was still brand new back then, but we realized we could stop paying for the other chat program and use Teams instead. It already came with Office 365, and unless it was terrible, it would work just fine for sending instant communications.

My story happened a few years ago when Teams had just been released. However, based on my work with many clients, their stories (and perhaps your story) are very similar to mine. Teams might have already been included with your organization's Microsoft 365 subscription, even though you hadn't used it before. You might need to use Teams now because the coronavirus pandemic in 2020 forced everyone in your office to start working from home and you need a way to communicate virtually with your coworkers. Regardless of how you start using Teams, you will likely spend your initial interactions sending messages to other people on your team.

Instant messages in Teams happen in *channels.* A channel is a place where people can type messages, add files, and share links. I like to think of a channel like a virtual water cooler. You go there to communicate with colleagues, learn and share gossip, and generally stay in touch with your social circle.

A channel lives inside of a team, and a team can contain multiple channels. You can name a channel anything you want. I recommend using a name that describes the purpose of the channel. For example, you could name your channels channel01, channel02, channel03, and so on, but these titles aren't descriptive. Are you creating a channel that people in your team will use to discuss carpooling to and from work? Name the channel Carpooling. Or do you want to create a channel for accounting and another for human resources? Name them Accounting and Human Resources, respectively. Or perhaps a group of people want to discuss the new policy of allowing pets in the office. Create a channel called Pets. You get the point.

A channel can contain multiple conversations happening at the same time. To try to make these conversations easier to follow, Teams groups them together in what are known as *threads.* A thread is simply a topic of conversation. When someone types a brand-new message, it appears in the channel, and any replies to that original message are placed underneath. If someone else types a different message for a different topic, it will become its own thread and any responses to that message will be grouped under the original message.

In Figure 4-1, you can see that I am creating a brand-new topic of conversation in the General channel ("Hello"). If I want to reply to the existing topic, I will click the Reply link at the bottom of the "Hello" thread. If I want to start another new topic, I will click the New Conversation button at the bottom of the message window to open the primary text box to begin a new conversation.

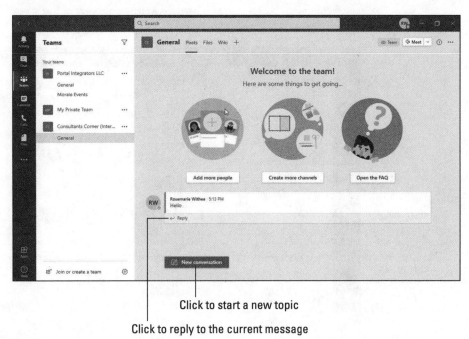

FIGURE 4-1: Starting a new topic of conversation.

Click to start a new topic

Click to reply to the current message

Sending Messages in Channels

Whenever you create a new team, a channel is created for that team automatically. Called "General," this channel is perfectly acceptable to use to start chatting with others on the team. (See Chapter 3 for a reminder on how to create your first team.)

To send a message in the General channel, follow these steps:

1. **Select the Teams icon in the left navigation pane to view all your teams.**

Under each team, you will see a list of channels that are available to you. If this is a new team, you will only see the General channel until more channels are created.

TIP

In addition to the channels available to you, there may be private channels in the team that you don't have access to. There could also be channels that are public but that you have not joined. The list of channels you see under a team might not be inclusive of every channel that team contains.

2. **Select the General channel, as shown in Figure 4-2.**

When you click a channel, it opens in the main part of the screen.

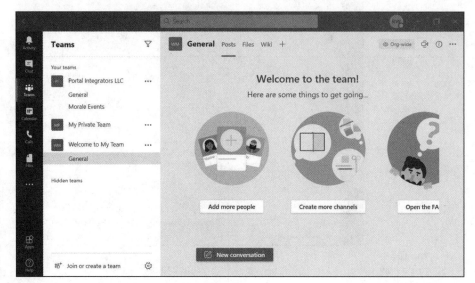

FIGURE 4-2:
Selecting the General channel that was automatically created when the Team was created.

3. **Click the New Conversation button that appears at the bottom of the screen.**

4. **Type a message in the text box that appears and click the Send icon, which looks like a paper airplane (or press the Enter key).**

Your message appears in the General channel screen.

Congratulations! You are sending messages!

TIP

Notice above your message that Microsoft Teams is giving you some hints about adding more people, creating more channels, and opening the Frequently Asked Questions (FAQ). These buttons that appear in new channels are shortcuts for you. You can achieve these same tasks without using these shortcuts, and you will find out how later in this chapter.

LEVELS OF COMMUNICATION

One of the reasons AOL Instant Messenger and IRC may have been so popular in the early days of the Internet is because chat fulfills a critical communications role when people are not located in the same room. And really, who is these days!? I like to think of communications as existing on different levels. The first level of communication is being face to face in the same room. Remember those days? The second level is voice communication (think of using the phone). And the third level is digital communication (think of email or instant messaging).

Email was tremendously popular from the inception of the Internet as well, but it was not instantaneous. Email has more in common with sending a postal letter (though a lot faster) than it does with chatting with someone over the phone. Instant messaging on the other hand, is similar to having a phone conversation with someone but in digital form, and it can happen asynchronously and with multiple people at the same time. Instant messaging doesn't replace email, just like sending a postal letter doesn't replace having a phone conversation. It is just a different form of digital communication.

A benefit digital communication has over both face-to-face and phone conversations is that it is inclusive. As an example, one of my neighbors is both hearing impaired and sight impaired. I can communicate with him just fine though digital communications. He has software on his computer that turns my communications into braille, and we stay in contact about the goings-on in our neighborhood. This would not be possible without digital communications.

Creating a New Channel

As you use Teams more, you will want to create chat channels for other topics so that everything does not happen in one "general" channel. For example, you might want to create a channel for your team to discuss finances, another for car-pooling, and another for team morale events. Team conversations can be organized in endless ways. The only thing that matters is what works for your team.

To create a new channel in your team, follow these steps:

1. **Select the Teams icon in the left navigation pane to view all your teams.**

2. **Click the ellipsis to the right of the team to which you wish to add a channel.**

   The More Options drop-down menu appears.

3. **Choose Add Channel, as shown in Figure 4-3.**

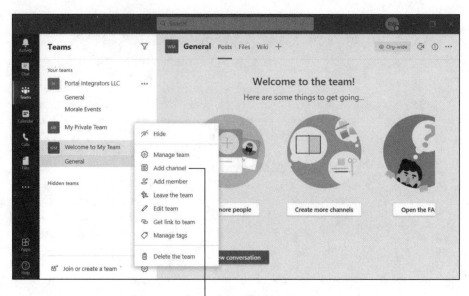

FIGURE 4-3:
Choosing Add
Channel from the
settings menu for
a team.

Click to add a new channel

WARNING

If this option isn't shown in the drop-down menu, you don't have permission to create a new channel. If you are a guest to a team, your ability to create teams and channels can be limited. I discuss setting team member permissions in Chapter 13.

4. **Enter a name and description for the channel in the dialog box that appears and then click Add, as shown in Figure 4-4.**

   The new channel appears under the team as shown in Figure 4-5.

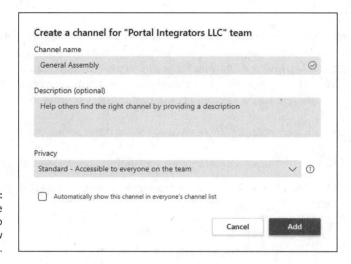

FIGURE 4-4:
Filling in the
dialog box to
create a new
channel.

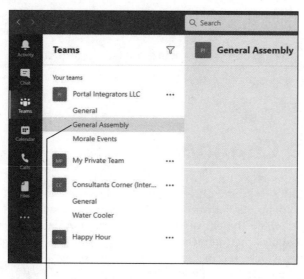

FIGURE 4-5:
A new channel in
a team.

The new channel

TIP

Note that when you create a new channel, you can set a few options. First, you can set the privacy settings as shown in Figure 4-4. The options include Standard and Private. A standard channel is accessible to everyone on the team by default. A private channel is only accessible to a specific group of people. When you select Private you then have the option on the next screen to add members to the channel. You can always add additional people to a private channel at any point in the future.

Second, you can also select the box to have this channel automatically show up for every person in the team. If you don't select this box, the channel will show up as hidden, and people will need to click a button to see it in the list of channels in the team. I cover hiding and unhiding channels in Chapter 8.

REMEMBER

A channel is part of a team. A team can contain multiple channels, and each channel can contain its own threads of conversation. You can create chat channels for any topic you want. I have seen teams have a lot of success breaking out work-related channels from non-work-related channels, such as morale events in one channel and budget discussions in a different channel.

Some things to keep in mind with channels are:

>> Each team can have a maximum 200 standard channels.

>> Each team can have a maximum of 30 private channels with a maximum of 250 members each.

>> Making a copy of a private channel doesn't copy over the channel's members.

>> You can search using keywords in standard or private channels.

>> Guest users cannot create private channels.

Configuring a Channel

You can configure many different settings for a channel via the More Options drop-down menu. As shown earlier in Figure 4-3, you access these additional options by clicking the ellipsis next to the channel name you wish to manage. Figure 4-6 shows the More Options drop-down menu that appears next to the new channel we created in the previous section. The options that appear for a channel you add include the following:

>> **Channel notifications:** You can configure the notifications you receive for this channel. This is important as your organization's use of Teams increases. Teams can quickly become noisy with everyone chatting about all manner of topics. You can use this setting to turn down the noise for channels that are less important to you and turn up the volume for topics you need to pay close attention to. The channel notifications submenu is shown in Figure 4-7.

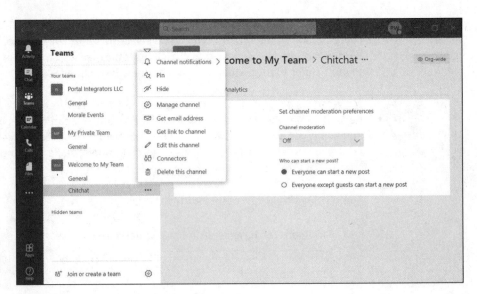

FIGURE 4-6:
The More Options menu for a team's channel.

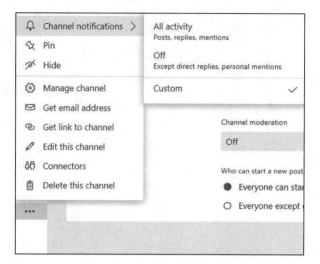

FIGURE 4-7:
Setting channel
notifications.

>> **Pin:** Select this option to keep a channel at the top of your list of channels. You can pin multiple channels and arrange them in any order you want.

>> **Hide:** Select this option to hide the channel from the list of channels you have in the team. You can always unhide the channel at any time. You will see a little message that lets you know how many channels you have hidden, and you can click it to see those hidden channels. I cover this behavior in more detail in Chapter 8 as it is something you will need to become familiar with as the number of teams and channels grows and start to become overwhelming.

>> **Manage channel:** This option allows owners of the channel to manage the permissions for the channel, as shown in Figure 4-8. You can allow others to moderate the channel and control who can post new messages to the channel. See "Adding Moderators" later in this chapter for more on adding moderation to a channel.

>> **Get email address:** A cool feature I use all the time is the ability to send an email message directly to a channel. You can configure the channel so that if you send an email, the message appears in the channel. (I send a copy of my email messages to my channels all the time!) Figure 4-9 shows the email address for the private channel I created in Chapter 3. Whenever I send an email message to this address, it appears in the channel, as shown in Figure 4-10.

>> **Get link to channel:** You can quickly get overwhelmed with the number of teams and channels in your organization. When you want to tell people about a channel, you can send them a direct link to the channel. You can get the link by using this option.

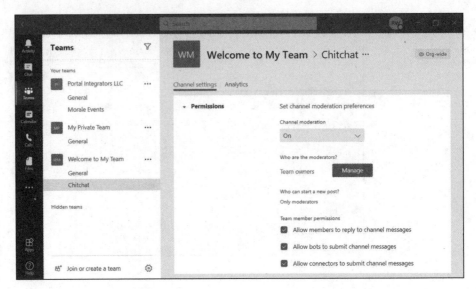

FIGURE 4-8:
Managing the moderators and permissions for a channel.

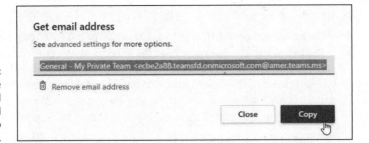

FIGURE 4-9:
Obtaining the dedicated email address to send email directly to the channel.

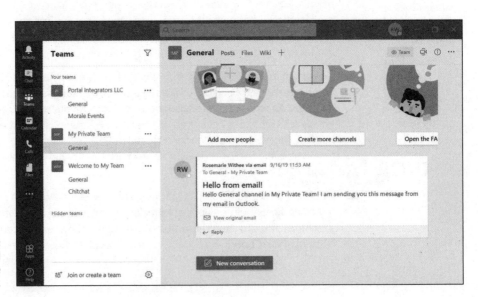

FIGURE 4-10:
Viewing an email sent to the channel.

>> **Edit this channel:** When you first created the channel, you set the title and description. You can change those settings with this option.

>> **Connectors:** Connectors are add-on apps. Think of them as custom extensions to Teams that you can add to a channel in order to connect with other software services. They allow you to connect other apps to your channel. There are many types of connectors, as shown in Figure 4-11. For example, you can connect your channel to GitHub or Zendesk or seemingly any other app out on the Internet. Check out Chapter 5 for more detail on adding apps and using connectors in Teams.

>> **Delete this channel:** When you are ready to remove a channel, you can choose this option to delete it.

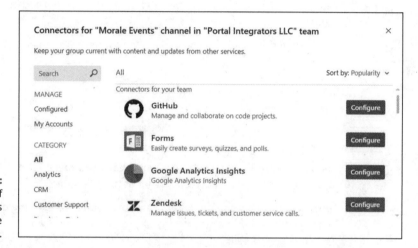

FIGURE 4-11:
Viewing some of the connectors that are available for a channel.

TIP

Be careful of the ellipsis you click to open the More Options drop-down menu. Figure 4-3 illustrates opening the menu for a team, while Figure 4-6 illustrates opening the menu for a channel. Channels appear underneath the team name, but it is easy to select the wrong ellipsis because they appear very close to each other.

Adding Moderators

One way to keep the team channel organized is to assign moderators. Moderators may only be assigned by team owners. With moderation, only an assigned moderator is able to start new posts and decides whether members are able to reply to posts or not. Using moderation allows you to leverage subject matter experts for a channel and ensure that their voices are heard. Think of a moderator as an air traffic controller. They can help things keep moving and avoid collisions.

The General channel and private channels do not have moderators by default. To turn on moderation for a standard channel, follow these steps:

1. **Click the ellipsis next to the channel name to which you want to add a moderator and choose Manage channel.**

2. **On the Channel settings tab, select On for Channel moderation as shown earlier in Figure 4-8.**

3. **Click the Manage button to select who can be a moderator and then select which options require moderation.**

   You can allow or disallow members to reply in the channel and bots or connectors to submit messages.

   Your changes are saved as you make them so there is no need to click a save button.

A team moderator can do the following:

» **Start new posts.** Note that only moderators can start new posts when moderation is turned on.

» **Add and remove team members as moderators to a channel.** Moderators, however, cannot remove a team owner as a moderator.

» **Control whether team members can post replies to existing channel messages.** The moderator can also control whether bots and connectors can make changes as well.

Moving from a Channel to a Chat

The various ways you can communicate within Teams can quickly become confusing. As a quick recap, a *team* is a group of people, and a *channel* is an ongoing conversation within the team. You can be in multiple teams and each team can have multiple channels.

The nice thing about this system of communication is that it has structure. You can always select a team from the left navigation pane and see the channels in that team. However, you might also need to just chat with someone or with groups of people, and you don't want to go through the process of setting up a new team or channel. Teams has you covered with a concept called *chat*. You find the Chat icon in the left navigation pane just above the Teams icon, as shown in Figure 4-12.

Chat icon

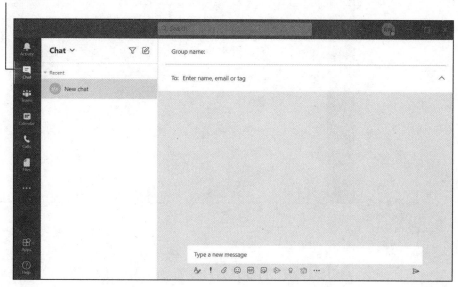

FIGURE 4-12:
The Chat feature
of Teams.

TIP

A chat is an ad hoc conversation between two or more people.

Click the Chat icon to see a list of all your open chats. If you remember using AOL Instant Messenger, Skype, or most any other chat application, you may recognize that each chat item is like a window. However, instead of a new window for each chat, each chat appears as an item in the list. Click a chat and you see the main window refresh to show that conversation.

Starting a private chat

You can start a private chat by selecting the New Chat icon, which is located to the right of the Filter icon at the top of the chat list. The New Chat icon looks like a piece of paper with a pencil on it (see Figure 4-13). When you select the icon, a new chat appears in the main pane of the Teams workspace. You type in the name of the person you want to send a chat message to in the To: field, and then click that person's name to add that person to the chat. Once you have added the person to the chat, you can send a message just like you do in a channel. You type your message in the text box at the bottom of the chat area and press the Enter key on your keyboard or select the Send icon, which looks like a paper airplane.

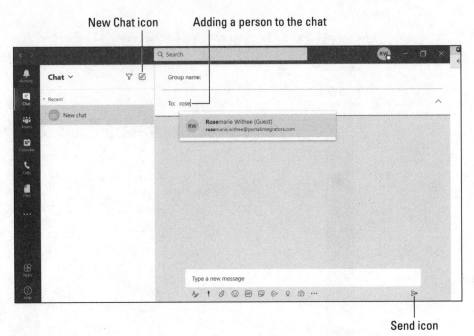

New Chat icon   Adding a person to the chat

Send icon

FIGURE 4-13:
Starting a new
chat in Teams.

Adding multiple people to a chat

The previous section covers how to start a new chat. You can chat with multiple people by adding them in the To: line when you start the chat. However, you may find that you want to add more people to an existing chat.

To add more people to a chat that has already started, select the Add People icon that appears in the top-right corner of the chat window (see Figure 4-14). Then, type in the names of the people you want to add in the Add dialog box. If you are chatting with only one person and you add another person, a new chat will appear with the three people in the chat. If you already have three people in a chat and you add a fourth person (or more), you will be presented with the option of including the chat history for the new people you are adding.

**TECHNICAL
STUFF**

If you are chatting with one person, you cannot add another person to the same chat and share the history of the personal chat with the new third party. The feature of adding people and keeping the history of the chat only appears when there are at least three people already in the chat. Microsoft has said that this is done for privacy reasons and the expectation that if there is a one-on-one chat happening, Teams should not allow one person to share that confidential chat with other people.

Add People icon

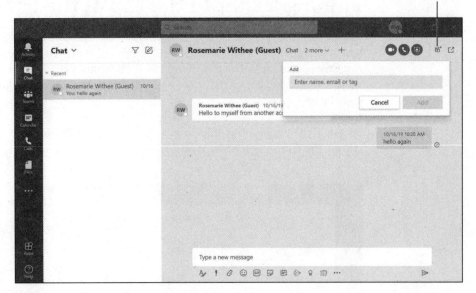

FIGURE 4-14:
Adding additional
people to a chat.

Giving a chat a title

By default, a chat is listed in your chat list with the names of the people in the chat. Often a chat will take on a life of its own as more and more people are added, and the chat becomes the central point of communication for a topic. When this happens, I find it helpful to give the chat a title so that when I am looking through my list of chats, I can quickly remember the topic of that chat.

To add a title to a chat, click the pencil icon at the top of the chat and type in a name, as shown in Figure 4-15.

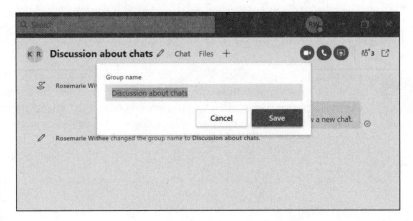

FIGURE 4-15:
Adding a title
to a chat.

Pinning a chat to the top of the list

In addition to giving a title to a chat, you can also pin a chat so that it always appears at the top of the list. By default, chats are listed in order with the most recently used chat at the top. What I will do is pin a chat to the top of the list so that I can quickly get to that chat even if it has been a few days since anyone has added a message to it.

To pin a chat, select the ellipsis next to the chat in the left navigation pane and choose Pin from the More Options drop-down menu, as shown in Figure 4-16.

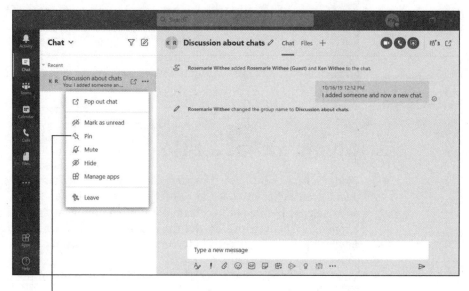

FIGURE 4-16:
Pinning a chat to the top of the list for quick access.

Select to pin a chat

Sending More than Text When Chatting

Entering text into a channel or chat is the most common way of sending your message to others on the team. However, you can send more than just text. You can send emojis, GIFs, stickers, and even attach files. These options appear at the bottom of the text box where you type in your message, as shown in Figure 4-17.

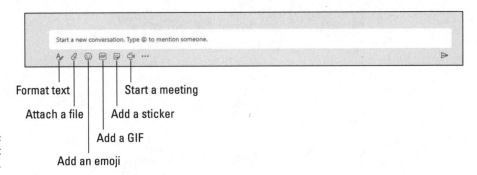

Format text

Attach a file

Start a meeting

Add a sticker

Add a GIF

Add an emoji

FIGURE 4-17:
Additional chat
options.

Adding emojis, GIFs, and stickers

Emojis are little icons that display an emotion. For example, a smiley face shows happiness and a sad face shows sadness. You will find emoji icons of all shapes and sizes and meanings. You can send an emoji by clicking the emoji icon and then selecting the emoji you want to use (see Figure 4-18).

FIGURE 4-18:
Adding an emoji
to your message.

TIP

Teams includes text shortcuts you can type so that you don't have to select an emoji with your mouse from the list of options shown in Figure 4-18. For example, to send a happy face, you can type a colon (:) followed by a closing parenthesis ( )). When you type this sequence of characters, the happy face emoji will automatically be added to your chat. You can also type a keyword inside of parenthesis in order to create an emoji icon. Some of the common emojis and their shortcut words are shown in Figure 4-19. The entire list can be found at https://365trainingportal.com.

Emoji	Description	Shortcut
	Smiley	(smile)
	Big smile	(laugh)
	Heart	(heart)
	Kiss	(kiss)
	Sad	(sad)
	Smiley with tongue out	(tongueout)
	Winking	(wink)
	Crying	(cry)
	In love	(inlove)
	Hug	(hug)
	Crying with laughter	(cwl)
	Kissing lips	(lips)

FIGURE 4-19:
Microsoft Teams
emoji shortcuts.

A GIF is an animated picture. Microsoft Teams includes several GIFs that are popular. For example, there might be a cat yawning or a reaction of a character from a popular television show. You can include these short video clips in your chat message as GIFs by clicking the GIF icon at the bottom of the text box.

Stickers are short little comic strip–type images. For example, a drawing with a speech balloon over the person. If you have ever read the *Dilbert* comic strip, then you can picture what these stickers look like. Microsoft Teams includes a lot of popular stickers, and you can add your own as well. Adding a sticker to your message is shown in Figure 4-20.

Adding a file

In addition to fun emojis, GIFs, and stickers, you can also add a file to the chat message. For example, you might be working on an Excel spreadsheet and you want to include it in the chat. You can add the file to your chat message using the paperclip icon, as shown in Figure 4-21. You can choose a recent file you have been working on, browse the files already uploaded to Teams, choose a file from OneDrive, or upload a file from your local computer.

TIP

When you attach a file to a channel, the file appears in the Files tab at the top of the channel. The Files tab is a SharePoint site behind the scenes. You can spot the Files tab at the top of Figure 4-21 in between the Posts tab and the Wiki tab.

FIGURE 4-20:
Adding a sticker
to your message.

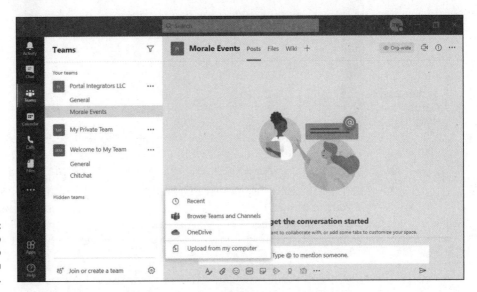

FIGURE 4-21:
Attaching a file to
a message to
send to a
channel.

@ TAGGING

If you want to get someone's attention in a chat, you can mention them with an @ tag (pronounced "at tag"). When you type the @ character, a list of people in the channel appears, and you can select the appropriate person's name. When you @ tag someone, that person is notified, based on their notification settings, that you are trying to get his or her attention. I cover setting your notifications in Chapter 8.

Reacting to chat messages

When someone types a message, you can react to it instead of or in addition to responding to it. To *react* to a message means to acknowledge you've seen the chat. For example, you can react with an emoji such as a thumbs up, a surprise emoji, or many others. To react to a message, you either hover your mouse over the message or select the ellipsis if you are using a mobile device and touchscreen, and then select the reaction. In Figure 4-22 I am reacting to a message with a thumbs up emoji to indicate that I like the message and acknowledge it.

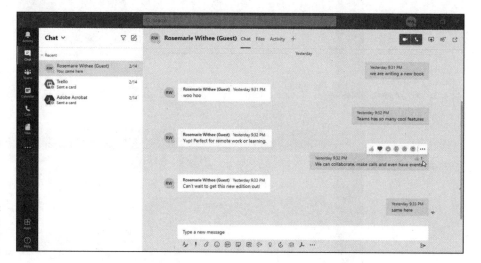

FIGURE 4-22:
Reacting to a message with a thumbs up.

If someone else has already given a reaction, such as a thumbs up, then your reaction will increase the number that appears next to the same reaction. For example, if your coworker gave a thumbs up, and you reacted with the same thumbs up, then a small number 2 will appear next to the thumbs up emoji. Reactions can be important to acknowledge a message without having to type out a response.

IN THIS CHAPTER

» Discovering apps in Teams

» Finding connectors to your favorite services

» Installing and using popular apps

» Exploring the Power Platform apps

» Getting chatty with your favorite bot

Chapter **5**

Extending Teams with Apps, Bots, and Connectors

The world today is more interconnected than at any other time in human history. On the Internet, these connections take the form of software applications communicating with each other. Microsoft Teams embraces integration with all types of software in the form of add-on apps, bots, and connectors. Apps come in many flavors. You can find apps for personal use, for adding tabs and bots to your channels, for adding connections to other software services, and for enhancing your messaging experiences.

In this chapter, you discover how to find, install, and use apps in Teams. You learn about the apps created for Microsoft Office such as SharePoint, Word, Excel, PowerPoint, Planner, and OneNote and how they integrate with Teams. You also find out about some of the most popular apps developed by companies other than Microsoft such as Asana, Zendesk, Dropbox, Box, and Google Drive, and how you can add these apps to Teams as well. Finally, you discover how bots can help your

Teams conversations as well as how Teams is becoming the primary hub for productivity with its integration with the Microsoft Power Platform.

That's quite a lot! Let's dive into the expanding world of Teams apps.

Discovering Apps Already Installed

If you are reading this book in order and created a new channel in Chapter 4, then you already have experience with apps. You might just not realize it yet because apps are designed to feel like part of Microsoft Teams. Every new channel you create includes two apps that show up as tabs at the top of the main Teams screen, as shown in Figure 5-1. These are the Files app and the Wiki app.

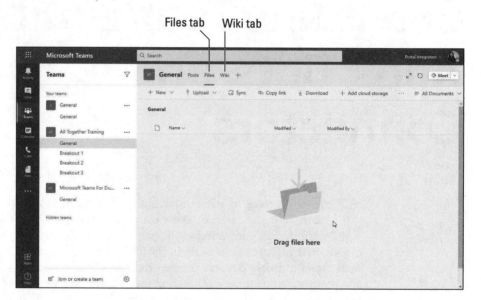

FIGURE 5-1: The Files and Wiki tabs in a channel.

The Files tab

The Files tab is an app that shows the files you have created and saved to a Teams channel, which is actually a SharePoint site that sits behind the scenes. And the Wiki tab is a Wiki page that also lives in the same SharePoint site. Did I mention that every team in Teams has an associated SharePoint site? You might never need to access it directly, but it is there behind the scenes offering up SharePoint functionality to Teams.

When you click the Files tab, you see a view into a SharePoint library. You can create new files, upload existing files, get a link to the library, add an additional cloud storage location (more on this shortly), and even open the library in SharePoint. Figure 5-2 shows the same library shown earlier in Figure 5-1, except it is open in SharePoint instead of Teams. If you add a file to either location, you will be able to see it instantly in the other location.

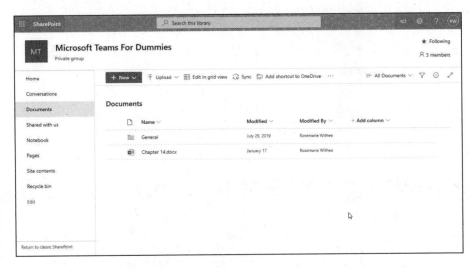

FIGURE 5-2:
Viewing the Files of a Teams channel in SharePoint.

SharePoint is a product unto itself, and it requires its own book. If you are interested in learning more about SharePoint, check out *Microsoft SharePoint For Dummies* (Wiley).

The Wiki tab

When you click the Wiki tab, you see a page that you can customize for notes or documentation or pictures or whatever you want to add to it. The page is a SharePoint Wiki Page, and it lives in the same SharePoint site where your files in the Files tab live. Figure 5-3 shows the Wiki page of the General channel in the Portal Integrators team.

Both the Files tab and Wiki tab are apps that you can add to Teams. These apps provide integration with SharePoint, and there are other apps that provide integration with just about any other software you can imagine. Let's look at those apps next.

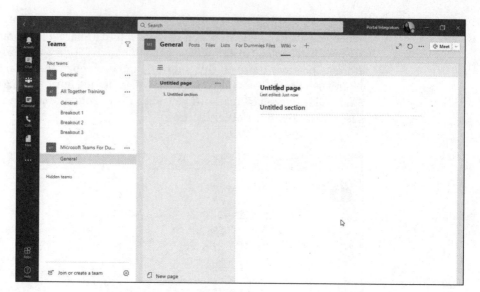

FIGURE 5-3:
Viewing the Wiki
tab in a Teams
channel.

Browsing and Adding Apps

An app store is built right into Teams, and you can access it in several different ways. The easiest way is to open the settings for a team and browse to the apps. However, you can also view the available apps, bots, and connectors on a channel within a team. First let's look at how to view and install the available apps via a team's settings.

To view and install the apps available for Teams, follow these steps:

1. **Select the Teams app from the left navigation pane to view a list of your teams.**

2. **Open the More Options drop-own menu by clicking the ellipsis to the right of one of the teams in the list.**

3. **Choose Manage Team.**

    The settings screen for the team appears.

4. **Select the Apps tab at the top of the settings screen, as shown in Figure 5-4.**

    You will see all the apps that are installed in Teams by default. Notice that the app for SharePoint is already installed. (You used SharePoint in the previous section when you clicked the Files and Wiki tabs in a channel.)

5. **Select the More Apps button to view the app store, as shown in Figure 5-5.**

    Notice that the apps are categorized for you and that you can also search for apps.

Apps tab

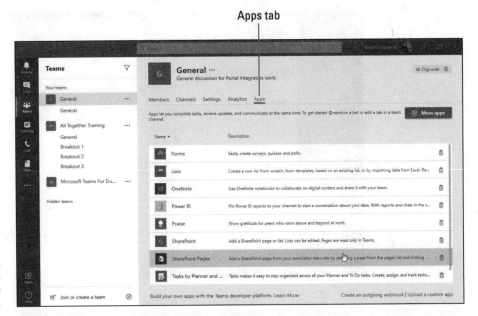

FIGURE 5-4:
The Apps tab on
the settings page
for a team.

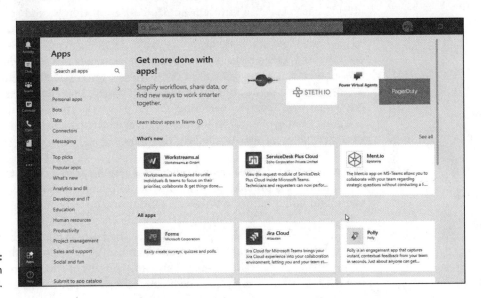

FIGURE 5-5:
The apps store in
Microsoft Teams.

6. **Select an app to learn about it, and then select the Add button to add it to a team or channel.**

Figure 5-6 shows adding the Trello app to a team. Trello is a task management service that can be found at https://trello.com.

FIGURE 5-6:
Adding the Trello app to a team.

When you add an app, you might not notice anything different about Teams right away. That is because different apps do different things, and some of that functionality is not obvious. For example, the Trello app allows you to add a special tab to your channels that is dedicated to Trello. Or you can use the Trello bot to interact with your Trello tasks by having it send messages in a channel. If you are using Trello, then you know to look for these things, but if you are not using Trello, you might not even be aware that the app was added. You can see exactly what apps are added to a team by selecting the ellipsis next to the team name and then selecting Manage Team. In the Manage Team settings, select the Apps tab to see exactly what apps are installed for the team.

You can also install an app as a tab or as a connector in a channel. The tabs at the top of a channel provide quick navigation to people in the channel. For example, you might add a tab for a Wiki or a tab for an app and the people in the channel can click on the tab to navigate between the channel discussion and the tabs you have added. To install an app as a tab, click the plus (+) sign next to the tabs at the top of the channel. The tabs that are included by default are the Files and Wiki tabs, but you can click the plus (+) sign to the right of those and add more. When you click the plus (+) sign, the Add a Tab dialog box appears, where you can choose which tab you want to add to the channel. (You learn more about this shortly, but you can skip ahead and check out Figure 5-10 to see the Add a Tab dialog box.)

To install a connector for a channel, click the ellipsis next to the name of a channel to open the More Options drop-down menu and choose Connectors from the list, as shown in Figure 5-7. The Connectors screen appears, as shown in Figure 5-8. You can connect a Teams channel to just about any popular software service out there on the Internet.

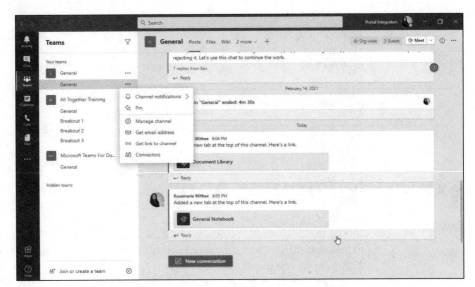

FIGURE 5-7:
Accessing the
Connectors
option from the
More Options
menu in a
channel.

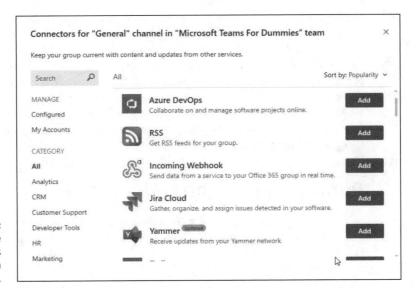

FIGURE 5-8:
View the
connectors
available in a
channel.

REMEMBER

A *connector* is a connection to some other software service that allows that service to provide updates directly to Teams and into your channel. For example, if you add a connector for Twitter, you can see tweets directly in the channel. I like to think of a connector as a way to stay up to date with things that are happening outside of Teams. Connectors let me stay connected with other software services without having to leave my Teams channels.

When you open the Connectors option for a channel, you get a filtered view of the app store. You can see the apps that are already installed that have connector options (notice the Forms app), and you can also add others.

TIP

Covering all the apps available for Teams is beyond the scope of this book. I cover a few of the most popular in the next section. Go ahead and install some and explore them. I find new apps all the time that I didn't even know existed!

Exploring Popular Apps

One of the best ways to understand how apps can extend Teams is by diving right in and installing and using them. In this section you discover some of the popular Teams apps Microsoft has developed. Next, you see some of the popular Teams apps that third-party companies have developed for Teams. (Note that these companies are called "third party" because they are not your organization and they are not Microsoft.) In addition to these apps, you can build your own Teams apps and upload them and use them, too.

TIP

An app can provide many forms of integration with Microsoft Teams. An app can provide a tab or connector to a channel, extend messaging capabilities, introduce a bot to channels (which I discuss later in this chapter), and even provide an immersive experience like the Word app I outline in the next section. As you are browsing the Teams' app store, you can read about the app to understand what type of functionality it provides to Teams.

Popular apps from Microsoft

Microsoft ships several apps for Teams that are enabled by default. You can also add more as you need them. I cover some of the most popular, and some of my favorites, next.

Office

Teams includes apps to integrate with Microsoft Office (Word, Excel, PowerPoint, and OneNote) by default. You don't need to install anything. One of my absolute favorite integrations is with Microsoft Word. When I wrote this book, I wrote it within Teams using Microsoft Word. Figure 5-9 shows what this chapter looked like in draft form in Teams! So, where does the Word document that I am working on live? It lives in a SharePoint library in my Portal Integrators subscription of Microsoft 365. I added the SharePoint library using the SharePoint app for Teams, which I cover how to do next.

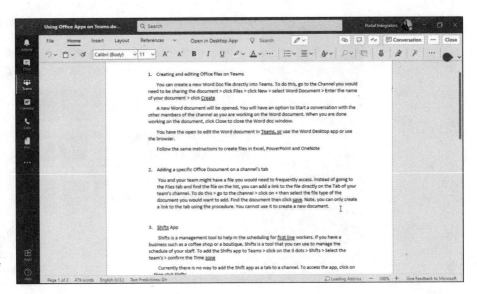

FIGURE 5-9:
Using Microsoft
Word inside of
Microsoft Teams.

TIP

You can open a Word document that lives in other locations besides SharePoint. For example, you can store your documents in Dropbox, Box, or even Google Drive and use the associated apps to integrate those services with Teams. Check out the discussion later in this chapter for details on installing these and other third-party apps.

SharePoint

The SharePoint app for Teams lets you integrate SharePoint sites, libraries, and lists into Teams. As I mention in the previous section, I wrote this book using Microsoft Word inside of Microsoft Teams. But the files themselves live inside a SharePoint site in my Portal Integrators subscription of Microsoft 365. So how did I add the files from the SharePoint site into Teams? I used the SharePoint app. It is installed in Teams by default; all you need to do is use Teams to integrate with SharePoint.

One handy tip for working with SharePoint in Teams is to add a tab to a specific SharePoint library to a Teams channel. Here's how to do so:

1. **Select the Teams icon in the left navigation pane to view all your Teams.**

2. **Click the channel you want to integrate with SharePoint to open the channel in the main part of your screen.**

3. **Click the plus (+) sign to the right of the Files and Wiki tabs to add a tab.**

   The Add a Tab dialog box appears, as shown in Figure 5-10.

FIGURE 5-10:
Adding a
SharePoint
Library as a tab in
a channel.

4. **Choose the Document Library option.**

   Notice you can also choose other popular apps that provide tab support, such as Excel, Forms, OneNote, PDF, and many others. If you don't see what you are looking for right away, you can search for a particular app or select the More Apps link to see all the apps in the app store.

5. **In the Document Library dialog box, choose the relevant SharePoint site and click Next, as shown in Figure 5-11.**

   The SharePoint sites that are in your same Microsoft 365 subscription show up by default. If you are adding a SharePoint site that lives somewhere other than in your Microsoft 365 subscription, you can enter the site link in this dialog box.

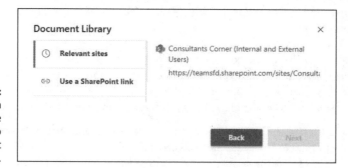

FIGURE 5-11:
Choosing a
SharePoint site
from which to
add a Document
library as a tab.

6. **Choose the library from those that are available in the SharePoint site and then select Next.**

   In Figure 5-12, I am choosing the SharePoint library called Documents.

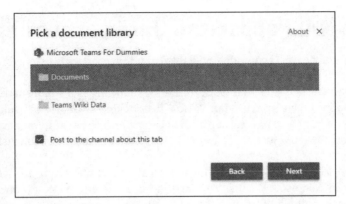

7. **Enter a name for the tab and then select Save.**

A new tab is now available in the channel, and clicking on it shows the files in the associated SharePoint library (see Figure 5-13). You can click an Office file and it will open inside of Teams and you can work on it. Pretty cool, don't you think?

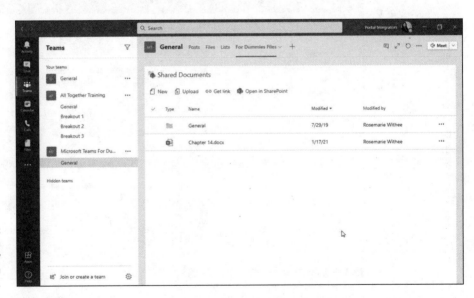

In addition to Office and SharePoint, I often use app integrations for Excel, Planner, OneNote, PowerPoint, OneDrive, Lists SharePoint Document Library, and Forms. Each of these has similar integrations as you just saw with Word and SharePoint.

Popular apps from third-party companies

The number of Teams apps available from third parties is astounding. As a consultant, I work with many different software services daily. Each of my clients seem to have their favorites that work for them. Following is a small spattering of some of the apps I have seen used in Teams. Just looking at the list of available apps in the Teams app store (see earlier in the chapter for information on how to find it), you will realize that just about anything you would want is probably listed in the store.

TIP

Each of the apps I describe have dedicated documentation for working with the app in Microsoft Teams. To learn more about any of them, open your favorite search engine and include the name of the app along with Microsoft Teams. For example, to learn about the Trello app, search for *Trello integration with Microsoft Teams.* Figure 5-14 shows the documentation Trello provides for its Microsoft Teams app.

FIGURE 5-14:
The documentation page for the Trello app for Microsoft Teams.

Freshdesk and Zendesk

Freshdesk (`https://freshdesk.com`) and Zendesk (`www.zendesk.com`) are popular support ticketing systems. For example, if you have a problem with a website, you might open a support ticket. Freshdesk and Zendesk are software products that manage those tickets. Both have a Teams app that allows you to get notified of tickets assigned to you and your team. The notifications come in the form of a bot that sends a chat to your channel. You can reply to the bot and send a message back to them to update the ticket. (Check out the section, "Getting Chatty with Bots" later in this chapter for more about working with bots in Teams.)

Asana and Trello

Asana (`https://asana.com`) and Trello (`https://trello.com`) are services for managing work. You can do things like managing your group's work, projects, and tasks. When you install the Asana or Trello app in Microsoft Teams, you can view your projects directly in Teams and turn your conversations into Asana or Trello items. For example, while you are having a chat with your team, you might decide that there is an action item that needs to be done. You can use the Asana or Trello app to add this action item into Asana or Trello directly from the chat.

Dropbox, Box, and Google Drive

Teams integrates SharePoint and OneDrive behind the scenes to store your files, and you can add apps to integrate other cloud storage locations, too. Three of the popular cloud storage locations to add are Dropbox (`www.dropbox.com`), Box (`www.box.com`), and Google Drive (`www.google.com/drive`). When you add one of these apps to Microsoft Teams, you can work with the files stored in them just like how I work with Word files in SharePoint. Figure 5-15 shows the documentation Dropbox created for its Microsoft Teams app.

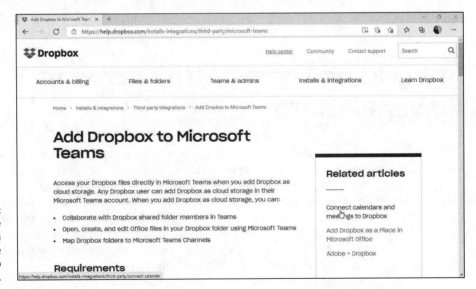

FIGURE 5-15:
The documentation page for the Dropbox app for Teams.

Salesforce

Salesforce (`www.salesforce.com`) is a popular customer relationship management (CRM) service that lets organizations track their contacts, sales, and many other things. When you install the Salesforce app for Microsoft Teams, you can interact with Salesforce items without leaving Teams. I have seen companies that use Salesforce really love this app because they can be chatting and working with Salesforce without ever having to switch out of Microsoft Teams.

Kronos

Kronos (www.kronos.com) is a software company that makes popular work management software. I have seen companies use it to track time and other human resources items. When you install the Kronos app for Microsoft Teams, you can interact with Kronos using a bot, handling basic Kronos tasks right from Teams.

As I mention earlier in this chapter, there are many more apps you can install to integrate Teams with other software services. The rate at which companies are developing apps for Teams is astounding. Teams seems to be taking center stage as the software where people spend their time at work, and being able to integrate with it has become a priority. I am noticing a trend where other software, especially other Microsoft software, fade into the background and Teams becomes the gateway to use them. I experienced this firsthand when I used Microsoft Word to write this book never leaving the Teams app. I know from experience that the book files lived in SharePoint and the editing I did happened in Word. However, if I were brand new to Teams, I might never know nor care about the apps behind the scenes; I might just think everything happened in Microsoft Teams.

Integrating Teams with Microsoft Power Platform

The Microsoft Power Platform is a collection of software that helps users and organizations analyze data, build custom business functionality, automate workflows, and create custom bots called *virtual agents.* The collection consists of Power Business Intelligence (Power BI), Power Apps, Power Automate (formerly known as Flow), and Power Virtual Agents. These apps can be connected together, or to Microsoft 365 and hundreds of other apps, to build end-to-end business solutions. The Power Platform doesn't require extensive coding skills, which makes it user-friendly and easy to roll out. Check your Microsoft 365 subscription to see if it is already included.

Microsoft integrated the Power Platform apps into Teams right away, as Teams is becoming the primary hub for productivity with Microsoft tools. So, it is a good thing you bought this book and are diving into Teams!

Power BI

Power BI is a data analysis and visualization tool from Microsoft. It is available both as a self-service app or as an enterprise solution. Check your Microsoft 365 subscription to see if Power BI is already included. If not, you can subscribe to it as an add-on for a monthly fee.

The amount of data businesses collect and use is growing exponentially. The data is also changing rapidly. Being dependent on a spreadsheet that might change daily, or weekly, and that needs to be shared in email, is inefficient. Power BI allows you to connect to nearly any type of data source, including Excel and Share-Point, and pull it into a single collection. Data can be updated and shared in real time. Power BI has robust data visualization capabilities. There are numerous pre-made graphs and charts available to choose from. With Power BI, not only is data updated in real time — so are the visuals. This combination allows decision-makers to have important data available to them right away.

TIP

One handy way to think about Power BI is as a centralized spreadsheet on steroids.

Power BI is available as a Teams app for easy integration with Teams. You find Power BI in the app store. Select the Apps icon on the lower-left side of your Teams screen and search for *Power BI*. If you already have a Power BI account, you won't need to log in again. If you don't yet have a Power BI account, you will need to sign up for one before you can log in.

Power Apps

Almost every business uses some type of software, and it is usually customized to meet specific needs. Hiring developers to develop and customize the software you need is expensive, and it is not always easy to keep the developers and business people on the same page.

Microsoft created Power Apps as a no-code solution for building software. The idea behind Power Apps is that business people can build their own software without the need of a professional developer. Microsoft focused on making Power Apps integrate with the rest of the Microsoft products — most especially with Teams.

Power Apps is an add-on to your Microsoft 365 subscription. Currently, it is priced at $10 a month per app or $40 a month for unlimited apps.

You can integrate the apps you build with Power Apps into Teams. You will find Power Apps in the app store. Select the Apps icon on the lower-left side of your Teams screen and then search for *Power Apps.*

Power Automate

The third power to the Microsoft Power Platform is Power Automate. (Power Automate used to be known as Microsoft Flow.) Microsoft created Power Automate to help with the repetitive and mundane tasks everyone knows as *grunt work*. We have all been there where we wished someone could just automate a mind-numbing task. Much like Power BI and Power Apps, Power Automate was created for you to use and automate your mundane tasks.

Power Automate is another add-on to your Microsoft 365 subscription. Check your licensing to see if you already have it.

You can integrate the automations you create with Teams. As with the other Power Platform apps, Power Automate is in the app store. Select the Apps icon on the lower-left side of your Teams screen and then search for *Power Automate*.

Power Virtual Agents

Power Virtual Agents is a fancy name for chatbots. A *chatbot* is an artificial intelligence (AI) software application designed to simulate conversation with a live person over an instant messaging platform. Chatbots have increased in popularity in the last couple of years. Organizations and businesses have started to use chatbots as the first line of customer support. In the beginning, chatbots could only be programmed to answer simple if/then scenarios. But with the advances in artificial intelligence, the chatbots are literally getting smarter!

To use Power Virtual Agents, you need to add it to your Microsoft 365 subscription. As of this writing, the subscriptions costs $1,000 a month for 2,000 chatbot sessions. But as usual with Microsoft licensing, be sure to check current pricing.

HUMAN OR BOT?

Let me know if this has ever happened to you: Once when I was chatting with a company's customer service department via a messaging app, I was not sure if the entity I was conversing with was a human being or a chat bot. When the customer service representative asked if I had any other questions, my only question was whether I was conversing with a human or a bot! The customer service representative laughed and confirmed that I was indeed talking to a human, but that many people wonder the same thing. What would have been scary is if the person responded that they were in fact, an AI bot!

You can integrate the Power Virtual Agents with Teams by adding it from the app store. Select the Apps icon on the lower-left side of your Teams screen and search for *Power Virtual Agents.*

Setting Permissions for Apps

You can limit the access the apps you add to Teams have to each of your devices. For example, you can turn on and off access to your microphone, speakers, and camera. You can allow apps to open links in external applications or access your geographic location. You can also allow apps to send notifications or even access the MIDI format for sending sounds between devices. App developers can specifically request these permissions and when they do, you will see a notification when you install the app asking for the permissions. You can explicitly turn off these permissions however, as outlined below. You can set these permissions for every app across the board or you can customize them per app.

TECHNICAL
STUFF

You can think of the apps that you add as tabs to your device as a mini web browser embedded into Teams. The tab can interact with your computer, like a web browser, but it must be provided permission to do that. If you open a website that wants to use your webcam and microphone, the web browser will ask you if the site has permission to do that. It is the same concept in Teams.

To set the permissions the Teams apps have for your device, follow these steps:

1. **Log in to Teams and select Settings from your profile drop-down menu.**

2. **On the Settings screen, select Permissions in the left navigation pane.**

   The Permissions screen appears, as shown in Figure 5-16.

3. **Set the toggles next to the Permissions settings you want to turn on and off.**

4. **Close the window by selecting the X in the top-right corner of the screen.**

   You don't need to save the settings; they are saved automatically as you adjust them.

FIGURE 5-16:
Setting the permissions that Teams apps you install have to your device.

Getting Chatty with Bots

A *bot*, short for *robot*, is a software program you can interact with by sending messages to it in a channel. Bots have been around a long time, becoming popular with Internet Relay Chat (IRC) back in the 1990s.

When you install a Teams add-on app, you might be installing the bot and not even realize it. A bot is just a type of app you can use in your channels. You can send messages to it in order to have it do things for you. For example, when you install the Freshdesk app, you are also installing the Freshdesk bot.

I like to think of the bot as the face of the app I am using in a channel. The bot will send messages to the channel, maybe a Freshdesk ticket update, and I can reply and interact with the bot, which can then send my ticket updates back to Freshdesk. Even though the bot is just a software program, I like to think of bots as a virtual concierge to the services they represent.

TIP

Teams uses the Microsoft Bot Framework (https://dev.botframework.com) to make bots possible. The types and purposes of the bots that can be created are mind-numbing. Chatbots are used to answer simple yes/no questions, provide links to websites or provide contact information. If you have an idea in mind for a bot or other Teams app, then rest assured: There is a developer out there that can build it for you. If you are a developer yourself, check out App Studio for Microsoft Teams in the app store to get started.

Chapter **6**

Unshackling Yourself with the Teams Mobile App

I f you are like me, you have a mobile device or smartphone on or near you at all times. I can't remember the last time I didn't work for a day without using my smartphone. There will always be a need for a laptop or desktop computer, but more and more often a smartphone is the tool of choice for modern information workers.

In this chapter, you discover how to use Microsoft Teams on your mobile device and smartphone. You get Teams installed and learn about some of the ways working with Teams on your phone can make you a lot more productive. You also take a look at how Teams makes it easy to keep in touch with family and friends by using it to help keep your personal life organized in addition to your work life. You discover how to use Teams to chat, make phone calls, plan events, share files, and even share your location with others.

Installing the Teams Mobile App

You can install Teams on your mobile device in a few different ways. The easiest way is to open the Google Play Store (on Android devices) or the Apple App Store (on iOS devices) and search for the Teams mobile app. Another way is to use your mobile web browser and sign into `https://teams.microsoft.com`, and then tap the icon for installing the mobile app.

TIP

The icon on the website to install the mobile app is a shortcut that takes you to the relevant app store. I find it easier to just go straight to the iOS or Android app store and search for Microsoft Teams instead of trying to navigate my mobile web browser to the Teams website.

Installing on iOS

To install the Teams mobile app on your iPhone or iPad:

1. **Open the Apple App Store on your iOS device.**

2. **Tap the Search icon in the store and type** Microsoft Teams **in the search box.**

3. **Click search.**

   Make sure you choose the Microsoft app from the options that appear (see Figure 6-1).

4. **Tap the download icon to install the app on your device.**

5. **Once the app has finished downloading and installing, tap the Open button.**

Installing on Android

To install the Teams mobile app on your Android phone or tablet:

1. **Open the Google Play Store on your Android device.**

2. **Tap the Search icon in the store and type** Microsoft Teams**.**

3. **Click search.**

   Make sure you choose the Microsoft app from the options that appear (see Figure 6-2).

4. **Tap the Install button to install the app on your device.**

5. **Once the app has finished downloading and installing, tap the Open button.**

Tap to download and install the app

FIGURE 6-1:
Installing the
Teams app from
the Apple App
Store.

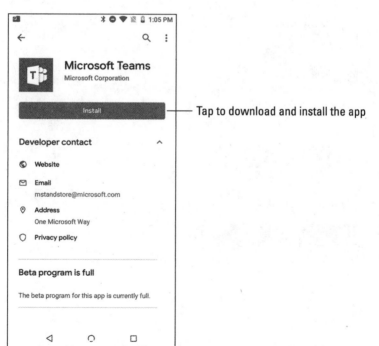

Tap to download and install the app

FIGURE 6-2:
Installing the
Teams app from
the Google Play
Store.

When you first open the Teams mobile app, you are presented with a sign-in screen where you can choose to sign in to Teams, as shown in Figure 6-3. Tap the Sign In button and then enter your Microsoft 365 credentials you created when you signed up for the Microsoft 365 trial in Chapter 1. Teams loads and walks you through some tips on using the app. Once you get through the tips, you can start working with Teams, as you will see in the next section.

TIP

If you have already signed in to any other Microsoft 365 app on your mobile device, such as Outlook, you can just select that account and Teams will automatically log you in using the credentials that are already cached on the device.

TIP

If you want to skip signing up for Microsoft 365, you can also sign up for a free account just by downloading the app on your mobile device and then tapping the Sign Up for Free button shown earlier in Figure 6-3.

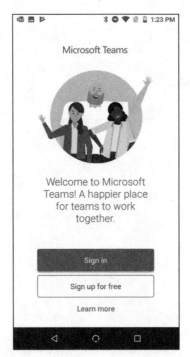

FIGURE 6-3:
Signing in to the Teams mobile app.

Finding Your Way Around the Teams Mobile App

Something I really love about Teams is that it doesn't matter what client I am using — the desktop and laptop version or the mobile app — the concepts and options are all the same. I have used the Teams client on my Mac, iPad, Android phone, Windows laptop, and my iPhone. Because Teams is a new application that was only created in the last few years, Microsoft took the opportunity to build all the clients at the same time. The interfaces are slightly different because they are optimized for the device you are using, but once you get familiar with the concepts in Teams, you can use any client and feel comfortable in how to use it.

TIP

If you are a Linux fan, you will be happy to learn that Microsoft Teams is now also available for Linux.

Throughout the previous chapters, I discuss the left navigation pane in the Teams web and desktop and laptop apps. The Teams mobile app is similar, except instead of accessing the Teams icons in the left navigation pane, the app includes tabs across the bottom of the screen, as shown in Figure 6-4. You get to your profile settings (see Figure 6-5) by tapping the Settings icon, which is also called the hamburger menu because the icon's three layers look like a hamburger. Here you can do things like set your status and status message, turn on or off notifications, learn about new features, and access additional settings specific for the mobile app.

Three settings control the settings for the Teams mobile app in general, as shown in Figure 6-6:

» **Dark theme:** When you enable this feature, the colors of the app switch to dark colors. By default, Teams uses lighter colors, but you may prefer the darker colors when using the app in low-light situations.

» **Notifications:** Use this setting to update how you get notified by Teams. You can set the hours you want Teams to be quiet and not send you notifications; set if you want the Teams mobile app to only send notifications when you are not active on the desktop app; configure notifications for incoming calls, missed calls, ongoing calls, chats, likes, and reactions; and set other notification-related settings.

» **Data and storage:** It would be nice if everyone had unlimited data on their mobile devices, but unfortunately this is not the case (as I can attest). Using these settings, you can set the quality (size) of images you upload, clear temporary files and app data, and clear your chat history to help manage the data load on your mobile device.

Tap to open the Settings menu

FIGURE 6-4:
Viewing the
navigational tabs
across the
bottom of the
Teams
mobile app.

Teams navigational icons

Additional settings may be set for each specific team, as shown in Figure 6-7:

» **Profile:** You can set your profile picture and view your activity, organizational chart, email address, and phone number with this setting.

» **Messaging:** Use this setting to show channels in your chat list. When you tap the Chat tab at the bottom of your mobile screen, you will then see your channels in addition to your private chats.

» **Shifts:** Shifts is a new feature that stems from a service called StaffHub. The Shifts functionality is designed for shift workers. You can set up reminders for your work shifts, set timing on when notifications should appear before your work shifts, and clear shifts app data.

» **About:** This setting provides information about the mobile app, such as the version, privacy and cookies, terms of use, and third-party software notices and information.

» **Help & feedback:** Click this setting to view Help information and provide feedback to Microsoft about the app.

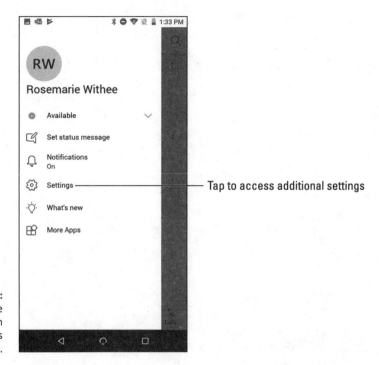

Tap to access additional settings

FIGURE 6-5:
The profile
settings menu in
the Teams
mobile app.

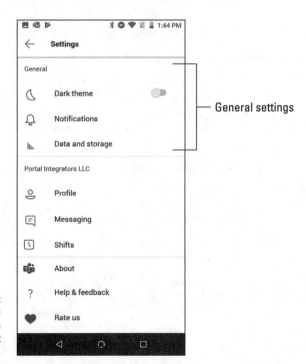

General settings

FIGURE 6-6:
The general
mobile Settings
for Microsoft
Teams.

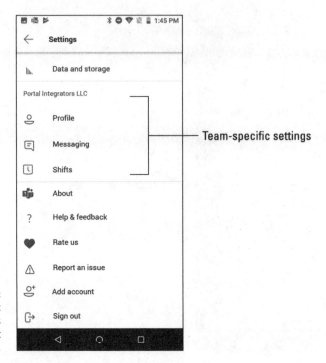

FIGURE 6-7:
The team-specific
mobile settings
for Microsoft
Teams.

>> **Rate us:** Use this setting to rate the app on the relevant app store.

>> **Report an issue:** Use this setting to report an issue about the app to Microsoft.

>> **Add account:** With this setting, you can add an additional account to use the app. I do this when I work with clients that set up an account for me in their Office 365 subscription. I can use multiple accounts with my Teams app on my phone.

>> **Sign out:** Use this setting to sign out of the Teams app. This is useful if you work in more than one organization. For example, I have a Teams account where I use my @portalintegrators.com email account. I use this for any work related to Portal Integrators. I have another Teams account specific to this book.

Tapping Your Way through Teams

The Teams mobile app, like any other mobile app, is designed to be used by tapping your fingers on the screen of your phone or tablet. I have found Teams to be intuitive; however, there are a few differences between using your keyboard and mouse and using your fingers.

Interacting with messages

In Chapter 4 you learn about reacting to messages in channels and chats. Using reactions, you can add a happy face, a thumbs up, or any number of different emojis to your chat messages. In addition, you can interact with messages in a number of different ways. You can:

>> Save a message so that you can quickly find and review it later.

>> Mark a message as unread so that it continues to show as new in Teams.

>> Copy a link to the direct message.

>> Open the message in the immersive reader, which will read the message for you and show you each word as it is read.

>> Turn on notifications for the message thread.

>> Create a new poll that will be attached to the message. (This is handy when someone brings up a topic that needs input from others.)

TIP

If you are reacting to your own message, then you have additional options such as being able to edit or delete the message. If you don't see these options for your own messages, then your administrator has turned off your ability to edit or delete messages.

When you are using Teams with your keyboard and mouse, you can hover your mouse over a message or click the ellipsis to see these interactions. However, when you are using Teams on your mobile device, hovering your finger isn't an option. Instead, you need to tap and hold on the message in order to bring up the same menu, as shown in Figure 6-8.

TIP

If you get stuck and cannot find a menu when navigating Teams on a mobile device, try tapping and holding as an option. Using a mouse, you can hover your mouse over elements of the interface to see menus, but hovering is not an option when using your fingers!

TIP

If you are reacting to a message in a chat, you must tap and hold to access the reaction options, but if you are reacting to a message thread in a channel, you will see a tiny ellipsis and you can tap that, too. I find it easier to just tap and hold a message in either a chat or a channel in order to bring up the menu shown in Figure 6-8.

FIGURE 6-8:
Reacting to a
message using
Teams on a
phone or tablet.

Getting used to navigation

As mentioned earlier in this chapter, navigation through the Teams mobile app is slightly different than when using your keyboard and mouse. Rather than clicking navigational icons along the left side of the app, in the mobile version these icons are found along the bottom of the app (refer to Figure 6-4).

The experience is optimized for mobile devices, which means the flow is slightly different in the mobile app because the amount of space on a mobile device is much smaller than a laptop or desktop computer screen. One key difference in navigation is that the screens you navigate may require more taps to the screen than the associated clicks with your mouse. For example, when you tap the Chat icon at the bottom of your mobile app, you will see all the chats you currently have going on.

Navigating into your chats on your mobile device is very similar to the keyboard behavior. However, if you tap the Teams option, you will be presented with all the teams and channels you have. You then you need to tap again to open one of those channels, as shown in Figure 6-9. On a large monitor you can see all the teams and channels at the same time you see the associated messages in the channel. With the mobile app, you need to make another tap in order to get into the channel, and if you want to change channels, you need to tap the back icon and then select a different channel.

FIGURE 6-9:
Tapping a
channel in the list
of teams on a
mobile phone.

TIP

Navigating Teams on a mobile device can take more taps than the associated clicks when using Teams on a laptop or desktop. Even though the mobile app takes more work to navigate, it is worth the effort because the experience on a mobile device is designed for smaller screens and using your fingers instead of a mouse.

Organizing Your Home Life

Raise your hand if you've ever had to plan a birthday party or a vacation with extended family and/or friends. Emailing the plans back and forth between all interested parties and then using text messages to follow up can get cumbersome. Not to mention all of the different messages can make it difficult to keep track of all the details. Having a single place to hold conversations and share documents will make planning and executing any party or family vacation feel much easier.

The Microsoft Teams app lets you do just that: with text messaging, voice and video calling, the ability to share files between contacts, and the ability to share your location in real time, you can keep the busyness of life at bay under one umbrella, er, app.

TIP

If you already have the Microsoft Teams app downloaded on your mobile device or desktop, you do not need to download another version to use it to organize your home life. All you need to do is to log in to Microsoft Teams using your personal account.

Using the mobile app for chatting

To use the Teams mobile app to chat, follow these steps:

1. **Open the Teams mobile app on your smartphone.**

2. **Select your Personal Teams account from the Accounts and Orgs list.**

3. **Select the Chat icon from the navigation bar at the bottom of the screen.**

   The Chat screen opens.

TIP

4. **Select the note icon that appears in the upper-right corner.**

   This icon looks like a piece of paper and a pencil.

   On the next screen, you will see a search box that starts with To:, a link for New Group Chat, and list labeled "Suggestions." The suggested names are contacts from your contacts list who are using Microsoft Teams.

5. **Select the name of the contact (or the group name if you created a group).**

   The contact appears in the To: field of the chat screen.

6. **To send a chat, tap in the text box labeled "Type a message," and type your message as you would for any chat application, as shown in Figure 6-10.**

7. **Tap the paper airplane symbol to send your chat when you're done.**

TIP

Creating a specific group can help keep your chat conversations organized. To create a group chat, select the note icon on the upper-right corner to start a new chat as described earlier in Step 3. Select the "New Group Chat" link and add a name for the group. Click Next and then add the names of the contacts you want to be added to the group chat. If your contact has not joined Microsoft Teams yet, that contact will get an invite and will be added to the group when they accept the invitation.

FIGURE 6-10:
Using chat on a mobile phone.

Using the mobile app for calling

To use the Teams mobile app to make phone calls, follow these steps:

1. Open the Teams mobile app on your smartphone.

2. Select your Personal Teams account from the Accounts and Orgs list.

HELP! MY CONTACT ISN'T USING TEAMS!

If the person you want to send a chat message to isn't using Microsoft Teams yet, no need to panic. You just need to invite that person to join Teams. Instead of selecting the name of the person from the list of suggestions Teams offers when you click the note icon, start typing the name or the email address of the person you want to invite to Microsoft Teams in the To: field. If the email address is already saved on your device, it will appear in the search results. Select the email address and it will appear in the To: field, along with a Send Invite button. Tap the Send Invite button to send an email invite. Once your contact accepts your invitation and logs in to Teams, you will see that person's contact information on the main Teams screen and you can chat away!

3. **Tap the Calls icon at the bottom of the screen on an iOS device; tap More and then Calls on an Android device.**

4. **Search for the name of the person you want to call and select that person's name.**

   Note that you can only call someone who is already in your Microsoft Teams contacts list.

5. **On the pop-up menu that appears, select phone icon to place a voice call or the camera icon to place a video call.**

TIP

Some of the call features you can use are putting someone on hold, sharing your screen, raising your hand, using a blurred background, and turning off incoming video if you need to save bandwidth. Access these options by tapping the ellipsis icon on the call screen.

Sharing files with contacts or groups

The chat and calling features discussed so far are par for the course for any messaging app like Viber, WhatsApp, Facebook Messenger, and so on. What sets Microsoft Teams apart from the others is that it lets you share documents with your contacts. Here's how:

1. **Open the Teams mobile app on your smartphone.**

2. **Select your Personal Teams account from the Accounts and Orgs list.**

3. **In the Search bar, search for the contact or group you want to share files with.**

   At the bottom of the screen, you will see an Activity icon, Chat icon, Calendar icon, Files icon, and the ellipses for more options.

4. **Select the Files icon.**

   A list of the available locations where you can select the file you want to share appears (see Figure 6-11).

5. **Select the storage location from this screen and navigate to the file you want to share.**

6. **Select the file you want to share.**

   Teams gives you the option to type a message.

7. **When you are ready to send the file, click Send.**

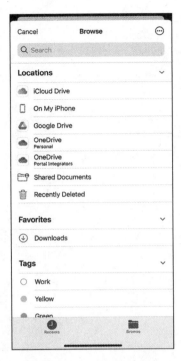

FIGURE 6-11:
Selecting the location of the file you want to share.

Planning events

Now that you know how to chat and share files on Microsoft Teams, you can use it the next time you plan an event. Create a group chat with the people you need to collaborate with and name the chat the name of the event. Doing this can help everyone to stay focused on the subject matter. Any conversations not related to the planning of the event can be had in a different group chat. Easily share a task list on a spreadsheet or that PowerPoint file for that slide show.

To create an event invite, follow these steps:

1. **Select the group chat you created for the event.**

2. **Select the Calendar icon.**

3. **Select the plus (+) icon in the upper-right corner to add a new event.**

   The New Event screen appears, as shown in Figure 6-12.

4. **Enter the information for the event.**

5. **Select Done.**

   The new event is added to your calendar and an invite is sent to the group you selected.

FIGURE 6-12:
Creating a new
event.

Sharing your location

Ten years ago, I went on vacation with my family to Disneyland in Hong Kong. Like anyone who has been to a Disneyland park, I know all too well how easy it is to lose track of someone in the park. One person decides to go one way, while others go another way, and then like that the person is out of sight. But Teams provides a way to help prevent this. Before you go on vacation, make sure every member of the entourage is using Microsoft Teams. If you have not already, create a group, and add all the members of the entourage to that group. Then, share your locations between the group members and voila! You can keep track of everyone without needing to make several phone calls to keep confirming locations.

To share your location within Teams, follow these steps:

1. **Select the name of the contact or group you want to share your location with.**

2. **On the bottom of the screen, select the location icon.**

3. **Select Share your live location.**

   You have the option of how long to share your location.

4. **Choose either 30 mins, 1 day, or Always On.**

5. **Choose Send Location.**

   Your location will appear on the chat screen. Any member of the group chat can click the link and see your location.

6. **To stop sharing your location, click the map you shared and click Stop Sharing.**

   Once you stop sharing, a message will appear on the chat window informing the members of the group that you have stopped sharing your location.

Chapter **7**

Working with People Outside Your Organization

I spend most of my time working online with people from many different companies, with freelancers, and with other consultants. Rarely are we all in the same organization and on the same Microsoft 365 subscription. Microsoft has built features into Microsoft Teams that enable people to work together even if they aren't a part of the same company or organization. Most of this functionality is built into features known as *guest access*, and that is the focus of this chapter.

In this chapter, you learn about guest access in Microsoft Teams and how to add people to your team who are outside of your organization and Microsoft 365 subscription. You learn how to configure the access guest users have and how to limit their access based on the level of comfort and privacy needed for your situation. You also look at the differences between a guest user and an external user and configure the permission settings for both.

Understanding How Teams Works with People Outside Your Organization

If only the world were nice and neat, and you only needed to communicate and collaborate with people inside your organization. If you are like me, that isn't the case. You probably work with people inside and outside your organization to get your work done. The good news is that if you work with consultants or freelancers or vendors or other companies, you can add them as guests to your team in Microsoft Teams.

How guests are added to your team depends on whether or not Teams considers them members of your organization:

>> When you add people to your Microsoft 365 subscription, they are considered part of your organization and you can add them as members to your teams and channels in Teams. (Yes, the wording can be awkward!)

>> Anyone you add to Teams who is *not* part of your Microsoft 365 subscription gets added as a guest user.

There may come a time when you need to be able to communicate and collaborate with another Microsoft 365 organization. For example, suppose your organization is called Contoso, and another separate organization is called Acme. Both Contoso and Acme have different Microsoft 365 subscriptions, so their users are separate from each other. Both organizations are part of the Microsoft cloud, however, and can view each other there. Acme users see Contoso users (and vice versa) as *external users.* In other words, the users in each organization are still in different organizations, but both are part of the Microsoft cloud.

TECHNICAL STUFF

Microsoft has started calling these users *Azure Active Directory business-to-business users,* which is really a mouthful! I prefer *external users* even though it is easy to confuse with the term *guest users.*

Let's dive into the differences and get a feel for guest users and external users in Teams.

REMEMBER

A *guest user* can be anywhere in the world. All the person needs is an email address to be invited to your teams as a guest. Guest users do not need to have a Microsoft 365 subscription. An *external user* is someone who is part of another Microsoft 365 subscription — their subscription is separate from yours.

Working with Guest Users

For someone to be able to see your channels and chat with you in Teams, that person needs to be part of your team in Teams. The way you add people to your team as a guest is by inviting them. Once the person has joined your team, you can chat, share files, and collaborate.

Enabling guest access

Before you can add guests to your team, the subscription administrator must turn on the Guest Access feature in the Teams Admin Center. You must also be the owner of the team in order to add and remove members or guests.

TIP

An easy way to know if you have the ability to add guest users is to click the ellipsis to the right of one of your teams in the left navigation pane to open the More Options drop-down menu. Select the Add Member option. If you can add guest users, the text in the Add Members dialog box will say "Start typing a name, distribution list, or security group to add to your team. You can also add people outside your organization as guests by typing their email addresses."

To enable guest access in the Teams Admin Center, follow these steps:

1. **Open your web browser and log in to the Teams Admin Center at** https://admin.teams.microsoft.com.

   Note that you need to be a Teams administrator in order to access the Teams Admin Center. If you signed up for the Microsoft 365 subscription (see Chapter 1), then you are an administrator by default.

2. **In the left navigation pane, select Org-Wide Settings and then Guest Access.**

   The Guest Access screen appears, where you can toggle this option on or off.

3. **Toggle the setting to allow guest access to Teams, as shown in Figure 7-1.**

   Once you toggle on guest access, additional settings appear, as shown in Figure 7-2. There are settings for calls, meetings, and messaging, and you can toggle them on or off based on your preferences.

4. **Click the Save button to save your changes.**

   Guest access is now enabled for Teams.

WARNING

I have seen Teams take up to 24 hours for changes to take effect. If the changes don't happen within 48 hours though, it's time to open a support ticket and find out what is going on.

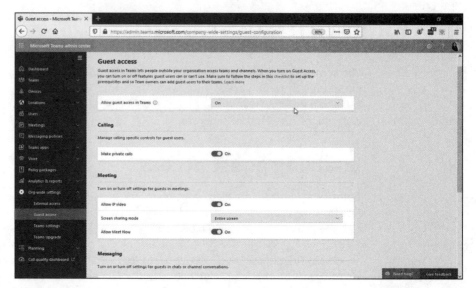

FIGURE 7-1:
Turning on guest
access for Teams.

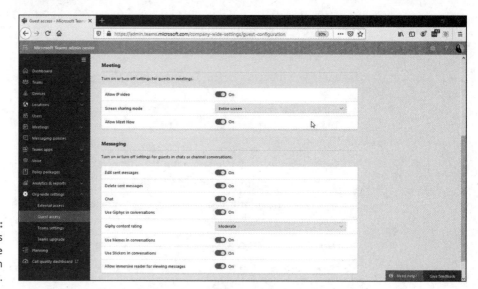

FIGURE 7-2:
Guest access
settings in the
Teams Admin
Center.

Configuring guest settings

When you turn on guest access in Teams (see the previous section if you still need to do so), you allow users to invite guests to their teams. In the Guest Access screen shown in Figure 7-1, you can fine-tune the settings for guest users with settings for calling, meetings, and messages.

Calling settings

>> **Make private calls:** This setting allows guests to make peer-to-peer calls using the Internet through Teams. This doesn't mean guests can make actual phone calls; in order to have a phone number assigned and make phone calls, they must be a full member of your Microsoft subscription and have the appropriate license in place. (See Chapter 11 for more about making phone calls through Teams.)

Meeting settings

>> **Allow IP video:** This setting lets guest users include video in team meetings, chats, and calls. I have found some companies don't allow video with guests for compliance reasons. Perhaps they are afraid of inappropriate video communication using company resources.

>> **Screen sharing mode:** Similar to allowing video or not, this setting allows users to screen share or not. *Screen sharing* is when you share your computer screen with the other members of the team during a meeting. You can configure this setting to disable screen sharing all together, allow sharing of only a single software application at a time, or allow sharing of the entire computer screen. Compliance reasons are the usual cause for turning this setting off. I can imagine someone innocently sharing their screen to a guest user when the internal company earnings email comes out. Oops!

>> **Allow Meet Now:** The Meet Now functionality provides a quick way to create an ad hoc meeting. The alternative is that a Teams user needs to create a calendar meeting and include the guest users in the meeting. When this happens, the meeting is part of the calendar system and it is clear who is attending. The Meet Now functionality, on the other hand, is an ad hoc meeting; think of it like making a phone call. This setting gives you control over whether you will allow guest users to start Meet Now ad hoc meetings or not.

Messaging settings

>> **Edit sent messages:** This setting turns on or off the ability for guests to edit the messages they have sent in Teams. If this setting is disabled, you have to be prepared for some random messages and mistyping or mis-sending of messages. However, often for compliance reasons, you may want a record of every message a guest has sent. This can help prevent the tricky situation when someone said he said one thing but then when you go back and look at the message, it says something different because it had been edited.

>> **Delete sent messages:** For similar reasons you might not want to allow guests to edit their messages; you can use this setting to disallow guests from deleting messages they have sent.

>> **Chat:** Sending messages in an official channel is a lot different than sending personal chat messages to individual users. You can use this setting to allow guests to use official Teams channels but not send private messages to individual users.

>> **Use Giphys in conversations:** A Giphy is an animated image in the GIF format. Teams uses an online database of these animated images, and you can choose to let guest users send them in messages or not. Some of the popular Giphys I have seen include everything from lighthearted scenes from popular sitcoms to violence from the latest blockbusters. The online database Teams uses can be found at https://giphy.com.

>> **Giphy content rating:** If you do choose to let guest users send Giphys, you can fine-tune how strict you want to be with the content they include. The online Giphy database includes content ratings, and you can decide if you want to disallow content based on those ratings.

>> **Use Memes in conversations:** Like a Giphy, a Meme is a way to include more emotion and connection in messages. A Meme is a short comic book–type depiction of a popular theme. You can allow guests to insert Memes in messages or not with this setting.

>> **Use Stickers in conversations:** A sticker is another way to show emotion and create connection and shared experience using messages. Just like a physical sticker, a virtual sticker might be an image or a drawing or a picture. You can choose whether to allow guests to include stickers or not with this setting.

>> **Allow immersive reader for viewing messages:** The Windows immersive reader opens a message and reads it aloud with a line appearing under each word as it is pronounced by the computer. You can decide if you want to allow guest users to open messages in the Windows immersive reader or not.

Inviting guests to the team

To work with guest users, you need to first add them to one of your teams. It is important to remember that guest users can be anyone outside your organization.

TIP

As a best practice, I like to make sure the title of the team to which I am inviting guest users includes the wording "Internal and External Users" so that it is clear to everyone that the discussion happening in the channels is not confidential.

To add a guest user to your team, follow these steps:

1. **Select the Teams icon in the left navigation pane to see a list of all your teams.**

2. **Next to the team you would like to add a guest user, click the ellipsis and select Add Member from the More Options drop-down menu, as shown in Figure 7-3.**

   The Add Members dialog box appears. Make sure the message at the top of the dialog says that you can also add people outside your organization. If you don't see this, refer back to "Enabling guest access" earlier in the chapter to turn on the Guest Access feature in the Teams Admin Center.

FIGURE 7-3:
Choosing Add
Member from the
More Options
drop-down menu.

3. **Type the email address of the person you would like to add to the team.**

   Once the email is verified as valid, you can select it from the drop-down menu that appears (see Figure 7-4).

4. **Enter as many email addresses as you would like to add and then click the Add button, as shown in Figure 7-5.**

5. **Click the Close button to close the dialog box.**

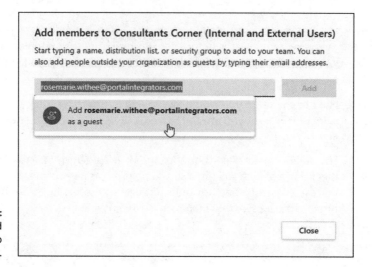

FIGURE 7-4:
Choosing a valid
email address to
add as a guest.

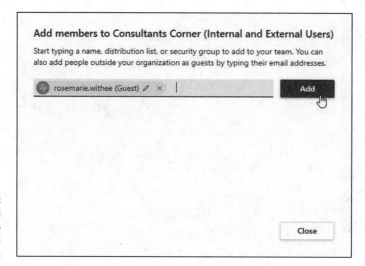

FIGURE 7-5:
Adding email
addresses as
guest users in
Teams.

REMEMBER

Once you have added guest users, you can send them chat messages in the channel. And don't forget that you can mention them using the @ ("at") symbol. When you @ tag someone, that person is notified, based on their notification settings, that you are trying to get his or her attention. (I cover setting your notifications in Chapter 8.)

On the guest user side, that person will receive an email message that invites them to join the team. If that person's email address is already associated with a user in Teams, then that user can immediately start chatting with you. If the guest user is brand new to Teams, they will be guided through a setup process and can start chatting with you using the web version of Teams. The guest user experience is refreshingly straightforward. I have been sitting next to people who have never heard of Teams before get the email invitation to join a team and they are able to start chatting in minutes. Hurray for Microsoft getting this part of the process right!

In addition to adding guests using their email addresses, you can also get a URL link to the team and send that link to anyone you want to invite to join the channel. When invitees click the link, they can log in with their Microsoft accounts and they are automatically joined to the team as a guest, as shown in Figure 7-6. You can get a link to the team by going to the More Options drop-down menu next to the team and selecting the Get Link to Team option. You will find the link on the drop-down menu when you click the ellipsis next to the name of a team.

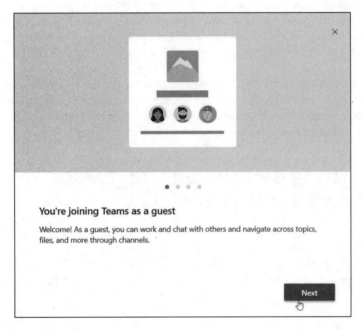

You're joining Teams as a guest

Welcome! As a guest, you can work and chat with others and navigate across topics, files, and more through channels.

Next

FIGURE 7-6:
A guest can join a team using a special link.

WARNING

When using the link to invite people to join a team or channel, make sure you keep the link a secret. Anyone with the link will be able to join the team as a guest, so treat it like a special ticket and only give it to people you want to be able to join the team.

Understanding the guest user experience

The general experience of collaborating with a guest user is almost identical to working with colleagues on the same Microsoft 365 subscription. However, there are some differences.

If you choose to allow it, you can let guest users create channels, participate in channel conversations and private chats, post and edit messages, and share channels. However, guest users cannot create teams, join public teams, view org charts, share files from a private chat, add apps, create meetings, access schedules, access OneDrive files, or invite other guests. There are also many limitations for guests regarding using voice and calling features in Teams. If you are interested in learning more about this topic, Microsoft has an excellent article titled "What the guest experience is like," and you can search for it using your favorite search engine. It goes into all the nitty-gritty detail of working with Teams as a guest, and I refer to it and the tables it contains whenever I am working with a guest user and we are trying to figure out why something works for me but not for them.

TIP

You can fine-tune the permissions guest users have in your teams. Earlier in the chapter, I describe the settings you can configure that affect your entire Microsoft 365 subscription, which is also known as a *tenant*. In the next section, I cover the settings you can configure for your individual teams.

Setting permissions for guest users at the team level

Earlier in this chapter, you discover how to enable guest access in the Teams Admin Center, and how to configure the various guest settings. However, those settings affect every team in Teams in your Microsoft 365 subscription. To fine-tune settings further, you can configure guest settings for each individual team.

WHAT IS A TENANT?

When you create a new Microsoft 365 subscription, you are creating a new *tenant*. Think of a tenant like you would think of a tenant in an apartment complex. An individual apartment might have multiple people living in it, but each unit is a separate space and on a separate contract from the other apartments. Similarly, your Microsoft 365 subscription can include many teams that are part of your same Teams service.

WARNING

Microsoft is adding features to Teams at a feverish pace, and additional guest settings are added to Teams all the time. So, you might see more settings than I discuss here depending on when your Microsoft 365 tenant receives them.

To configure guest settings for a team, follow these steps:

1. **Select the Teams icon from the left navigation pane to see a list of all your teams.**

2. **Click the ellipsis next to the name of the team you want to manage to open the More Option drop-down menu.**

3. **Select Manage Team.**

4. **Select the Settings tab at the top of the screen (see Figure 7-7) and then expand the Guest Permissions option.**

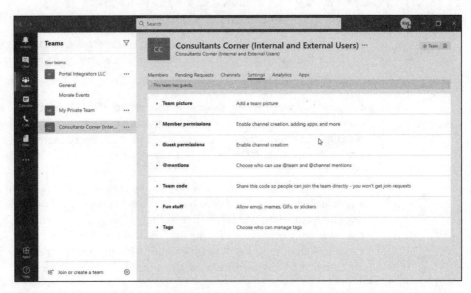

FIGURE 7-7:
Configuring guest permissions in a team.

5. **Select the options to allow guests to create or update channels or to delete channels.**

   - *Allow creating and updating channels:* This setting is used to allow guests to create new channels or update existing channels. If you have a team with a lot of guests, you might want to allow them to create new channels within the team. The number of channels in a team can quickly grow out of control, though, so I recommend coaching your guest users on your preferences if you let them create their own channels. I have seen teams with guest users that have more channels created than I ever thought possible. In the end, I suppose it depends on how well-behaved your guests are.

- *Allow guests to delete channels:* With this setting, you can allow or not allow guests to delete channels they created. This setting is often used as a compliance measure when you don't mind guests creating new channels and sending messages in them, but you don't want them to delete any of those channels.

After you make your selections, your changes are saved automatically.

Interacting with External Users

As you have seen in this chapter, you can collaborate and interact with guest users in much the same way you work with people within your organization. However, there is one more case to consider.

Suppose you work with people at Acme frequently. You need to be able to chat with them, and they need to be able to chat with your organization. However, you don't want to add every single user as a guest user for every team. You can use a feature in the Teams Admin Center called *external access.*

External access gives you the ability to approve users based on the domain in their email address. Let's say Acme has the Internet domain acme.com. You can add the domain to the external access list so that anyone with an email address @acme.com can chat with members of your organization. External access is flexible, too. You can allow all domains on the Internet and block specific domains, or you can block all domains on the Internet and allow only specific domains.

Some of the key differences between guest user access and external user access are outlined in Table 7-1 and available in the Microsoft Teams documentation at https://docs.microsoft.com/en-us/microsoftteams.

TABLE 7-1 **Key differences between guest user access and external user access in Teams**

Feature	External user access	Guest user access
User can chat with someone in another company	Yes	Yes
User can call someone in another company	Yes	Yes
User can see if someone from another company is available for call or chat	Yes	Yes
User can search for users across external tenants	Yes	No
User can share files	No	Yes
User can access Teams resources	No	Yes
User can be added to a group chat	No	Yes
User can be invited to a meeting	Yes	Yes
Additional users can be added to a chat with an external user	No	N/A
User is identified as an external party	Yes	Yes
Presence is displayed	Yes	Yes
Out of office message is shown	No	Yes
Individual user can be blocked	No	Yes
@mentions are supported	Yes	Yes
Make private calls	Yes	Yes
Allow IP video	Yes	Yes
Screen sharing mode	Yes	Yes
Allow Meet Now	No	Yes
Edit sent messages	Yes	Yes
Can delete sent messages	Yes	Yes
Use Giphy in conversation	Yes	Yes
Use memes in conversation	Yes	Yes
Use stickers in conversation	Yes	Yes

Source: https://docs.microsoft.com/en-us/microsoftteams/communicate-with-users-from-other-organizations

You will find the external access settings in the Teams Admin Center listed under Org-Wide Settings, as shown in Figure 7-8. I cover the Teams Admin Center in depth in Chapter 13.

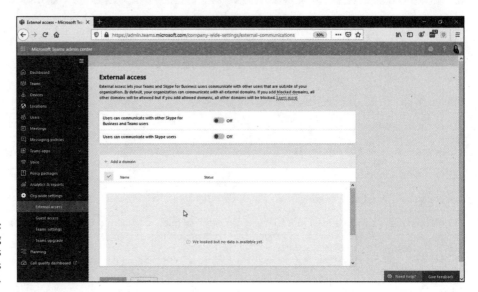

Chapter **8**

Taming the Noise and Staying Focused

When I work with organizations to adopt Microsoft Teams, I usually make the same observation: There seems to be a point when an organization goes from having a few people using Teams here and there, to everyone using Teams for all communication. When this happens, Teams becomes very noisy very fast! This is more evident as more and more people are doing work remotely and online these days. Luckily, some of the features of Teams have been designed specifically to help you get a handle on all this activity.

In this chapter, you find out how to use Teams to focus on the communication that matters to you and ignore the rest. More than ever, it is good to feel some control when even your conversations on Teams can be chaotic. You learn how to set the Activity feed to filter conversations and set up notifications for the topics important to you. I also share some of the tips I have learned over the years that help me stay focused yet be available for critically important communications.

Embracing the Activity Feed

The Activity feed is a one-stop shop for all things that are happening in Teams. I have heard Microsoft describe the Activity feed as your "inbox for Teams," and I agree. I tend to start my workday by looking at the Activity feed just like I used to start my day by looking at my email inbox.

To view your Teams Activity feed, select the Activity icon in the left navigation pane, as shown in Figure 8-1.

Click to open the Activity feed

Click to filter the Activity feed

FIGURE 8-1:
Viewing the Activity feed in Teams.

The @ symbol next to a chat

The Activity feed lists the activities that happen in Teams that you might want to pay attention to. For example, you will see the activity in the teams and channels you are following, private chats, locations where people @mention you, replies to your chats or chats you have liked, calls you have received, voicemails, and notifications from apps. You will also see activity such as someone adding you to a channel or team, chats that are trending, and chats that Teams thinks you might want to check out.

TIP

Each notification in the Activity feed includes an icon that describes the type of notification. For example, notice the @ ("at") symbol in Figure 8-1 next to a chat. The @ symbol means someone mentioned you by name in a chat.

The Activity feed includes a filter option to limit the types of activity you see in the feed. For example, suppose you want to only pay attention to when someone has @mentioned you. You can click the Filter icon (refer to Figure 8-1) and then select the @ Mentions filter, as shown in Figure 8-2.

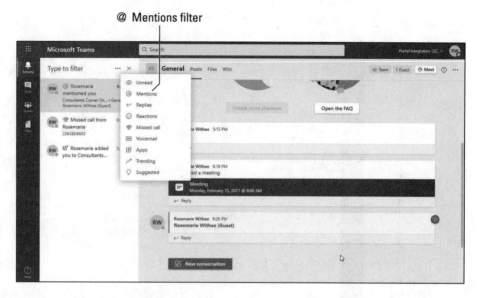

TIP

When you click an event in the Activity feed, the event changes from unread to read status. Any event you have not looked at is listed in bold text, and any event you have looked at (in other words, you have read it), is set in regular text.

Hiding and Showing Teams and Channels

The concept of a team in Teams is a grouping of people. And any person can be in multiple teams. You might be in a team that is putting together a fund-raising event, while at the same time be in your working team in finance, be part of another team that is working on a special project, be in a team that involves everyone in the company, be in a team for people who like cats, and so on.

The number of teams you can be in is only limited by people's imaginations. As Teams becomes popular in your organization, you will likely be in more teams that you ever thought possible. In addition, as you read in Chapter 4, each team can contain multiple channels. When you combine the multitude of teams you are in with the multitude of channels in each team, you can quickly see how the information can get out of control.

Fortunately, you can show or hide certain teams and channels to reduce the number of teams that show up in your navigation. To hide a team, click the ellipsis next to the name of the team and select Hide from the More Options drop-down menu, as shown in Figure 8-3. To hide a channel, you do the same thing, but click the ellipsis next to the channel you want to hide.

Click to hide a team or channel

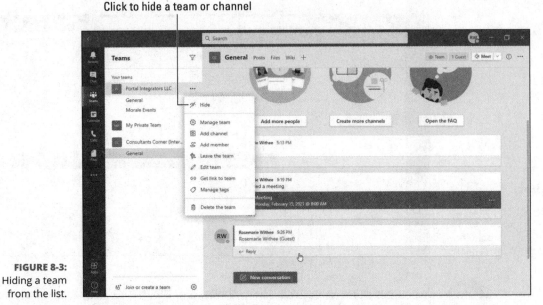

FIGURE 8-3:
Hiding a team
from the list.

When you hide a team, it moves to a collapsed section in your list of teams. When you hide a channel, it moves to a section at the bottom of the channels in a team.

When you click "Hidden Teams" or "Hidden Channels," the list expands to show the teams or channels you have hidden. To unhide a team, click the ellipsis next to the hidden team and select Show from the More Options drop-down menu. To unhide a channel, click Hidden channel, and then in the fly-out menu that shows all of the hidden channels, click Show next to the channel you want to see (see Figure 8-4).

TIP

Activity in teams or channels that is hidden will still show up in your Activity feed unless you adjust your notifications. I usually keep teams hidden when I don't need to actively follow all the conversations happening in those channels. And likewise, if there is a team I usually like to keep shown, but it has channels I don't need to actively follow, then I hide those channels. However, if I want to read and keep up on the conversations, I don't hide the team or channels so that I can actively stay in the loop.

Click to show a hidden team or channel

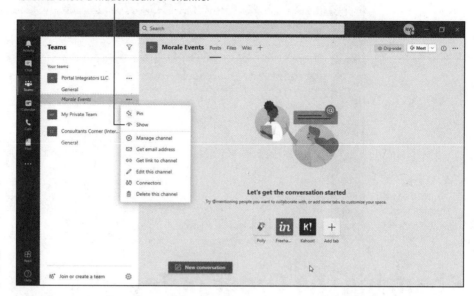

FIGURE 8-4:
Showing a hidden
channel.

Filtering by Team or Channel

As you discovered in the previous section, you can hide and show teams and channels. Even with this ability, you may also want to filter the list of teams and channels to find one in particular you are looking for. This might sound crazy until you find yourself with over a hundred teams and thousands of channels. I never realized how many teams and channels were possible until I found myself searching for a channel I know exists but cannot find in the list.

To filter the list of teams and channels, click the funnel icon at the top of the teams list, and then type in a word to filter by the name of the team or channel. In Figure 8-5 I am filtering my list of teams by the word "private."

TIP

I use the filtering feature frequently when I have a large list of channels that scrolls down past the end of my screen, and I want to jump to a team or channel without having to scroll and search.

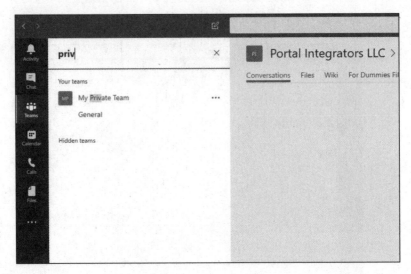

FIGURE 8-5:
Filtering the list
of teams and
channels.

Changing the Order of Teams in Your List

In general, people scan through their teams and channels from the top to the bottom. As such, you might find it helpful to keep the most important teams at the top of the list so that you spot them first. You can drag and drop teams in your list to change the order. To do this, just click and hold a team name and then drag and drop it at the location you want to move it, as shown in Figure 8-6.

Muting Channels to Decrease Notifications

You can mute a channel to stop notifications from appearing in your Activity feed if you find yourself bombarded with the constant pinging of new messages. You can still click on a channel that is muted and follow along with the conversation; however, muting it makes the process more proactive — you decide when to pay attention to and/or respond to notifications. For example, I usually mute channels that I like to keep track of but don't need to respond to frequently. Then, when I have time, I click through the channels to keep up with those conversations.

1. Click and hold the channel you want to move.

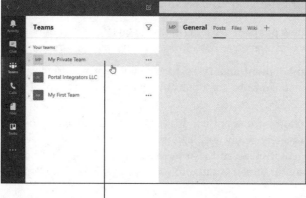

FIGURE 8-6:
Drag and drop
teams in your list
to change the
order.

2. Drag and drop the channel in the desired location.

To mute a channel, follow these steps:

1. Click the ellipsis next to the channel name you want to mute.

2. Select Channel Notifications from the drop-down menu that appears.

The Channel Notifications Settings dialog box appears, where you can adjust the settings to be notified for All Activity, turn off notifications, and set custom settings.

3. Select Off to mute the channel.

You will not be notified of new activity, except if someone directly replies to you or mentions you in a message.

TIP

For information on custom notification settings, check out the next section.

Tracking Important Activity with Custom Notifications

Even with all the features you have seen thus far in the chapter, the amount of information coming at you can quickly become overwhelming. One of the most important features you can use to sift through the mountain of chatter is the custom Teams notifications settings, where you can set how often you receive notifications of new activity in your channels.

To access the custom notifications settings, click the ellipsis next to the channel you want to adjust, select Channel Notifications, and then select Custom. Two settings appear in the Channel Notification Settings dialog box:

>> **All new posts:** This setting enables you to adjust your notifications for any new message posts (also known as new message *threads*), in a channel.

>> **Channel mentions:** This setting enables you to designate when and how you are notified when someone @mentions you in a channel.

You can choose three options for each setting. You can choose to turn off notifications completely, show notifications only in your Activity feed, or show notifications in your Activity feed and also in the Teams banner that pops up at the bottom of your computer screen (similar to when you get a new email and are notified about it).

TIP

I like to keep notifications for Channel mentions on because if someone is @mentioning me, I like to be notified right away. One area where I have had to turn this off is when someone @mentions the entire channel instead of me in particular. If you find this happening a lot in a channel and it is disrupting your work, you can turn these notifications off or only allow them in your Activity feed but not in the pop-up banner that draws your attention to them immediately.

Searching for Past Conversations

One problem I always seem to have is that I remember having a conversation, but I may not always remember the specific details such as dates, times, locations, and conclusions. If I don't write it down when I am having the conversation, then I will likely not remember it down the road. The nice thing with digital communications is that there is a record of the conversation (assuming the conversation was held in chat and not voice). Using the search functionality of Teams, you can search through all the digital conversations that have happened to jump right to the conversation you want to remember.

The search functionality takes the shape of a search box. You find the search box at the very top of the Teams application, as shown in Figure 8-7.

Click to select what you want to search

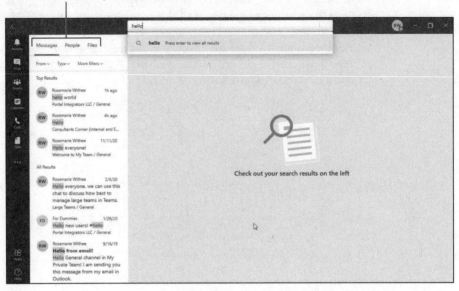

FIGURE 8-7:
Using the search
functionality in
Teams.

When searching Teams, you can search for more than just digital communications. You can also search for people who are part of the teams in your organization, and you can even search for files. Click the appropriate tab at the top of the left navigation pane to change between the results (refer to Figure 8-7).

TIP

The same textbox you use to type in search terms can be used for shortcuts as well. For example, you can type **/whatsnew** to see a listing of what is new in the app. There are many shortcuts you can type in to make routine tasks faster. If you type a slash (/) in the command window, a drop-down menu appears that lists all the available commands and a short description of what they do.

Getting Creative with Search and Hashtags

If you have used Twitter or Slack or Yammer, then you are probably familiar with the concept of a hashtag. A *hashtag* is comprised of the pound symbol (#) immediately followed by a series of characters or words. For example, #CompanyPicnic is a hashtag.

On Twitter you could click this hashtag and see any tweet that someone sent that includes this tag. In other words, a hashtag is a way to add keywords to a message in order to group it with other similar messages.

As of this writing, Teams doesn't include the functionality of hashtags. However, I use the concept of hashtags all the time in Teams. The way I like to use hashtags is to tie topics of conversation or concepts together by adding a hashtag to them. Then I can easily type the hashtag in the search bar and see all areas throughout Teams where I have added the hashtag. I use this within wikis, OneNote files, channels, and private chats.

3
Staying in Sync with Meetings and Conferencing

Discover how Microsoft Teams integrates with Outlook and shines when you use Outlook to manage and conduct your Teams meetings.

Learn how to schedule a new meeting and join an existing meeting.

Take a look at how breakout rooms and Together Mode can help create an atmosphere of togetherness in a remote work environment.

Explore Teams' built-in conference call and video call capabilities that enable you to make video calls through the Teams portal.

Explore the hardware you can use with Teams, including headsets, speakerphones, and cameras, as well as gear designed for large meeting rooms and conference calls.

Chapter **9**

Working Remotely: Embracing Teams to Make Meetings Better

The year 2020 was the year of remote work. Companies and organizations that weren't used to conducting business remotely suddenly had to adapt to working from home as the coronavirus pandemic caused many governments to issue stay-at-home orders. Although working from home provided the convenience of having no commute, it also meant that so many were now working by themselves. The lack of social interaction during a workday can be isolating.

In this chapter, you take a look at how two Teams features — breakout rooms and Together Mode — can help create an atmosphere of togetherness with your coworkers. You also take a peek at Teams Live Events, which are productions unto themselves.

But first things first. The chapter starts with an introduction to the different types of meetings Teams offers — scheduled meetings, ad hoc meetings, and private meetings — and you discover how to schedule each one of them. You also learn how to start a meeting and join an existing meeting, and you explore Teams' built-in conference call and video call capabilities, which enable you to meet with people from all over the world.

Whew, that's a lot about meetings! Let's get started.

Getting Up to Speed with Teams Meetings

A *meeting* is a general term that encompasses everything from a one-on-one chat with a friend to a presentation to hundreds of colleagues. Teams accommodates a variety of meeting types, and the way you set up a meeting in Teams depends on the frequency of the meeting and how many people need to be involved in the meeting.

The three types of Teams meetings include:

>> **Regular or recurring meetings:** Think of this type of meeting as a traditional meeting in an organization. For example, you might have a recurring team meeting that happens every Monday at 11:00 a.m. Or your colleagues might have a regular meeting to go over the latest financial reports with various people throughout the organization. These types of meetings are meetings that are scheduled on your calendar.

>> **Instant ad hoc meetings:** This is a meeting that happens instantly. For example, you might be communicating with a group of people and someone decides that it would be better to call a quick meeting to decide on something.

>> **Private meetings:** A private meeting involves a discussion with another person. I equate this meeting type to picking up the phone and calling someone.

As you work with Teams, keep in mind the type of meetings you can initiate. You can schedule a meeting, start an instant meeting with a group of people, or start a private meeting with another person.

TIP

Use the types of meetings in order to build your mental model of becoming more efficient with Teams. For example, if you need to meet with five people right away, you don't need to schedule a new meeting on everyone's calendar. You can use the Meet Now functionality to start an ad hoc meeting, which I discuss how to do later in this chapter.

Viewing Your Calendar in Teams

If you are a veteran of Microsoft Office, you are surely familiar with Outlook. Microsoft Outlook is an app that is part of the Office suite of products that you can use to manage your email, calendar, and contacts. Microsoft Teams integrates with Outlook and shines when you use Outlook to manage and conduct your Teams meetings. If you are like me, you welcome any help you can get to make your calendar and meetings schedule more organized and streamlined.

Just as you can view your calendar in Microsoft Outlook, you can view your calendar in Microsoft Teams. Your calendar is where your meetings are scheduled and where you can view what meetings you need to attend. Click the Calendar icon in the left navigation pane, as shown in Figure 9-1, to open your Outlook calendar in Teams.

Click to open your calendar   Click to start an ad hoc meeting

FIGURE 9-1:
Viewing your
Outlook calendar
in Teams.

TIP

The Calendar navigational item only shows up as an option in Teams if you have Outlook installed on the same computer. If your Office 365 subscription includes the Office clients, you can install them by logging in at `https://office.com`. Once you log in, you should see a button that says Install Office on the main landing page. The process is covered in detail in *Microsoft Office 365 For Dummies* (Wiley).

You can view your calendar in Teams in several ways. You can view by the day, by the week, and by the workweek. You can change the view with the selector in the top-right corner of your calendar. By default, the view selector is set to Work Week.

Creating a New Meeting and Inviting People

With Teams, you can create an instant or ad hoc meeting to connect with someone right away, or you can schedule a meeting for the future that will appear as a meeting on the invitee's Outlook calendar. To create an ad hoc meeting, click the Meet Now button in the top-right corner of your calendar (shown earlier in Figure 9-1). When you click the Meet Now button, a meeting will be created, and you are instantly able to join it, as shown in Figure 9-2.

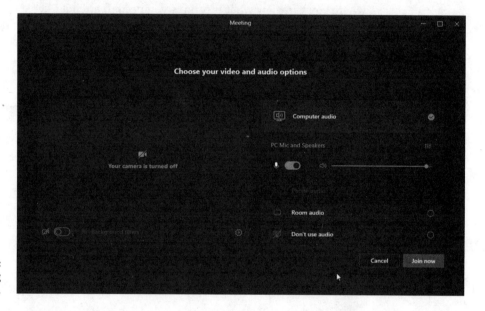

FIGURE 9-2:
Joining a meeting
in Teams.

TIP

When you join a meeting in Teams, you have the option of turning on or off your video and microphone before you join.

When you first create a Meet Now meeting, you will be the only one in the meeting. You can invite others to join your meeting by selecting Meeting Participants from the icons that appear in the middle of the meeting window and then writing the name of the person you want to invite.

TIP

You can also start an ad hoc audio or video call directly from a chat by clicking the video camera or Phone icon. You will find these icons in the top-right corner of the screen when you are chatting with someone, or when you hover your mouse over the name of a person in a channel. The icons will appear, and you can start an audio or video call with them or even send them a chat or email. I cover chat functionality in Chapter 4.

Meeting instantly is a nice feature, and I use it often. However, many of my meetings are also scheduled in advance and booked on other people's calendars. This is a task I used to do in Outlook but find myself using Teams for nowadays.

To schedule a new meeting in Teams, follow these steps:

1. **Click the Calendar icon in the left navigation pane to open your Outlook calendar.**

2. **Select the New Meeting button, which is just to the right of the Meet Now button.**

   Both buttons are shown in Figure 9-1. You are presented with a New Meeting dialog box to set up the meeting, as shown in Figure 9-3.

   You can also browse your calendar and click on a day and time to open the New Meeting dialog box.

TIP

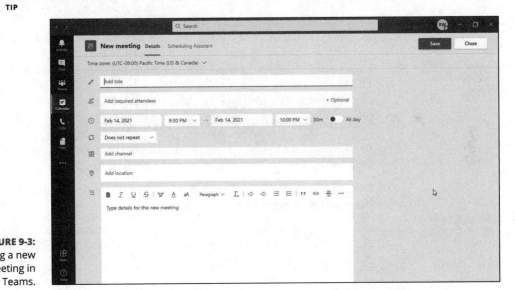

FIGURE 9-3:
Scheduling a new meeting in Teams.

3. **Provide a title, location, date, time, and details for the meeting.**

4. **Invite people to your meeting by typing the name of a person into the Invite People textbox.**

   As you type, Teams offers suggestions of team members based on the name you start to type.

5. **Select the person or people you want to invite from the list of team members.**

You can also invite people who are external to your organization if you have that feature enabled. See Chapter 7 for more information about working with external users.

TECHNICAL STUFF

(Optional) One nuance of a Teams meeting is that you can make the meeting available and open to anyone in an existing Teams channel. To do this, choose the channel you want to access from the Select a Channel to Meet In drop-down menu. When you do this, the meeting will appear in the channel. When the meeting starts, anyone in the channel can join it. In addition, all the chat conversations of the meeting and recording appear in that Teams channel.

I like to think of this option as a transparency feature. Even though I might only need to meet with three people, I can give everyone in the channel the option of joining the meeting. This also lets everyone in the channel view the recording, the chat logs, and any files that were shared. In other words, the meeting is transparent to everyone in the channel, even if only a few were invited. Because I am unable to meet in person with the people I am working with, this has become a lifesaver. We get to be on the same page without much effort.

Once you have added people to the invitation, Teams shows you their availability. The scheduling assistant will also kick into gear and you will see common times when people are available based on their Outlook calendars. To see more detail, you can click the Scheduling Assistant link to view the calendar availability for each attendee. This meeting functionality has been a part of Outlook for a long time, and it is now integrated with Teams.

6. **Select the Schedule button to create the meeting.**

A summary of the meeting is displayed, and you can edit it if you made any mistakes.

7. **Once you are satisfied with the meeting, select the Close button to close the New Meeting dialog box.**

The meeting is now scheduled on your calendar, as shown in Figure 9-4. In addition, if you selected a Teams channel for the meeting, it will appear in the channel as well (see Figure 9-5).

REMEMBER

The calendar in Teams is tied to Microsoft Outlook. If you open Outlook and look at your calendar, you will see the meeting you just created in Teams, as shown in Figure 9-6. You can also schedule a Teams meeting directly from Outlook. When you are in Outlook, and you want to schedule a Teams meeting, click the button that says New Event in the upper-left corner.

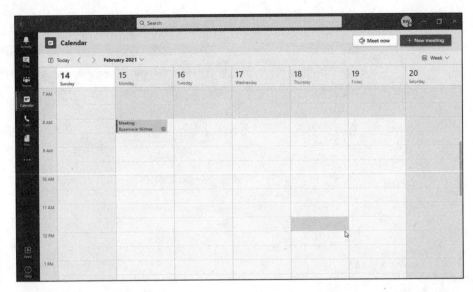

FIGURE 9-4:
A meeting on your calendar in Teams.

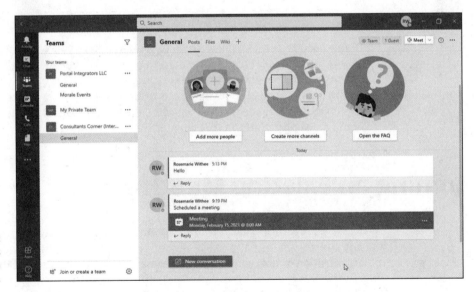

FIGURE 9-5:
A meeting that is shared with a Teams channel.

Outlook integrates with many different types of meeting software. Because Teams comes with many of the Office 365 subscriptions, I see most organizations quickly adopt Teams. However, if your organization uses other meeting software, such as GoToMeeting, you will have a similar experience in Outlook.

Click to schedule a new meeting

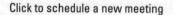

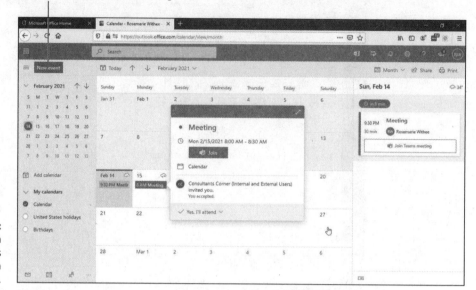

FIGURE 9-6:
FIGURE 9-6:
Viewing a
scheduled Teams
meeting in
Outlook.

TIP

If you need to broadcast an event to many people, you can use a feature called Teams Live Events. This feature used to be called Skype Meeting Broadcast, and it is designed for presentations to a very large audience. If your Office 365 subscription includes Teams Live Events, you will see the option to create a regular meeting or create a live event when you click the Schedule Meeting button. (See "What Are Live Events?" later in this chapter for more about Teams Live Events.)

Joining an Existing Meeting

One of the features that has made Teams the fastest growing product in Microsoft's history is its ease of use in joining meetings. Whether you are part of the organization or not, you can join a Teams meeting with a few clicks of your mouse.

The most straightforward way of joining a Teams meeting is when your organization already uses Microsoft Office. If you are familiar with the meeting reminders that pop up from Outlook, then you already know how to join a Teams meeting. Those Outlook meeting reminders include a Join Online button that connects you to the meeting. When you join a meeting this way, you have the option to turn on or off your web cam or mute your microphone.

You can also find the link to join the Teams meeting by opening the meeting from your Outlook calendar. Click the meeting in your calendar, and the link to join appears in the meeting description, as shown in Figure 9-7. If you are signed in to Teams, you will also get a notification when a Teams meeting starts. The notification lets you know that someone has started the Teams meeting and that you can join.

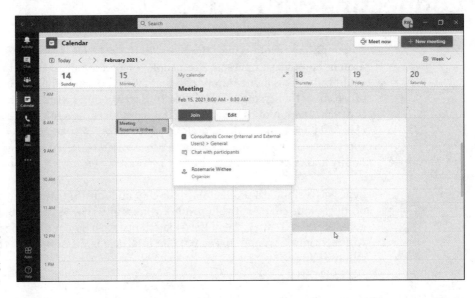

FIGURE 9-7:
Joining a Teams meeting by opening an Outlook meeting in your calendar.

REMEMBER

You can install Teams on Windows, Mac, and Linux. If you are using a temporary computer, you can use the web version of Teams. You can also install Teams on your mobile device running iOS or Android. However, I find attending meetings to be more productive when I am sitting at a desk using a full keyboard, video camera, and microphone on my laptop or desktop computer. Installing the Teams client is discussed in Chapter 3.

Using Teams for Conference Calls

If you expect people to call into the meeting using a traditional phone number, you can set up Audio Conferencing. Setting up Audio Conferencing requires you to obtain a phone plan, which I cover how to do in Chapter 12. When you set up the Audio Conferencing feature in Teams, a traditional phone number will be assigned to the meeting. Participants will then be able to dial into the audio portion of the meeting using a traditional phone. However, these attendees won't get the full meeting experience of sharing files and video.

The Audio Conferencing feature is not available in every country. You can check if it is available in your country by using your favorite search engine and searching for *Audio Conferencing in Microsoft Teams.* You can also search the official Microsoft site at `https://docs.microsoft.com`.

Connecting with Video

Meetings have evolved over the years. In the old days, everyone would crowd into a room and meet in person. For people who were not in the same location, they could call into a phone number so that everyone could share a line and hear each other. All of that changed when meetings went online with Lync and Skype. Teams is a continuation of these tried and true products, and Microsoft has evolved and consolidated its meeting technology with Teams. In 2020, we saw the explosion of everyone making video calls whether for work, school, or staying connected with family and friends.

Lync was a standard product used for chat and meetings for many years. Then the product name changed to Skype for Business and now Skype for Business has been gobbled up by Teams. If you have experience with any of these past products, you will feel right at home in Teams. The interface is different, but the concepts are still the same.

MEETING CHATTER

Often a Teams meeting will have a chat going during the meeting, and everyone in the team can enter messages and follow along. The presenter can review the chat conversations and answer questions as time permits. In addition, people can share links and files in the chat portion of a meeting. One of the things I like about the chat portion of Teams is that I can always catch up later and see any of the discussions and chatter I might have missed if I am late to a meeting. If I miss the entire meeting, I can review the recording and catch up.

The chat portion of a Teams meeting is a great way to communicate information that is relevant to the meeting. For example, if someone is talking about a specific Excel spreadsheet, he or she can paste a link to that document in the chat so that everyone can access it immediately. Check out Chapter 18 in the Part of Tens to find out more about chatting with other team members during a meeting.

A Teams meeting can include many different features. At the most basic level, a Teams meeting provides an online chat group, a voice link, and a shared screen where people can present presentations, share their screens, and see each other through video.

A meeting is often more productive and inclusive when you can see the other participants and watch their reactions and facial expressions. Teams works especially well at making a meeting feel inclusive when the conference room also has video of the entire room. That way people offsite and the people in the room can see each other *and* the presentation at the same time. The people offsite see the presentation and the video of the room on their computer screens. The people in the room see the presentation and the video of those offsite projected on the wall. This functionality makes a meeting with a dispersed team feel very natural and efficient. When I am part of a meeting without video, I always feel like I am on the outside of the meeting and that everyone in the room is on the inside. When there is video, I feel very much connected to the rest of the people because I can see them and they can see me. In order to make this happen, you need to have special hardware designed for Teams, which I cover in Chapter 10.

To conduct a video call in a Teams chat, follow these steps:

1. **Click the Chat icon in the left navigation pane and then select the chat message for the person you want to call.**

   If you don't already have a chat going with the person you want to meet with, you can start one by clicking the New Chat icon (which looks like a pencil writing on a paper).

2. **To start a video call, click the video icon in the top-right corner of the chat, as shown in Figure 9-8.**

   The video call will start ringing the other person and, you can click the video icon or the audio icon to either turn off your video camera or mute your audio button, as shown in Figure 9-9.

TIP

   You can turn off your webcam and microphone at any time throughout the call as well. For example, maybe you have a child who runs into the room unexpectedly and you want to turn off your webcam for a moment, or your dog starts barking and you need to mute your microphone. Click the video icon or the audio icon and the webcam will be disabled, or the audio will be muted. To enable them again, simply click them again.

3. **When you are finished with the call, click the red hang-up icon and the call will end.**

Click to start a video call

FIGURE 9-8:
Starting a video
from a chat.

FIGURE 9-9:
Calling another
person with a
video call.

Click to turn the webcam on or off

TIP

You can start a video call from just about anywhere in Teams. Just hover your mouse over the name of the person you want to call and then select the video icon. You can find all your contacts by selecting the Calls icon in the left navigation pane and then selecting Contacts. I generally just hover over a person's name in a channel or start a call from a chat as outlined in the previous steps.

During a Teams meeting, most of the Teams window is usually taken up by the presentation someone is discussing. If a presentation is not active, then the screen fills with the video of the person speaking.

You can customize the way these components appear on your computer. To customize these components, all you need to do is hover your mouse over the main display screen to reveal the meeting control icons (see Figure 9-10). In addition to using these icons to turn your webcam and microphone on or off, you can also make adjustments to how your screen appears. For example, clicking the icon of a little monitor with an arrow pointing up into it will pop-out the video or the presentation so that you can view different aspects of the meeting on different monitors or on different portions of a large monitor.

FIGURE 9-10:
Use these icons to customize your meeting screen.

I generally find the defaults work well, and I don't change things most of the time. But just be aware that you can if you want to. The best way to discover this functionality is to hover the mouse over the meeting and test out the icons that appear.

Breaking Out into Breakout Rooms

When a meeting involves a lot of people, it is useful to break into groups for small group discussions. This is common in seminars or workshops. Doing this in person is easy when people can just walk toward each other to gather into groups. When meetings are virtual, however, it's a bit trickier. Teams' breakout rooms are designed to enable virtual meeting attendees to form subgroups within a larger group to facilitate smaller discussions. Think of breakout rooms as smaller meetings within one main meeting, or "meetings within a meeting."

TIP

Just like organizing an in-person seminar or training, advance preparation is recommended. This will help the organizer run the meeting smoothly. (It is possible to break out into breakout rooms after a meeting has begun, and I discuss how to do that later in this section.)

To create a meeting with planned breakout rooms, it's important to map out just how many breakout rooms you will need before you create the meeting invite.

Once you know how many subgroups you will need, follow these steps to set up breakout rooms for your meeting:

1. **If there isn't an existing team to use for your meeting, create one and add the participants to your channel.**

   Within this team, a General channel is created by default. This will be the main channel for your meeting.

2. **Create separate channels for your breakout groups.**

   Each separate channel is a different breakout room, as shown in Figure 9-11. Make sure you label each channel clearly. (See "Creating a New Channel" in Chapter 4 if you need a refresher on creating new channels.)

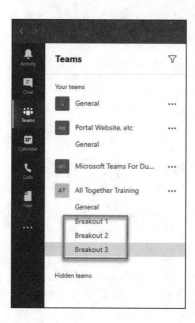

FIGURE 9-11:
Create a separate channel for each breakout room.

3. **Select the General channel and create a meeting invite to your meeting, as shown in Figure 9-12.**

   The General channel will be your main meeting room.

4. **Next, create a meeting invite for each of the channels you created (see Figure 9-13).**

   When you are done, the meeting, including all breakout rooms, appear on your calendar.

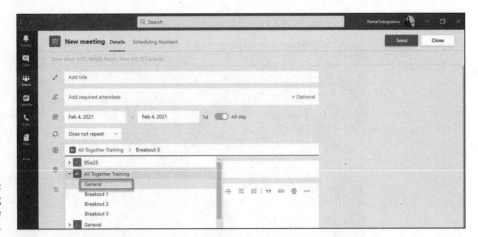

FIGURE 9-12:
Create a meeting invite for the main meeting.

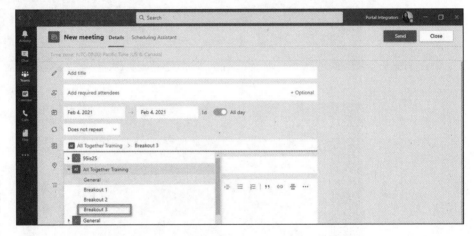

FIGURE 9-13:
Create a meeting invite for each channel.

TIP

You can create as many as 50 breakout rooms in a meeting.

What if you decide you want breakout rooms after a meeting has already started? No problem. Breakout rooms can also be used in ad hoc meetings. Here's how:

1. **Start the Teams meeting per usual.**

2. **Click the Breakout Room icon on your screen, as shown in Figure 9-14.**

REMEMBER

Only the meeting organizer can start breakout rooms, and the organizer must be present throughout the entire meeting to facilitate the breakout groups.

3. **Give a name for your breakout room meeting and select the audio options and then click Join Now.**

The Create Breakout Rooms dialog box appears, as shown in Figure 9-15.

Breakout Room icon

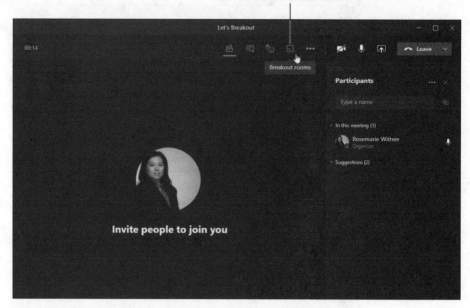

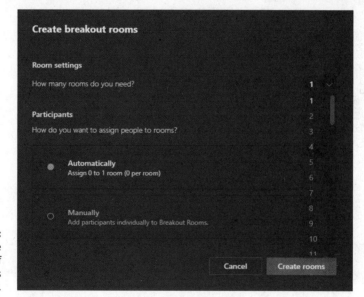

4. **In the Create Breakout Rooms dialog box, select the number of breakout rooms you need and how you want to assign people to rooms.**

   You have two options for assigning participants to rooms: automatically or manually. Selecting the automatic option tells Teams to create breakout assignments based on the number of participants and the number of rooms.

5. **Select Automatically to have Teams automatically assign the meeting participants into rooms.**

6. **Click the Create Rooms button to create your breakout rooms.**

   The rooms should all say Closed next to them. Participants are not available to join yet and won't be until you open them.

7. **Open each breakout room by clicking on the Closed button next to each room (see Figure 9-16).**

8. **To close the breakout rooms, select Close Rooms.**

   The participants will rejoin the main meeting.

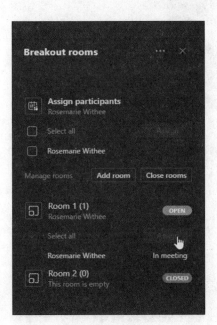

FIGURE 9-16:
Open each breakout room individually.

If you choose to assign participants manually in the Create Breakout Rooms dialog box, you will see the breakout rooms you have created and the participants in your meeting on the right side of your screen.

To manually assign these participants to breakout rooms, follow these steps:

1. **Select the name or names of the participants from the right side of your screen you want to assign to a room.**

2. **Select which room to assign your participant(s), as shown in Figure 9-17.**

FIGURE 9-17:
Assigning
meeting
participants into
breakout rooms.

3. **Once you are done assigning participants to breakout rooms, select the Start Rooms icon.**

   The participants will find themselves in the breakout room they have been assigned to.

4. **Select Close Rooms to end the meetings in the breakout rooms.**

   The participants will rejoin the main meeting.

Getting Together with Together Mode

In mid-2020, after months of having no live sports, the National Basketball Association (NBA) was the first professional sports league in the United States to start playing live competitions. The NBA created a safe "bubble" of players who quarantined and lived together in order to stay virus-free and able to practice and play basketball together. However, in adherence to safety protocols, teams had to play without a live audience. The once packed arena seats were now empty of fans. To help both player morale and promote fan excitement when watching games on TV or the Internet, the NBA had virtual audiences fill the seats. To do this, it used Together Mode on Microsoft Teams. With it, fans are able to watch and experience the game with other fans.

Together Mode is a new meeting experience that uses artificial intelligence (AI) technology to create virtual "cutouts" of meeting participants and place them in a virtual conference room, lecture hall, or sports stadium. It gives the feeling of sitting in the same room with everyone else in the meeting. It's another way to feel, well, together in virtual space.

Together Mode uses technology that knows where the participants are in the shared virtual meeting space. Instead of viewing each participant separately in a grid, you are interacting with each one in one space. Physical gestures are less awkward, since you are now sitting next to someone.

TIP

Together Mode requires at least four participants (including the host), and it will only be enabled if at least four participants have their video turned on.

Enabling Together Mode

To use Together Mode, you first need to ensure it is enabled in your version of Teams. Here's how:

1. **From the desktop app, select your profile picture in the upper-right corner and select Settings.**

2. **In the Settings screen, click in the box next to "Turn on new meeting experience" to turn it on.**

3. **Restart Microsoft Teams.**

Using Together Mode in your meetings

Once you are in a meeting, you can enable Together Mode in the meeting toolbar. Here's how:

1. **Join your meeting.**

2. **Select the three ellipses that appear in the meeting toolbar.**

3. **Select Together Mode from the drop-down menu.**

REMEMBER

Together Mode requires that there are at least four participants in the meeting, and that they have their video turned on. Together Mode uses Teams AI to create virtual "cutouts" of each participant, and does not work without video.

What Are Live Events?

By now you have attended your fair share of meetings online. You may have been in meetings with as few as two participants or as many as twenty or more. With a limited number of people in a typical meeting, most if not all attendees have an opportunity to have their say. But sometimes a meeting requires one person to many people at the same time. Examples include all-hands or town hall presentations, conferences, and seminars. Microsoft makes the distinction by calling such meetings *live events.*

Hosting a live event requires quite a bit of preparation, so much so that preparing for a live event is referred to as *producing* the event. The host does not just schedule a video call and talk in front of an audience. There is a literal producer to orchestrate the live event as it unfolds.

There are two types of Teams Live Events:

>> **Public event:** Any event where anyone who has a link can attend. There is no need to sign in to Microsoft Teams to attend a public event.

>> **Private event:** Any event where there is restricted access to join the event. Participants need to sign in to Microsoft Teams to attend the event. If the event is produced in Microsoft Teams, participants will need to download Microsoft Teams and sign in. If the event is produced externally, the participants would need to have a license for the Microsoft Stream video-sharing service.

TIP

To produce a Teams live event, you need an E1, E3, or E5 enterprise license to create a live event. As Microsoft often makes changes on what is allowed for the different tiers of licenses, always check with your administrator for any changes. For you to create events, your administrator should give you permission to do so. To be given permission you need to be a full member of the organization that is hosting the event. You cannot be a guest or a third party.

The various roles required to host a live event include the following:

>> **Organizer:** Much like a meeting organizer, a live event organizer creates the live event, sets attendees' permissions, sets the agenda, and sends invites to attendees. The organizer selects the production method and configures event options such as whether there will be a Q&A session at the end. The organizer also selects event group members and does the after-event reporting.

TIP

Microsoft created an organizer checklist that you can find at https://support.microsoft.com/en-us/office/teams-live-event-organizer-checklist-44a80886-0fd9-42e5-8e7c-836c798096f8. This is a handy guide to help you remember all the bits and pieces needed to organize a successful event.

>> **Producer:** Think of an event producer as someone who will orchestrate or direct what happens during the event. The producer starts and stops the event, can share video (both his or her video or participant video), shares an active desktop or window, and selects even layouts. Whatever happens during a live event is the responsibility of the event producer. The producer and organizer work closely together.

>> **Presenter:** A presenter or host is the face and voice of the event. This could be a keynote speaker at a conference, an instructor at a seminar, or a manager at an all-hands event.

Chapter **10**

Bringing Teams into the Physical World

eetings and communication underwent a revolution in the past couple of decades. The Internet and connectivity changed the game of global communications. I still remember calling friends in other parts of the world using a traditional landline phone and hearing a tinny echo in the background. They always sounded so far away, and this made sense at the time because they were. Then Skype came along, and I got used to calling friends anywhere in the world using the Internet and seeing them as we spoke.

Then came the coronavirus pandemic in 2020, which forced many more people to find ways to communicate with coworkers and loved ones over the Internet. Everyone from tech-savvy office workers to 4-year-old preschoolers found themselves online for meetings, school, or social get-togethers using Skype, Zoom, and Microsoft Teams.

As you discover in Chapter 9, you can make video calls directly through the Teams portal! Teams also includes a lot of features that are designed specifically for working with the groups of people in your teams. One area that has really accelerated in the past few years as Teams has come onto the scene is the hardware. Hardware companies have started designing gear optimized and designed specifically for Teams.

In this chapter, you explore some of the latest hardware you can use with Teams, including gear designed specifically for you as an individual, such as headsets, as well as gear designed for meeting rooms and conference calls. If you love gear like I do, then this chapter is for you!

Discovering How Teams Is More Than Software

It is easy to forget that a software product like Microsoft Teams can encompass more than just software. Teams is designed for communication with other people, and as a result, it requires physical devices such as phones, headsets, screens, and projectors to facilitate that communication.

These types of devices have been around for years, but manufacturers are starting to design them for specific scenarios and specific software applications such as Teams. Microsoft has a web page (www.microsoft.com/en-us/microsoft-teams/across-devices/devices) that describes these devices in detail and guides you on where to purchase them (see Figure 10-1).

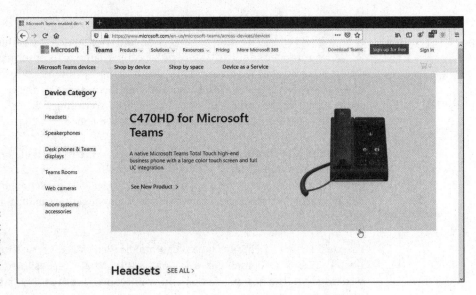

FIGURE 10-1: The Microsoft web page dedicated to hardware for Teams.

TIP

The devices Microsoft includes on its products page are designed specifically for conferencing and calling and are certified for use with Teams. For personal devices, like headsets and video cams, you can usually use just about any device that is compatible with your computer. For other devices, like room systems and conference phones, you are best to stick with the recommendations by Microsoft, or at least get a clear statement from the manufacturer that the device works with Teams.

Going Hands Free with Teams

Using your computer to make and receive phone calls is becoming the standard, especially when people have to work from home for long periods of time. Some organizations have embraced this practice fully, while others are sticking with the tried and true form factor of a traditional phone. In either case, you can find gear you can use to free up your hands while you are on a call or in a meeting.

The two primary categories of such gear are headsets and speakerphones. If you work in an open environment or in a shared space, a headset is probably the better choice. If you are fortunate enough to have an office with four walls, you might prefer a speakerphone. Microsoft has some featured headsets and speakerphones on its product web page as shown in Figure 10-2 and Figure 10-3.

FIGURE 10-2: The featured headsets on the Microsoft product web page for Teams.

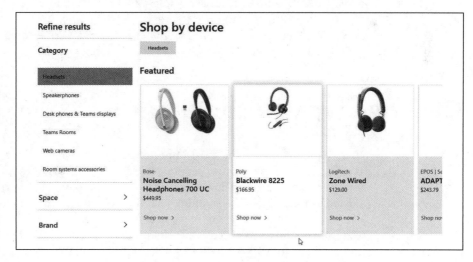

FIGURE 10-3:
The featured
speakerphones
on the Microsoft
product web
page for Teams.

My personal preference is a headset with full ear cover and an attached microphone. I find that I feel more immersed in the call when I use such a headset, and I can easily tune out distractions such as other conversations that might be happening around me.

When I need to include others in the conversation, I will switch to a speakerphone so that everyone around me can hear and participate in the meeting. Some nice speakerphone features I have seen include omnidirectional microphones so that audio can be captured from every angle including if you are tilting your head or not speaking directly into the microphone. Generally, any microphone will do, however. I have yet to see a microphone that works with a computer that Teams cannot use.

Getting Visual with Cameras

In my opinion, one of the most important aspects of a successful online meeting is being able to see the other people. The reaction of a person says more about the tone of the meeting and how it is going than most of what is said in the meeting. A good camera will make an online meeting feel like an in-person meeting.

The cameras Microsoft displays on its products page are top-notch and designed and certified to work with Teams. However, just like headsets, any camera that works with your computer will usually work with Teams.

WHAT? THAT CAMERA IS $10,000?

At the extreme high end, let's take a look at the EagleEye Director 2, which is featured on the Microsoft product web page. It is listed for upwards of $10,000! What is so special about it? Well, I have been in meetings that have used this camera, and it provides another level of interaction. This camera is meant for meetings with large groups of people. The camera connects to an intelligent microphone system, which means when someone in the room is speaking, the camera pans over to that person automatically and focuses in on them. The result is that the camera system takes over the role of a person running around the room with a microphone and a camera operator that pans around and focuses on whomever is speaking. Once you experience this level of immersive meeting, it is easy to wish it was available everywhere.

I have used very expensive cameras and very inexpensive cameras. The value that is added by adding a camera to a meeting is extraordinary. The value that is added by using more expensive cameras is debatable, but there is no doubt that the extremely high-end cameras are great when they fit your budget.

TIP
The featured products Microsoft includes on its product web page are some of the best, but you can also stop into your local electronics superstore or online retailer and pick up a camera that will work with your computer. I have found the best experience happens with a webcam that supports 4K video resolution and is capable of at least 30 frames per second (FPS).

TIP
The most important aspect to having a successful meeting is the speed of your network and Internet connection. You might have the best 4K webcam, but if your Internet speed is slow, the other person will appear choppy, and you won't hear the audio clearly because all that 4K data won't be able to reach the other person fast enough for it to make a difference. If there is one place to spend a little extra, it is on obtaining a very fast Internet connection.

Using Desktop Phones for Teams

Using a desktop phone with Teams provides an interesting new dynamic for communications. A desktop phone for Teams looks similar to a traditional phone; however, in addition to speaking voice to voice as you do with a traditional phone, a Teams-specific phone also includes a screen that can be used for presentations and video. The desktop phones Microsoft features on its product web page are shown in Figure 10-4. Desktop phones are the one type of device I recommend making sure it is specifically designed and certified for Teams.

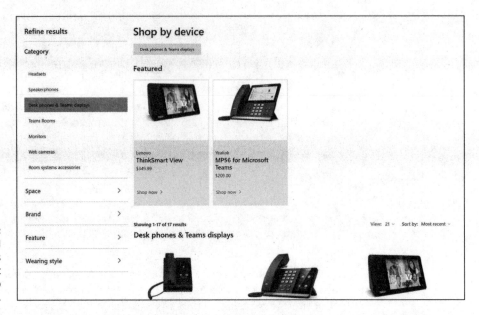

FIGURE 10-4:
The featured
desktop phones
on the Microsoft
product web
page for Teams.

These phones are not cheap, and that is because they are essentially a small computer designed specifically for online meetings. To set them up, you sign into the actual phone like you would normally sign into your computer.

I cover setting up a phone number and using Teams as your phone system in Chapter 11.

Turning a Conference Room into a Teams Room

A traditional conference room, also called a meeting room, generally has a table with chairs around it, a projector, and perhaps a speakerphone for remote participants to call into the meeting. Most organizations have some form of conference room at their locations. I have been in hundreds of them at clients all over the world, and it is remarkable how similar they are. You could drop someone into a conference room in Manila, Philippines, and then in Seattle, Washington, and they would likely be hard-pressed to tell the difference between them.

Teams has excelled with features and devices that augment these conference rooms and turn them into a digital space that is accommodating and inclusive of remote participants. One such device is a conference phone built for Teams that allows you to enter the room, push a button, and have the room automatically join the Teams meeting.

Another exciting development in conference room communication systems are the Teams room systems (see Figure 10-5). *Room systems* are a combination of conference phones, cameras, projectors, and microphones designed to transform communication.

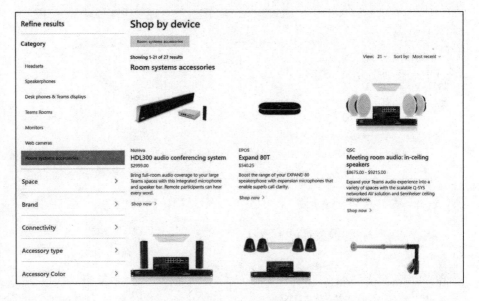

FIGURE 10-5: The featured room systems on the Microsoft product web page for Teams.

A Teams room system includes all the gear you need to transform a traditional conference room into a Teams room. It is important to make sure any system you purchase is designed and certified to work with Microsoft Teams.

There is nothing stopping you from buying all the pieces that make up a Teams room system and assembling them. The benefit of a room system package is that everything you need comes as part of the system, so you don't have to figure out what pieces work best with each other.

PEERING INTO THE FUTURE WITH SURFACE HUB

If you want to see into the future of what is possible with Teams, check out Surface Hub. Surface Hub is an all-in-one digital communications center. Think of it as a smart TV that has Teams built into it. Not only can you conduct meetings with it like a giant laptop, you can also draw on it and move it around as it is battery powered. You can see the Surface Hub on the Microsoft web page dedicated to it (www.microsoft.com/en-us/surface/business/surface-hub-2), and as shown in the following figure.

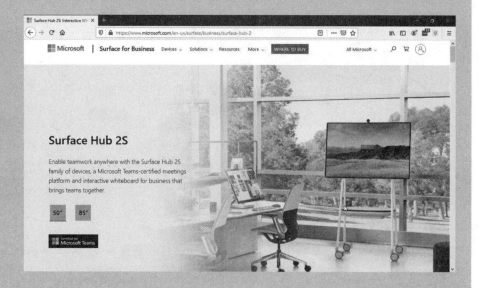

I recently had the opportunity to check out the Surface Hub and it feels like the future. The price tag is beyond many budgets, however, with each hub ranging from $9,000 to $12,000. Google has come out with a similar product called Jamboard (https://gsuite.google.com/products/jamboard), and these communications computers have been described as a new wave of computing. Instead of a personal computer, these are computers that belong to a communal and shared space and are meant to be interacted with as such. It is worth checking out and keeping an eye on these devices for future meeting needs.

4

Taking Communication to the Next Level with Voice

Discover how Teams can act as the phone system in your organization.

Learn how to make and receive calls through the Teams portal using a traditional phone number and how to make calls without one.

Find out how to set up Teams to route incoming calls and handle your voicemail, and how you can even set up phone trees and call queues using Teams.

Learn how to assign delegates who can work with Teams on your behalf, how to configure permissions, and how to set up notifications and privacy.

Chapter **11**

Making and Receiving Calls

Communicating with others using our voice is a basic human activity that began when man first walked the earth. Doing so with someone at a distance has only been an option for most people since the late 1800s with the advent of the telephone. Today, Internet apps such as Skype have changed the game for voice communication, and Microsoft Teams is the next evolution.

In this chapter, you discover how Teams can act as the phone system in your organization. You learn how to make and receive calls using Teams. You find out how phone numbers work in Teams and how you can make calls without them. Also, you learn a bit about the history of phone numbers and how you can set them up through Teams to work with the traditional phone system.

Making Phone Calls in Teams

In our office in Seattle, Washington, we don't have a phone system or even any traditional phones. Instead, we have a high-speed office network that is connected to a fast Internet connection, which we use to make calls through our computers and electronic devices. When we want to call someone else in the office, we use Teams. When we want to call someone outside the office using a regular phone number, we also use Teams.

TIP

To receive or make a phone call using a phone number over Teams, you must set up Teams with the correct licensing and assign a phone number. If you don't do this, you won't be able to dial a phone number or have someone else dial you using a phone number. I cover setting up phone numbers in Teams later in this chapter.

TECHNICAL STUFF

Modern communication networks can get confusing quickly. To understand them better, it helps to understand how the networks work. Entire volumes of books have been written on networks; however, understanding a few differences is rather straightforward. The Public Switched Telephone Network (PSTN) is a precursor to the Internet and used analog technology that created a route between your phone and someone else's phone over that network. To identify each device, so that the network knows about it, phone numbers were invented (see the sidebar, "Understanding How Phone Numbers Work" later in this chapter). If the circuit between your phones is cut, your call is dropped.

The Internet was invented to solve the problem of relying on a single route between two points on a network. In addition, the Internet uses digital information, known as *packets*, to send information over the network. To optimize voice communication over this digital network — the Internet — a special protocol was invented called Voice over Internet Protocol (VoIP). Today there is a weird mashup of these two networks, and the PSTN terminology still refers to using the traditional phone network, but today a mix of Internet connections is intertwined within it.

In general, you can use only VoIP technology if you call someone from Teams on your computer over the Internet, and the other person answers using Teams. No phone number is involved. When you need to use an actual phone number, you need to go through the regulatory system that was associated with the PSTN network, and this involves phone companies and the federal regulatory bodies. I can envision a day when everyone has high-speed Internet connections on all of their devices (think Elon Musk and his Starlink satellite Internet system) and phone numbers disappear. For the time being, though, we still need phone numbers to reach people who are not using a VoIP product such as Teams, Skype, Hangouts, Slack, Zoom, or countless others.

Calling another Teams user

If you have ever used a software app, such as Skype, to call another person using the same app, then you know how easy it is to communicate using voice over the Internet. Teams follows this same paradigm. You can initiate a call with another Teams user from just about anywhere in Teams. If you can see the name of a person in the Teams app, you can call that person. Just hover your mouse over the person's name and select the Phone icon, as shown in Figure 11-1.

FIGURE 11-1:
Calling another
Teams user.

TIP

When I am in the office working, I prefer to use a headset that has a built-in microphone for making all my calls. This allows me to free up my hands so that I can continue working on my computer. I cover using headsets with Teams in Chapter 12.

Finding the Calls dashboard

In the previous section, you see how communication, including voice calls, is built into the Teams interface (Figure 11-1). Teams also provides a dashboard called the Calls dashboard specifically for voice communication. You open the Calls dashboard by selecting the Calls icon in the left navigation pane, as shown in Figure 11-2. Note that you won't see the Calls icon in the navigation pane if you have not set up voice in Teams. This is an administrator task, which I cover later in this chapter and in Chapter 12.

The Calls dashboard includes navigational items for speed dial, contacts, history, and voicemail, as well as an area to make a call:

>> **Speed dial:** This screen is where you can set up the contacts you dial frequently. Just as the name implies, it is for speedily dialing a person. I find this particularly handy when I am working with very large organizations and the list of contacts might include hundreds or thousands of people.

The Calls icon

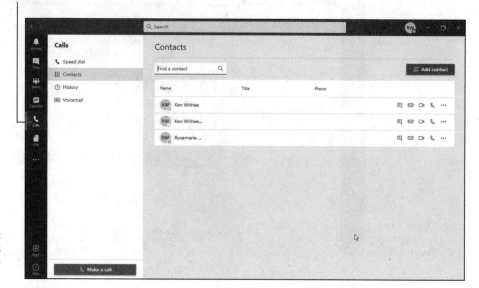

FIGURE 11-2:
Opening the Calls dashboard in Teams.

>> **Contacts:** This screen contains a list of all your contacts. You can add any type of contact you want here; it doesn't have to be another Teams user. You add a contact by selecting the Add contact button that appears in the top-right corner of the screen. You then type a name or phone number and Teams automatically starts searching through the other users within your organization and presents you with possible matches based on what you entered. If Teams doesn't find any matching possibilities, you are prompted to create a new contact.

>> **History:** Your history of incoming and outgoing calls is displayed on this screen.

>> **Voicemail:** Your voice messages are shown on this screen. You can listen to the messages as well as view transcripts of the messages that Teams has already transcribed for you. I use the transcription feature frequently since it takes time to listen to a message, but I can glance at the transcript and know instantly what the message is about and whether it is worth listening to and acting on now or waiting until later.

TIP

When adding a new Contact in Teams, just type the first letters or numbers of a person's name or phone number and Teams will search the organization's contacts and provide options in a drop-down menu based on what you entered. You can refine the search by continuing to type additional letters.

The Calls dashboard also includes an area in the left navigation pane titled "Make a call" (see Figure 11-2). In this area, you find a Phone icon next to each contact's name. Click the Phone icon to immediately call that contact. I find this area redundant since you can make a call to any contact by just clicking the Phone icon next to the person's name from anywhere in Teams. Most of my calls happen from within the channels and chat areas of Teams; I don't necessarily go to the Calls dashboard. I just hover over a user's name from wherever I am in Teams and select the Phone icon to start a voice call.

TIP

If you have a phone number set up in Teams, you will find your phone number on the Calls dashboard above the "Make a call" section. If a phone number is not assigned to the user signed into Teams, no phone number will appear.

Receiving a Call in Teams

On the surface, receiving a call in Teams happens the same way regardless of whether the other person initiated the call using Teams or a traditional phone. Your Teams app rings, and you can decide to answer it or ignore it.

Where Teams shines is in the ability to configure what happens when someone calls you. For example, you can set up Teams to route incoming calls to your desk phone between 9 a.m. and 11 a.m. on weekdays, and to your mobile phone at other times. Or you can set it up to ring at whatever device you are active on so that your calls follow you wherever you are. I cover the details of this digital operator functionality in Chapter 12.

Using Teams with Phone Numbers

In Teams, you can call anyone in your contacts list by clicking the Phone icon. However, not everyone uses Teams or the Internet, and so phone numbers persist. And Teams handles them just like you would expect. You dial a phone number from your Teams app, regardless of whether you are using a desktop, a laptop, a phone, or a tablet, and the phone you are dialing rings. Likewise, if someone dials the phone number set up with Teams, the Teams app rings.

I often use Teams to call people from my mobile phone. It is easy to forget that all I really need is Teams and Internet connectivity to make this work. My mobile phone plan has mostly become about getting connected to the Internet. Yes, I get a number from my mobile phone company, too, but I could just as easily get one from Microsoft with Teams or Google with Hangouts or any number of new services. My mobile plan has become my connection to the Internet when I am not at my desk. If Elon Musk carries out his plan to beam down high-speed Internet from satellites with Starlink, then I wonder if anyone will need a mobile plan anymore. Or perhaps cell towers and satellites will compete for our mobile Internet needs.

TIP

All you need to make a phone call is your Teams app and an Internet connection.

When a Teams user has a phone number set up, the phone number will appear in the lower-left corner of the Calls dashboard. When someone calls the phone number, Teams will ring, and the call can be answered. You can also dial a phone number by entering it into the "Make a call" section.

UNDERSTANDING HOW PHONE NUMBERS WORK

A phone number is a series of numbers assigned to one phone that when dialed by a user on another phone, enables a connection between the two devices. Parts of the number designate the country, the area, the region, and the specific device. The overall telephone system is known as the Public Switched Telephone Network (PSTN), and it was born in 1875 when Alexander Graham Bell invented voice communication over a wire. Bell then formed a company called Bell Telephone Company in 1877, and voice communication over a long distance became the norm. The mechanism to connect with others became the phone number.

Modern communication changes this paradigm. You can still use a phone number to connect to another device, but if you are contacting someone using the same communications app, such as Skype or Teams, you just select that person's name from your contacts list. Instead of your voice traveling over the PSTN, it is traveling over the Internet using the Voice over Internet Protocol (VoIP).

As you see in this chapter, you can use the Teams app to call other Teams contacts over your local network or even the Internet. However, if you want to make and receive calls using the PSTN, you will need to get a license for that and obtain a phone number, which I discuss how to do in this chapter.

Adding Phone Numbers to Teams

Many organizations use Teams *and* pay for a separate phone service. And the bill for phone service for even a small office can be shocking! Microsoft offers phone service through Teams that you can sign up for through the Microsoft 365 Admin Center and set up in the Teams Admin Center. (I cover the Teams Admin Center in depth in Chapter 13 and in Chapter 14.) In this section, I outline the steps to sign up for a phone service and start using phone numbers in Teams.

WARNING

To use Teams to receive and make calls using a phone number, you need to sign up for a phone service and license. If you don't sign up for a service, you will only be able to call other Teams users.

Obtaining a license and dial plan

Licensing is one area that often causes a huge amount of confusion and frustration with Microsoft products. The good news is that for small and medium-sized organizations, Microsoft has recognized this pain and is trying to reduce it. (Large organizations usually have a dedicated account representative.)

At the time of this writing, Microsoft has launched a cloud-based voice plan and license called Microsoft 365 Business Voice in Canada, the United Kingdom, and the United States. Microsoft 365 Business Voice includes all the pieces you need to get started using phone numbers in Teams. It integrates into Microsoft 365, giving you the ability to make phone calls in Microsoft Teams. The Microsoft 365 Business Voice documentation page is shown in Figure 11-3.

Without using the new Microsoft 365 Business Voice plan and license, you will need to obtain a phone system license and calling plan. When writing this chapter and Chapter 12, I purchased a Microsoft 365 E5 license and a calling plan. However, I am eagerly waiting for the Microsoft 365 Business Voice license to roll out in the United States. If your Microsoft 365 subscription does not include the correct license, you will see an error message when you start the wizard to obtain a new phone number.

TIP

It can take some time to procure a license that includes phone services. If you purchase a license and immediately try to create a new phone number, you will likely receive an error message stating you are missing the required license. Wait at least 24 hours and try again. If you keep getting an error, then open a service request (support ticket) with Microsoft. You can do that in your Microsoft 365 Admin Center under the Support option in the left navigation pane.

FIGURE 11-3:
The Microsoft 365
Business Voice
documentation
page.

You can obtain licensing for various Teams features such as conferencing, toll-free numbers, and calling plans. Check the service descriptions for each license to see what is included. You will find these licenses along with your other Microsoft 365 licenses on the admin site for those services. In Chapter 1, you learn about signing up for a Microsoft 365 subscription. After you log in to your Microsoft 365 dashboard, you will find license information under the Billing section in the navigation pane.

To add a phone number to a Teams user, you also need to obtain a calling plan. A calling plan is essentially a way to pay for time spent using the Public Switched Telephone Network (PSTN). You will find calling plans for domestic calling and for international calling. If you are familiar with traditional telecommunications, all of this may sound familiar. If this terminology is new, then be thankful you are just learning about it now, when it is becoming simplified with services like Teams.

Much of the appeal of Teams is that you can get up and running in a short amount of time without the need to hire expensive experts. However, Microsoft also offers many features and services specifically designed for large enterprise organizations. For example, Microsoft offers replacement functionality known as Phone System for traditional Private Branch eXchange (PBX) systems. A PBX is a system for routing phone traffic around your organization. A PBX system used to be a large physical device that would take up a small room. The offering from Microsoft is all virtual and lives in the cloud, even though it performs the same functionality.

TIP

If you are a decision-maker at a large organization, I recommend reaching out to Microsoft directly and having an account representative walk you through the features and add-on licensing for Teams.

Signing up for a new phone number

You can request a new phone number for a location and Microsoft will assign one from the available pool of numbers. To obtain a new phone number that you can assign to a Teams user, follow these steps:

1. **Log in to the Teams Admin Center and expand the Voice option that appears in the left navigation pane.**

2. **Choose Phone Numbers.**

   The Phone Numbers screen opens on the desktop, as shown in Figure 11-4.

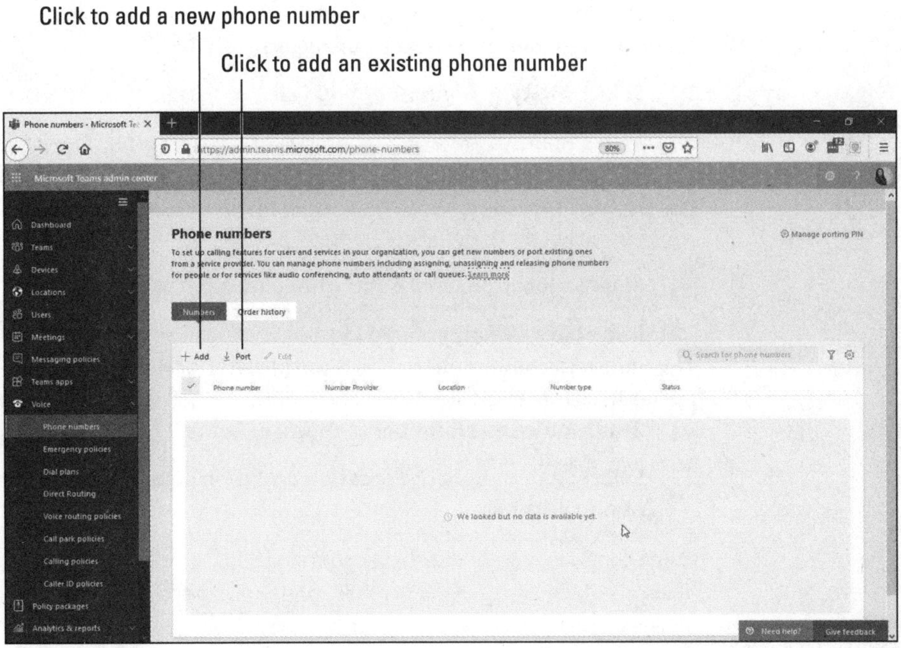

Click to add a new phone number

Click to add an existing phone number

FIGURE 11-4:
Opening the Phone Numbers page in the Teams Admin Center.

3. Select +Add in the Phone Numbers screen to start the New Phone Number wizard, as shown in Figure 11-5.

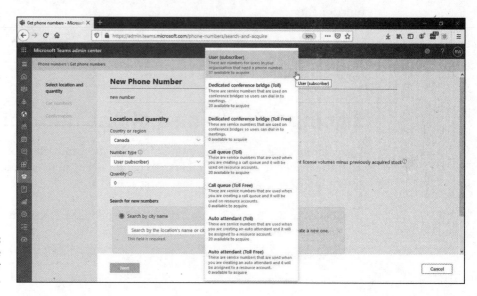

FIGURE 11-5: Selecting the type of phone number to obtain.

4. Provide a title for the order of the phone number, enter a description, and then select a country or region.

5. Select the type of number you want to assign.

In this example, I am choosing a basic user phone number (see Figure 11-5). The other options include a dedicated toll and toll-free conference bridge, a toll and toll-free call queue, and a toll and toll-free auto attendant. I cover these options in more detail in Chapter 12.

6. Select a location where this phone number will be based.

If you have already entered locations, you can search and find it in the list. If not, add a new location. This is the physical location for the phone number and is used for things like emergency services when you call 911. I entered our Seattle office as a location, as shown in Figure 11-6.

7. Select Save to save the location and then select it as the location for this phone number.

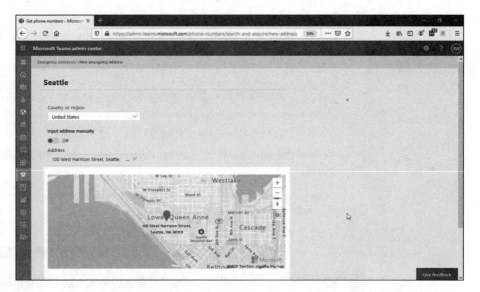

FIGURE 11-6:
Adding a location for a phone number in the Teams Admin Center.

8. **Select the area code from the available options, select the quantity of phone numbers you want to add, and then select Next to continue, as shown in Figure 11-7.**

I received an error message saying that there weren't any more 206 (Seattle) phone numbers available. I then entered a Redmond, Washington, address and obtained a 425 area code so that I could continue. I reached out to Microsoft and learned that new area codes are being added. If you run into issues, I recommend opening a service request in your Microsoft 365 Admin Center under the Support area in the left navigation pane.

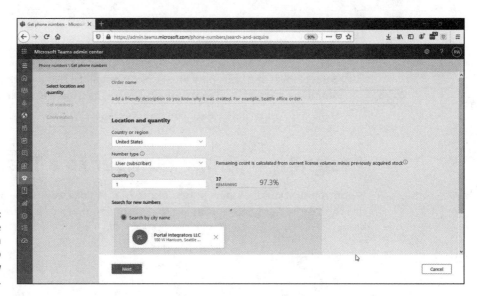

FIGURE 11-7:
Filling out the Teams Admin Center page to obtain a new phone number.

I experienced several problems and errors while trying to set up a new phone number. I had to open a service request support ticket in order to get it resolved. In general, when you run into problems, open a service request. Microsoft has always been fast to respond, in my experience, and the customer service representatives will work with you to get your problem resolved, usually with a same-day turnaround. You can open a service request on your Microsoft 365 Admin Center under the Support area in the left navigation pane.

9. **Review the number that is assigned and then select Place Order, as shown in Figure 11-8.**

   Once your new phone number has been provisioned, you will see a confirmation page that lets you know your order has been placed.

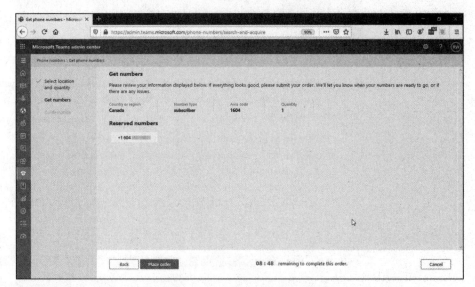

FIGURE 11-8: Placing an order for a new phone number.

10. **Select Finish and your new phone number will be listed on the Phone Numbers page in the Teams Admin Center, as shown in Figure 11-9.**

    You can now assign the phone number to a Teams user.

Assigning a phone number to a Teams user

When you first obtain a new phone number, it is not assigned to anyone. You can use the Teams Admin Center to assign a phone number to a Teams user.

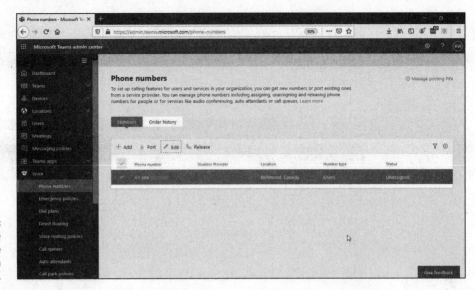

FIGURE 11-9:
A new phone
number in the
Teams Admin
Center.

To assign a phone number to a Teams member, follow these steps:

1. **Log in to the Teams Admin Center, expand the Voice option in the left navigation pane, and choose Phone Numbers (refer back to Figure 11-4).**

   The Phone Numbers screen appears where all your Teams phone numbers are listed.

2. **Select the phone number you wish to assign and then select Edit.**

   The Edit pane opens on the right side of the screen.

3. **Search for the user you want to assign to this phone number.**

   TIP

   If you don't see a specific user when you search, make sure that user has a Calling Plan license assigned. You can do this by selecting the user in the Microsoft 365 Admin Center, as shown in Figure 11-10, and then checking the box on the correct Calling Plan license.

4. **Select the location of this user and then click Apply.**

   The phone number is now assigned to the Teams user and any calls to it will be routed to that user.

Bringing an existing phone number to Teams

If you already have a phone number, you can move it into Teams. The process is similar to obtaining a new phone number; however, you select Port instead of Add in the Phone Numbers screen of the Teams Admin Center. You can see both options in Figure 11-4. Once you select the Port option, the porting wizard begins, as shown in Figure 11-11. Follow the wizard to bring your existing phone number into Teams. Once the porting is complete, you can then assign it to your Teams user.

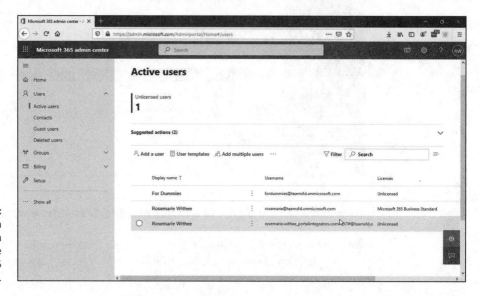

FIGURE 11-10:
Assigning a calling plan to a user in the Microsoft 365 Admin Center.

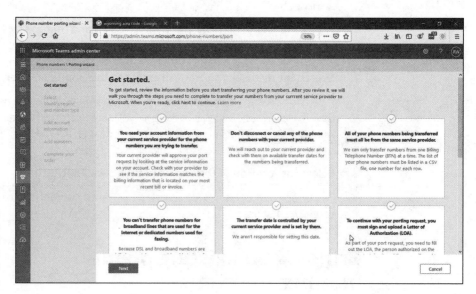

FIGURE 11-11:
Bringing an existing phone number into Teams with the porting wizard.

Unassigning or changing the phone number assigned to a user

You can unassign or change the phone number that is assigned to a Teams user. This is done on the same page in the Teams Admin Center where you assign a new phone number.

To unassign or change the phone number assigned to a Teams user, follow these steps:

1. **Log in to the Teams Admin Center, expand the Voice option in the left navigation pane, and choose Phone Numbers (refer back to Figure 11-4).**

2. **Select the phone number you wish to unassign from the Teams user and select Edit.**

   The Edit pane opens on the right side of the screen where you will see the current Teams user the phone number is assigned to (see Figure 11-12).

3. **Click the X next to that person's name to unassign the user, and then click Apply to save the changes.**

4. **To assign a different phone number, follow the same process and select the number you want to assign, select Edit, and then assign the Teams user.**

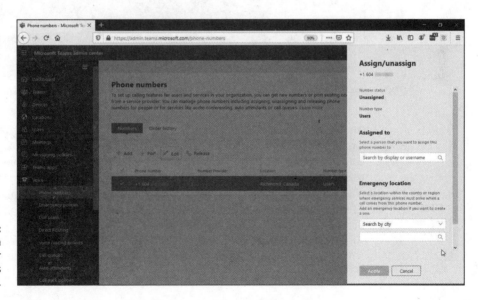

FIGURE 11-12: Unassigning a phone number from a Teams user.

Setting Up a Teams Phone

Many organizations I work with still prefer to use a traditional phone to make and receive calls. Several devices have been released specifically for these user preferences.

I cover phones built specifically for Teams in Chapter 10. A Teams phone looks like a regular phone with a display attached to it. One of the options from the Microsoft products web page is shown in Figure 11-13. The phone runs the Teams application, and you log in to Teams just like you would log in to the Teams app on your computer or mobile device.

FIGURE 11-13: A Teams phone displayed on the Microsoft products web page.

Once you have logged in to the phone, you can dial a phone number just like you would with any other phone. Or you can use the display screen to select a Teams contact and start a voice call with that person by tapping his or her name. The nice thing about these devices is that you can bring Teams communications to people who would rather use a traditional phone. There is no requirement for any other computing device. Teams is already pre-installed on the phone, and all the person must do is log in to his or her Teams account.

Chapter **12**

Letting Teams Be Your Personal Operator

In the past, only the most senior executives had administrative assistants who would answer their calls and route them appropriately. With Microsoft Teams, everyone can set up rules to route their incoming calls and handle voicemail. Teams will even transcribe voicemail for you so you can read the message and determine if it is worth getting to right away, or if it is something that can wait.

Also in the past, advanced voice-system features such as phone trees and call queues were the realm of only the largest organizations. Teams provides these capabilities to organizations of any size.

In this chapter, you learn how to tell Teams when and where to ring your incoming calls. You discover how to create rules to automatically forward calls and limit how and when you receive calls so you can maintain focus without getting interrupted. You also find out how voicemail works in Teams and how to get it set up. In addition, you learn how to assign delegates who can work with Teams on your behalf, how to configure permissions, and how to set up notifications and privacy, auto attendants, and call queues for your organization.

Setting Up Audio Devices in Teams

A traditional telephone is pretty straightforward. It usually includes a cradle and a handset that contains both the speaker and the microphone so that you can hear the call and speak to the person on the other end of the call. Using Teams for calls introduces many additional dimensions to this old way of using a telephone.

When using Teams to make and receive calls, you can set up multiple audio devices and configure them in several different ways. For example, you might have a speakerphone and a headset plugged into your computer. You might prefer the speakerphone to ring when you get a call so that you can hear it ring without wearing your headset. You might also prefer to answer the call and communicate with the other person only using your headset. Or, if there are others around you who need to hear the call, you might want to switch the call to use the speakerphone. You can configure all of this using Teams.

To set up the audio devices you use with Teams to make and receive calls, follow these steps:

1. **Log in to Teams and select Settings from your profile drop-down menu, as shown in Figure 12-1.**

   The Settings screen appears.

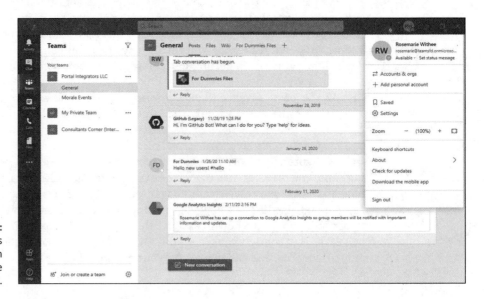

FIGURE 12-1:
Opening Teams settings from your profile drop-down menu.

2. **On the Settings screen, select Devices in the left navigation pane.**

   The speakers, microphones, and cameras that are attached to your computer are displayed, as shown in Figure 12-2. You can select which device to use for your microphone, your speaker, and your camera. You can also choose a secondary ringer, which allows you to direct the ring to a speaker or speaker-phone and still answer the call using your headset.

3. **To make a test call to test your settings, click the Make a Test Call button (see Figure 12-2).**

   You will hear a recording that guides you to say a few words to test your microphone and speaker. After the recording, a results page will be displayed, as shown in Figure 12-3. If any device is not working properly, you will see a red triangle next to that device. In this example, I didn't have a camera configured, but the microphone, speaker, and network were working fine.

TIP

   Since Teams uses the Internet, it is important you have a fast Internet connection. I use this test frequently to see if there are any network problems that might cause problems with my phone calls.

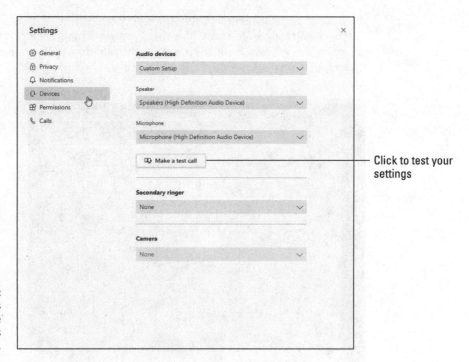

FIGURE 12-2:
The devices
section on the
Teams Settings
screen.

4. **After you have configured the settings, close the window by selecting the X in the top-right corner of the screen.**

   You don't need to save the settings; they are saved automatically as you adjust them.

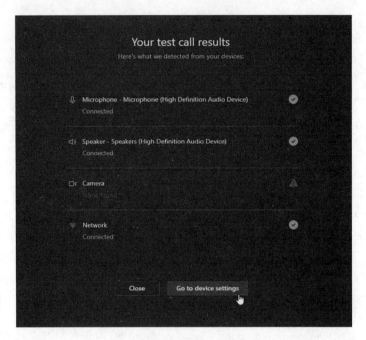

FIGURE 12-3:
Making a test call
in Teams.

TIP

If you are already in a Teams meeting, you can change your device settings by selecting the ellipsis from the meeting information toolbar and then selecting Show device settings, as shown in Figure 12-4.

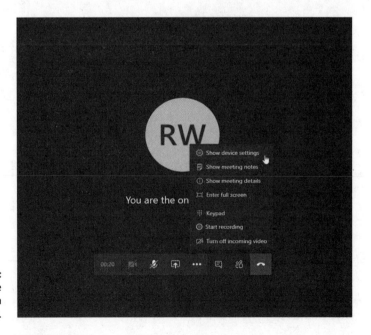

FIGURE 12-4:
Opening device
settings while in a
Teams meeting.

Customizing How You Receive Calls

You can customize Teams to receive calls in a way that makes the most sense to your circumstances. You can set rules that tell Teams what to do with incoming calls. You can have Teams ring you on the device you are currently using, or you can forward your calls to voicemail, to another phone number, or even to a group of people. You can even set Teams to do these things only after you don't answer.

TIP

One of the nice things about Teams is that it is a software app that you can install on many devices. I recommend installing it on multiple devices, such as your laptop or desktop computer, mobile phone, and tablet. When you set Teams to ring you, Teams will ring you on whatever device you are using when you are currently logged into Teams. So, to get your calls in Teams, all you need to do is log in to the app. Teams doesn't care which app you are using — you can even use the web app without installing Teams!

One rule I like to set up is to have my mobile phone number ring if someone calls my office number, which is in Teams.

To have another phone number ring if someone calls your Teams number, follow these steps:

1. **Log in to Teams and select Settings from your profile drop-down menu.**

2. **On the Settings screen, select Calls in the left navigation pane.**

3. **Make sure the Calls Ring Me radio button is selected, and then in the Also Ring drop-down menu, select New Number or Contact, as shown in Figure 12-5.**

You can also forward your calls in this screen by selecting the Forward My Calls radio button.

4. **Enter the phone number you want to ring at the same time someone calls your Teams number.**

You can also enter a Teams contact here instead of using a phone number.

5. **After you have configured the settings, close the window by selecting the X in the top-right corner of the screen.**

You don't need to save the settings; they are saved automatically as you adjust them.

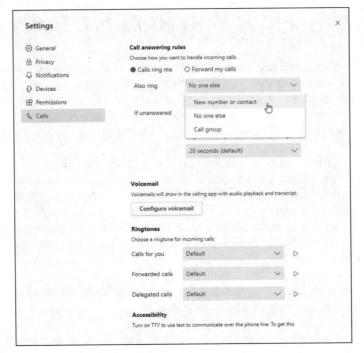

FIGURE 12-5:
Entering another phone number or contact to ring when your Teams number is called.

Restricting Calls with Do Not Disturb

When you set your status as Available, Busy, Do Not Disturb, Be Right Back, or Appear Away in Teams, it also affects how you receive phone calls. (See Chapter 3 for more details about setting your status.) There are times when I like to set my status to Do Not Disturb so that I don't receive phone calls. However, if there is an emergency, I want family members to be able to reach me.

To set your status to Do Not Disturb, click your profile image in the top-right corner of the Teams window. From the drop-down menu that appears, hover over your current status and select Do Not Disturb from the status options.

To allow someone to call even when you have Do Not Disturb set, follow these steps:

1. **Click your profile icon in the upper-right corner of the Teams app.**

2. **Select Settings from the available options in the drop-down menu.**

    The Settings dialog box appears.

3. **Select Privacy.**

4. **Under the Do Not Disturb section, click the Manage Priority Access button.**

5. **Add the person you want to be able to send you chats, messages, and calls while your status is set to Do Not Disturb.**

   Once the person is added to the list, you can close the dialog box. Your settings are saved automatically.

Delegating Access to Others

If you have an administrative assistant, or would otherwise like to delegate access to your Teams account to someone else, you can allow that person to access your Teams features on your behalf without sharing your password. This is handy when an admin needs full control over your calendar and communications system, for example. When you delegate access to your Teams account to someone else, that person can make and receive calls from your Teams phone number, and work with meetings on your behalf.

WARNING

When you add a delegate to your account, that person has full control of your Teams features and acts on your behalf in Teams.

To add a delegate to your Teams account, follow these steps:

1. **Log in to Teams and select Settings from your profile drop-down menu.**

2. **On the Settings screen, select General in the left navigation pane.**

3. **Select Manage Delegates, as shown in Figure 12-6.**

   The Delegate Settings screen appears where you will see the People You Support tab, which lists who you have delegate access for, as well as the Your Delegates tab, which shows the people you have designated as your delegates.

4. **Select Your Delegates and then type in the name of the Teams user you want to add as a delegate, as shown in Figure 12-7.**

5. **Set the permissions for the delegate.**

   You can choose to allow the delegate to make and receive calls on your behalf as well as change your call and delegate settings, as shown in Figure 12-8.

6. **Select Add to add the new delegate.**

7. **Close the window by selecting the X in the top-right corner of the screen.**

   You don't need to save the settings; they are saved automatically as you adjust them.

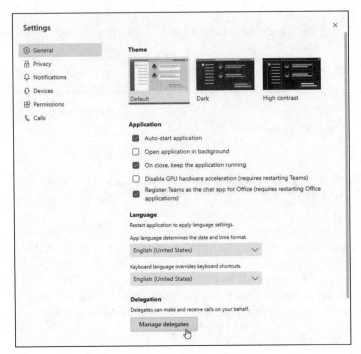

FIGURE 12-6:
Accessing the delegate management screen in Teams.

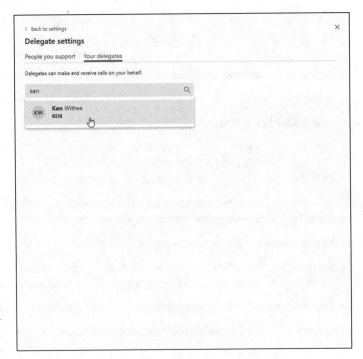

FIGURE 12-7:
Adding another Teams user as a delegate.

FIGURE 12-8:
Setting
permissions
for a new
delegate.

TIP

You can change the permissions for a delegate or remove them by navigating back to the same screen you used in the above procedure and then selecting the ellipsis next to their name in the list.

Digging into Modern Voicemail

If you are like me, you might find it a rare occurrence when someone calls you when you are not busy with something else and can answer the call. Voicemail provides a mechanism for people to leave a message when they call, and for you to retrieve the message when you have the time. Teams offers voicemail, but you must set it up before people can leave messages for you.

To set up voicemail in Teams, follow these steps:

1. **Log in to Teams and select Settings from your profile drop-down menu.**

2. **On the Settings screen, select Calls in the left navigation pane.**

3. **Select the Configure Voicemail button, which is shown in Figure 12-5 earlier in this chapter.**

   The setup screen for voicemail appears, as shown in Figure 12-9. You can record a greeting, set rules for when voicemail should be used, select the language of a default greeting, and set a custom out-of-office greeting. You can even trigger the out-of-office greeting to play based on events in Outlook, such as when you have an out-of-office message set for email or when you have a calendar event where you are listed as "out of office" on your status.

TIP

   When someone calls your phone and you don't answer, you can send the call to voicemail, send the call to another person automatically, or give the caller the option. I find that giving the incoming caller the option of leaving a voicemail message or being transferred to someone covering for me while I am out of the office is particularly valuable. You can see the options in Figure 12-10.

4. **Click OK to save your settings.**

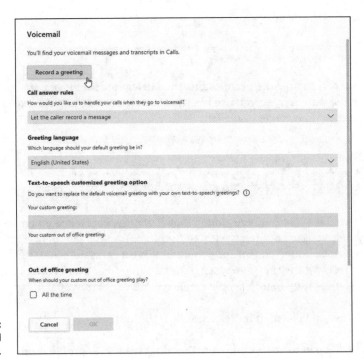

FIGURE 12-9:
The Voicemail
screen in Teams.

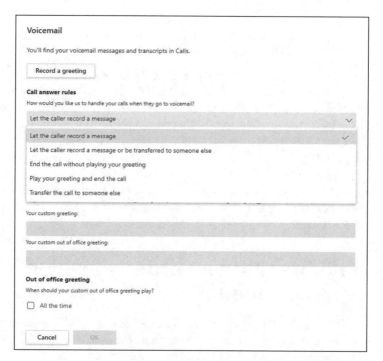

FIGURE 12-10:
Call answering
rules for
voicemail.

Understanding Phone Number Types

In Chapter 11, you discover how to obtain and assign a phone number in Teams. A phone number can be assigned for different uses. Teams offers four types of phone numbers for different uses: subscriber numbers, conference bridges, call queue numbers, and auto attendant numbers, each of which are described here:

>> **Subscriber:** This is the basic phone number you assign to a person. You can think of it as a regular phone number you would use to make and receive calls in Teams. (Chapter 11 walks you through assigning a subscriber number to a Teams user.)

>> **Conference bridge:** A conference bridge is a phone number you can use for large meetings. Multiple people can call into the same number and all talk together. When I signed up for the Microsoft 365 E5 plan, a conference bridge was automatically assigned for Teams use.

>> **Call queue:** A *queue* is a line in which the first in the line is the first out. A call queue works similarly, but the "line" is made up of people who have called into a particular phone number. For example, if you have a phone number that people will call for support, you want to use a call queue. Your support agents answer the phone as calls come in, and if there is a backup, the new

callers will be placed on hold in the queue. While on hold, the callers will listen to hold music until someone is available to take the call.

>> **Auto attendant:** When you need to route calls to different people and different departments, you want an auto attendant. An auto attendant provides phone-tree functionality. For example, when you dial the number, you might hear a recording that directs you to "press 1 for sales, 2 for support, and 3 for billing." The auto attendant feature is what makes this possible in Teams.

TIP

A conference bridge, call queue, and auto attendant phone number can be obtained as either a toll or toll-free number. (Refer back to Figure 11-5 in Chapter 11 to see these options.)

Taking calls in an orderly fashion with call queues

A call queue is a line of calls that you can answer in the order in which they were received. A call queue is a simple concept, but has always been considered a phone-system feature reserved for large organizations. Microsoft Teams brings call queues to organizations of any size. When a call comes into a call queue number, it is sent to a Teams user who can answer it. If everyone who can answer the line is already busy on another call, the person calling is placed on hold until someone is available.

WARNING

To set up a call queue, you must have a resource account. You can think of a resource account as an Office 365 account that is for resources instead of the usual accounts that are for people. You manage your resource accounts in the Teams Admin Center by selecting Org-Wide Settings in the left navigation pane. (Refer to Chapters 13 and 14 for more details about the Teams Admin Center and setting up resource accounts.)

To set up a call queue, follow these steps:

1. **Open your favorite web browser and log in to the Teams Admin Center at** `https://admin.teams.microsoft.com`.

   Refer to Chapter 13 for more details on logging into the Teams Admin Center.

2. **In the left navigation pane, select Voice and then select Call Queues.**

   The Call Queues screen is displayed, and you can see a list of any existing call queues.

3. **Select +Add to create a new call queue, as shown in Figure 12-11.**

4. Configure the new call queue and then select Save.

Figure 12-12 shows a portion of the call queue configuration screen. When you are finished configuring your call queue, your new call queue will show up in the list that was shown in Figure 12-11.

Click to add a call queue

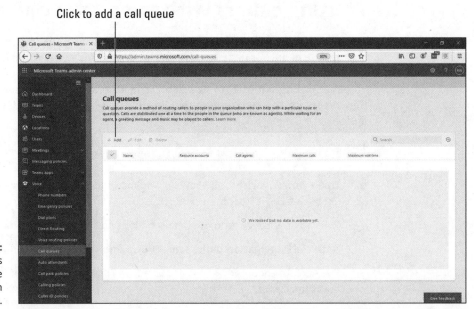

FIGURE 12-11:
The Call Queues screen in the Teams Admin Center.

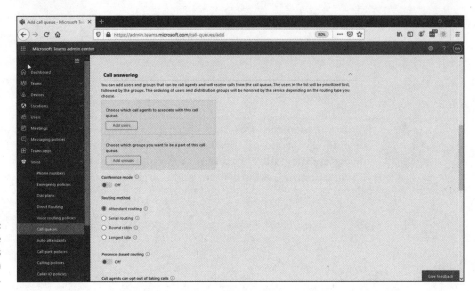

FIGURE 12-12:
A portion of the Call Queues configuration screen.

Call queues can quickly become complicated, and the details of them are beyond the scope of this book. A good place to learn more is the Microsoft documentation site for administrators located at `https://docs.microsoft.com`. Navigate to the Teams content and search for *call queues.*

Routing callers with auto attendants

An auto attendant is a phone-system feature that routes incoming calls to the appropriate people or departments within an organization. When a call comes into an auto attendant, the caller hears a recording that lists several options, such as "press 1 for English or 2 for Spanish." The auto attendant then routes the call to the correct person or group depending on how the caller navigates the tree of options.

To set up an auto attendant in Teams, follow these steps:

1. **Open your favorite web browser and log in to the Teams Admin Center at** `https://admin.teams.microsoft.com`.

   Refer to Chapter 13 for more details on logging into the Teams Admin Center.

2. **In the left navigation pane, select Voice and then select Auto Attendants.**

   The Auto Attendants screen is displayed, and you can see a list of any existing auto attendants.

3. **Select +Add to create a new auto attendant, as shown in Figure 12-13.**

4. **Configure the new auto attendant by navigating through the wizard.**

5. **Select Next to navigate each screen and then select Submit when finished.**

   Your new auto attendant will show up in the list that was shown in Figure 12-13.

Auto attendants can quickly become complicated, and the details of them are beyond the scope of this book. A good place to learn more is the Microsoft documentation site for administrators located at `https://docs.microsoft.com`. Navigate to the Teams content and search for *auto attendants.*

Click to add an auto attendant

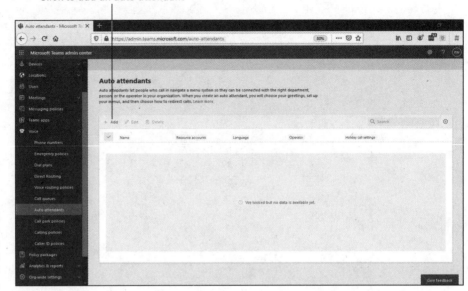

FIGURE 12-13:
The Auto
Attendants
screen in the
Teams Admin
Center.

5
Becoming a Microsoft Teams Administrator

IN THIS PART . . .

Discover where all the behind-the-scenes action happens in the Teams Admin Center.

Understand that you don't need to be a dedicated IT specialist to handle Teams administration.

Find out how to log in to the Teams Admin Center and become familiar with the layout and Teams settings you can control.

Add new users to Teams and configure their settings.

Learn how to perform common tasks such as configuring teams, messages, and other settings across your entire organization.

Find out how to configure policies for apps and Teams navigation as well as manage devices such as desk and conferences phones.

Chapter **13**

Getting to Know the Teams Admin Center

The Microsoft Teams Admin Center is where all the behind-the-scenes action happens. It is where you make decisions about what apps are available to the rest of the Teams users, configure settings for external access and guest access, add new teams and configure existing teams, configure meetings and voice settings, and set policies for individual users, among a whole host of other actions. Large organizations generally have dedicated IT departments that handle the configuration; however, if your organization doesn't have a specialized IT department, you just might find yourself working in the Teams Admin Center regardless of your job title. Fortunately, Microsoft seems to have recognized that most Teams administrators are not dedicated IT personnel by making its Admin Centers straightforward and easy to use. The Teams Admin Center is no different.

In this chapter, you discover where to find the Teams Admin Center and how to log in. Next, you take a quick peek around the Admin Center to become familiar with the layout and the settings you can control. You then learn how to add new users to Teams. In the next chapter, you dive into the nitty-gritty details of using the Admin Center to configure Teams to your liking.

Finding and Signing In to the Teams Admin Center

In Chapter 1, you find out how to sign up for a Microsoft 365 subscription. Microsoft provides an administrative website, or *Admin Center*, for each of the services included in Microsoft 365. For example, Teams has its own Admin Center, as do Exchange and SharePoint.

To find the Teams Admin Center via the Microsoft 365 administrative site, follow these steps:

1. **Open your web browser and navigate to `www.office.com`.**

2. **Sign in with your Microsoft 365 credentials.**

These are the same credentials you created in Chapter 1 when you signed up for Microsoft 365.

3. **Select the Admin app from the app launcher, as shown in Figure 13-1.**

The primary Microsoft 365 administration site opens. The Microsoft 365 administrative site, also known as the Microsoft 365 Admin Center, is where you manage your overall Teams subscription including adding users and assigning licenses for all the available services.

FIGURE 13-1:
Opening the Microsoft 365 Admin Center from the app launcher.

The Admin app

If you don't have administrative privileges for your organization, you won't see the Admin option listed in the app launcher.

4. **To open the Teams Admin Center, click Teams in the left navigation pane, as shown in Figure 13-2.**

When you click the Teams link, a new tab opens in your web browser and the Teams Admin Center loads, as shown in Figure 13-3. The default page that is loaded is the Dashboard, which provides a view into your Teams setup for your organization.

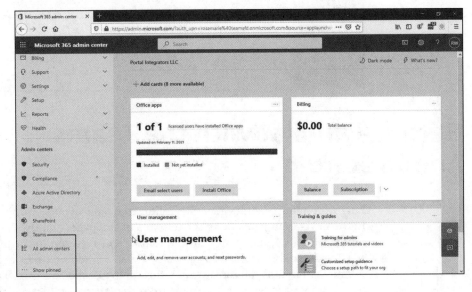

FIGURE 13-2:
Opening the Teams Admin Center from the Microsoft 365 Admin Center.

Click to open the Teams Admin Center

As a shortcut, you can also enter the address for the Teams Admin Center directly into your web browser to access the Dashboard:

1. **Open your web browser and enter** `https://admin.teams.microsoft.com` **in the address field.**

If you are already logged in to Microsoft 365, the Teams Admin Center Dashboard loads immediately.

2. **If you are not already logged in, enter your Microsoft 365 credentials to log in and be taken to the Teams Admin Center Dashboard.**

Microsoft has made progress in keeping track of authentication. If you have logged in to one Microsoft property, such as `https://www.office.com`, and then go to another one, such as `https://admin.teams.microsoft.com`, you will automatically be logged in to the site.

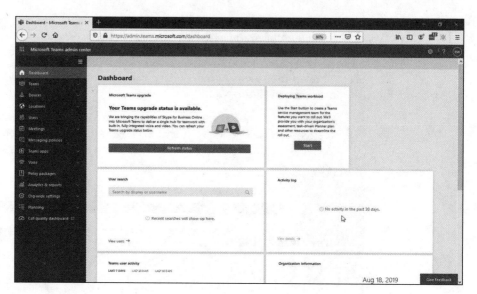

FIGURE 13-3:
The Teams Admin
Center.

Getting Familiar with the Teams Admin Center

Microsoft Admin Centers generally follow the same layout: Settings options appear in the navigation pane along the left side of the page, and the details of the currently selected option appear in the center. As I mention in the previous section, the Teams Dashboard screen opens by default when you first access the Teams Admin Center, and you can always return to the Dashboard from wherever you are in the Admin Center by selecting it from the left navigation pane. Following is a high-level overview of each of the options available in the Teams Admin Center.

Underneath the Dashboard option, the Teams Admin Center includes the following settings options:

>> **Teams:** Use these settings to manage teams and team policies. You can add new teams and configure existing teams. (Chapter 3 covers the process of creating a new team.) You can also set up policies that define which features and settings a team can use. The management page for the teams in your organization is shown in Figure 13-4.

>> **Devices:** These settings are used to set up and manage the devices on your network. You can set up configuration files that are used for devices you have approved for your organization.

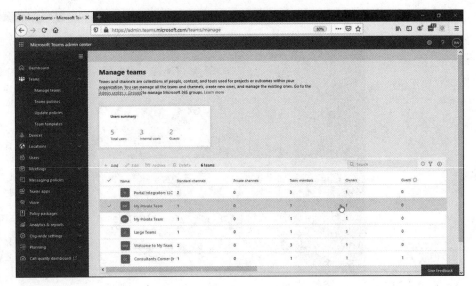

FIGURE 13-4:
The management page for all the teams in your Teams service.

>> **Locations:** Use these settings to set up physical geographic locations of your Teams members. You can set labels so that you can report on specific offices and set up 911 locations that are used by emergency services. These locations can be used for things like users and also for offices and buildings.

>> **Users:** In this section you can view information about Teams users and configure and set policies for individual users. The list of Teams users is shown in Figure 13-5, and setting a policy for an individual user is shown in Figure 13-6. Adding new users to Microsoft 365 and Teams is discussed later in this chapter.

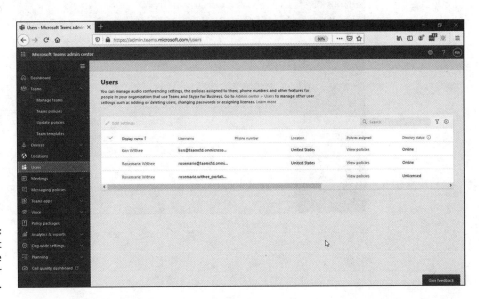

FIGURE 13-5:
The management page for all the users in your Teams service.

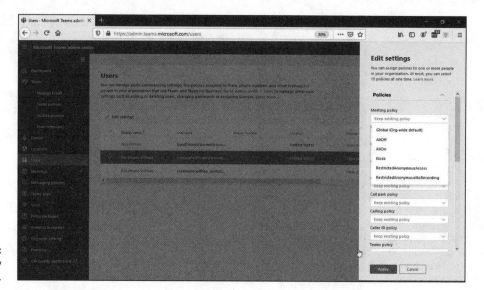

FIGURE 13-6:
Setting a policy
for a user.

>> **Meetings:** These settings are used to configure meetings in Teams. Here you can set up and configure conference bridges, meeting policies, meeting settings, live event policies, and live event settings. Figure 13-7 shows the settings page for meetings.

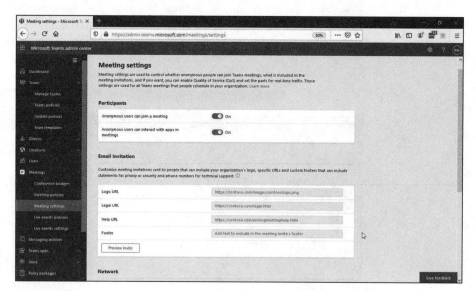

FIGURE 13-7:
The settings page
for meetings.

>> **Messaging policies:** Here you can set which features are available in chat and channels. A default org-wide policy is set by default, and you can add others.

>> **Teams apps:** These settings are used to set up policies and permissions for how Teams users can use apps. For example, Teams includes a default policy for people that have first contact with customers such as cashiers behind the checkout counter (often known as firstline workers). The Firstline Worker policy ensures that the Shifts app, which is used for tracking time for shift work, is pinned and available to everyone that has the policy assigned. The Firstline Worker app policy is shown in Figure 13-8.

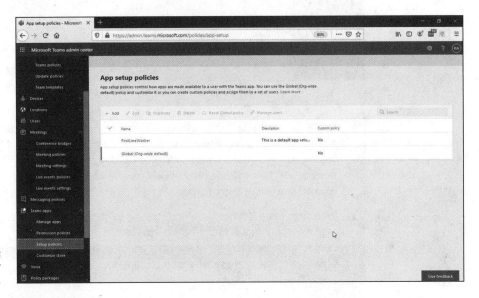

FIGURE 13-8: An app policy for firstline workers.

>> **Voice:** Voice call settings are configured with these settings. Chapter 12 covers the process of adding phone numbers and setting up auto attendants and call queues.

>> **Policy packages:** With these settings you can package up a group of pre-defined policies and apply them to groups of users. For example, for educational use, there are predefined policy packages for teachers and another policy package for students.

>> **Analytics & reports:** Here you can view and download reports about Teams usage. There are reports about user activity and usage. You will find usage reports for the Teams app, devices, live events, voice and text messages, and blocked users. I find these reports incredibly valuable for planning network capacity and understanding how an organization is adopting Teams. A user activity report is shown in Figure 13-9.

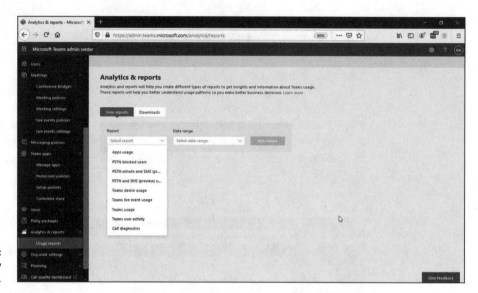

FIGURE 13-9:
A user activity report.

>> **Org-wide settings:** These settings affect your entire organization. You can configure settings for external access and guest access as well as general Teams settings. You can also configure holidays and set up resource accounts that are used for voice features like auto attendants. (See Chapter 12 for more information about auto attendants.)

>> **Planning:** Here is where you find tools to help with planning your Teams deployment. You will find a Teams advisor tool and a network planning tool. I expect Microsoft to continue adding tools to this section to help larger organizations with deployment and adoption.

TIP

Refer to Chapter 14 for specific information on working with each of these settings in the Teams Admin Center.

Adding New Users to Microsoft 365 and Teams

To add new users to Teams, you must first add them to Microsoft 365 and assign them a license that includes the Microsoft Teams service.

TIP

You can add guest users to your teams for free; however, guests have limited functionality. To learn more about the limitations of guest users, see Chapter 7.

To add new users to Microsoft 365 and assign them a Teams license, follow these steps:

1. **Log in to the Microsoft 365 Admin Center by navigating to www.office. com and signing in with your Microsoft 365 credentials.**

2. **Select the Admin app from the app launcher to open the Microsoft 365 Admin Center.**

3. **In the left navigation pane, select Licenses from the Billing option and confirm that you have licenses available that include Teams, as shown in Figure 13-10.**

   TIP

   To determine which Microsoft product licenses include the Teams service, use your favorite search engine and search for "Microsoft 365 licensing for Microsoft Teams" to access an article on the Microsoft documentation site that includes a nice table that lists the licenses that include Teams.

Click to check license availability

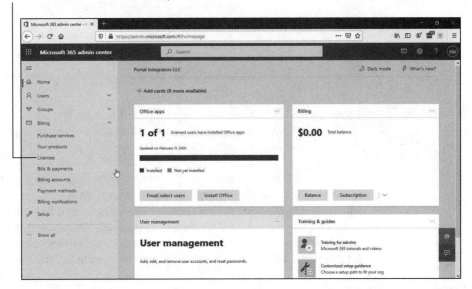

FIGURE 13-10: Checking license availability in the Microsoft 365 Admin Center.

4. **In the left navigation pane, select Active Users from the Users option and then select Add a User.**

5. **Follow the wizard to create a new user, as shown in Figure 13-11.**

   When you get to the screen to assign a license to the user, make sure you select a license that includes Teams. If you want to also assign the user a phone number, you should assign a calling plan to the account too. Refer to Chapter 12 for more information about phone numbers.

Once the user has been created, he or she can sign in to any of the Microsoft 365 services for which the license is valid.

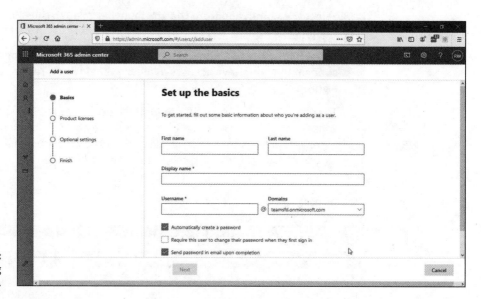

FIGURE 13-11:
Creating
a new user.

WARNING

I have noticed that it can take some time from when you add a user until that user shows up in the list of options when adding a person to a channel or chat in Teams, sometimes as long as 24 hours.

The Microsoft 365 Admin Center is where you manage users for all your Microsoft services. If you handle any type of administrator duties for your organization, you will likely spend a good deal of time in the Admin Center. For smaller organizations, it is often the person who happened to purchase Microsoft 365 who becomes the administrator. Microsoft has designed the Admin Centers to be user-friendly, and for the most part, you won't have any trouble figuring out what you need to get done.

Managing Teams Users

Once you have added a user to Microsoft 365, you will find Teams-specific settings for that user in the Teams Admin Center, as shown earlier in Figure 13-5. You can open the settings for a user by selecting his or her name in the list and then selecting the Edit Settings option, or you can click the user's name in the list. Once you select a user, you can configure that user's Teams settings. The settings for each user include account information, voice, call history, and policies. A user's account settings are shown in Figure 13-12.

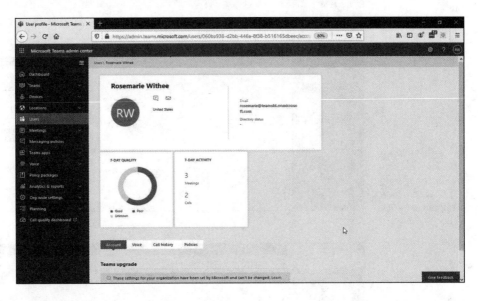

FIGURE 13-12:
The account settings for a user in Teams.

In addition, at the top of the user settings page is a dashboard that shows the user's phone number, address, and email address. You will also find information about the call quality a user has been experiencing in Teams and that user's activity.

TIP

You will find Teams-specific settings in the Teams Admin Center and general settings about the user in the Microsoft 365 Admin Center.

The Account tab includes information about a user's coexistence. *Coexistence* refers to moving users from Skype for Business to Teams. If you are new to Teams, you don't need to worry about this. If you are a veteran of Office 365 (now Microsoft 365) and have people using Skype for Business, then you can use this setting to transition your organization to Teams in an orderly fashion.

The Voice tab is where you configure a user's call-related settings. You can configure where people can dial out of your organization and set up group calls, call delays, and call delegation. Restricting a user to only being able to dial out to the same country is shown in Figure 13-13.

You can view the call history of a person on the Call History tab. The call history includes some very valuable information such as when the call was made, the people who were called, the duration of the call, the type of call, and how the call was made (see Figure 13-14).

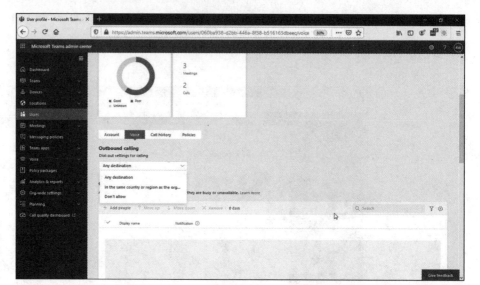

FIGURE 13-13:
The voice settings for configuring how someone uses call features.

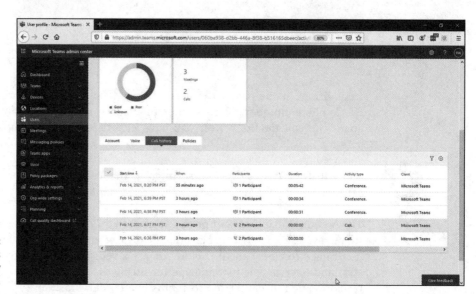

FIGURE 13-14:
Viewing a user's call history information.

Finally, the Policies tab is where you configure policies for the user. There are many types of policies in Teams. There are policies for the navigation that appears on the left side of a user's Teams client, policies for how messaging and channels work, policies apps, and policies for calling, just to name a few. I cover setting up a policy for apps in Chapter 14.

Chapter **14**

Digging into Teams Administration

Whether you've found yourself as an "accidental admin" or you signed up to be the Microsoft Teams administrator for your organization, you need to dig deep and get familiar with the Teams Admin Center. Even if you aren't an administrator, it is a good idea to be familiar with the settings and options that cause Teams to behave in a certain way. Are you not seeing what you expect to see in the navigation in Teams? There is a setting that controls that. Are you unable to delete messages in a channel? There is a setting for that, too. There are more settings than can possibly be covered in this book, but I cover some of the most useful ones in this chapter.

In this chapter, you dig deeper into the Teams Admin Center and learn how to perform common tasks such as configuring teams, messages, and other settings across your entire organization. You learn how to configure policies for apps and Teams navigation as well as manage devices such as desk and conferences phones.

Configuring Teams

It can be awkward to say that you are configuring a Teams team in the Teams Admin Center. But that is exactly what you are doing. As you have learned throughout the book, a *team* is a group of people in Microsoft Teams, and it is core to how you use and interact with others in your organization. You can manage how teams work and set policies for them in the Teams Admin Center via the Teams option in the left navigation pane.

To manage the settings for a team in your organization, select Teams from the left navigation pane and then choose Manage Teams. A listing of all the teams in your organization will be displayed. To view the settings for a team, click the name of the team you want to view (see Figure 14-1).

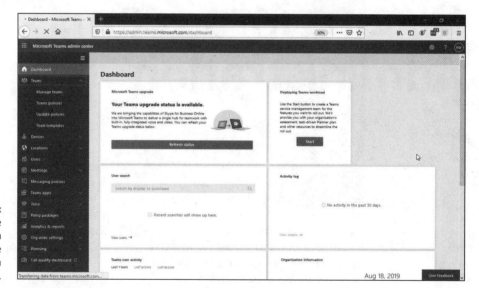

FIGURE 14-1:
Viewing the settings for a team in the Teams Admin Center.

TIP

By default, anyone in your organization can create new teams. You can keep an eye on how many teams are being created and if they are public or private via the Manage Teams option. When I am helping roll out Microsoft Teams to an organization, I work with the administrators to build a habit of keeping tabs on how many teams pop up across the organization.

TECHNICAL STUFF

Currently, there isn't a setting to disable the creation of new teams. In order to do so you have to go into the settings of the Microsoft 365 tenant and disable group creation.

When viewing the details about a team, you can select the Members tab to see the members of the team and the Channels tab to see channels associated with the team. There is also a tab for the team's general settings where you can view the configuration of channels and conversations. To edit these settings, click the Edit link that appears in the top-right corner of the screen. Alternatively, you can go immediately to these general settings by selecting a team in the main list (when you first open the list of teams) and then clicking Edit, as shown in Figure 14-2. Here you can allow people to be able to delete or edit their messages as well as be able to create or delete channels in the team.

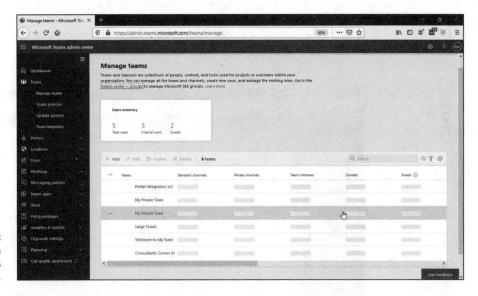

FIGURE 14-2:
Selecting a team to view a team's general settings.

TIP

An Archive button appears to the right of the Edit button. When a team is not needed anymore, you can archive it and then bring it back if you ever need it again. I cover how to archive a team in Chapter 16.

Making Configuration Changes for Meetings

You can fine-tune several settings to make Teams meetings fit the needs of your organization. Under Meetings in the left navigation pane, you will find options to adjust the settings and policies for conference bridges, meetings, and live events.

Conference bridges

A *conference bridge* is a phone number you can use for large meetings that allows people to call in using a traditional phone. You can add toll and toll-free numbers and require callers to record their names and announce themselves to everyone in the meeting if you choose. You will find conference bridge settings under the Meetings tab in the left navigation pane. However, if you have not signed up for a voice license then you won't see the conference bridge option in the navigation.

When you select Bridge Settings, a list of the conference bridges currently in use is displayed. Selecting Bridge Settings at the top of the list of numbers opens a dialog box where you can configure conference bridge behavior, as shown in Figure 14-3. Selecting Add lets you add a new conference bridge phone number.

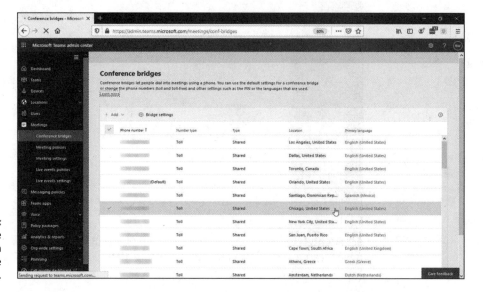

FIGURE 14-3:
Configuring the behavior of a conference bridge.

Check out Chapters 11 and 12 for more information about conference bridges and adding new phone numbers to Teams.

Meeting policies

Policies are a common theme in Teams. A *policy* is a grouping of settings that you create and then assign to teams, users, or channels. Throughout the Teams Admin Center, you will find areas where you can create policies. For example, in the Meetings section, you can create policies that relate to meetings. You will also find policies for teams, messaging, calling, and many others. Whenever you see an area of the Teams Admin Center to set a policy, think of it as a way to define a group of settings that you can apply in Teams.

Microsoft has already set several default policies for you, and you can tweak them or create new ones from scratch. I walk through creating a setup policy to change Teams navigation later in this chapter.

Meeting settings

One area you will want to review and spend time understanding is the Meeting Settings option. The Meeting Settings screen lets you set up exactly how meetings behave for Teams users. For example, you can allow or disallow anonymous people to join meetings, configure how meeting invites are formatted and sent, and configure how meetings work with the network. The Meeting settings screen is shown in Figure 14-4.

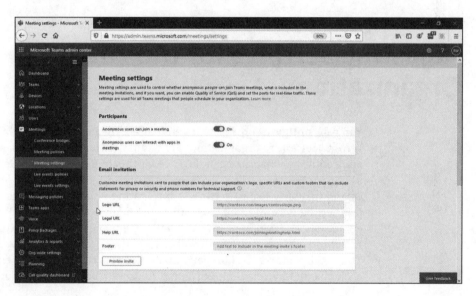

FIGURE 14-4:
Configuring how meetings work in Teams.

Live events policies

Live events allow you to broadcast meetings and presentations to many people at once. Think of giving a webinar where you have people sign up for the webinar and you demonstrate or discuss a product or service or walk through a presentation. Some of the well-known products that compete in this area are GoToMeeting (www.gotomeeting.com) and WebEx (www.webex.com). I have used other server products, too, but I prefer using Teams Live Events now because it is part of my existing subscription, and I have not had any issues with people being able to join my broadcast events from many different devices.

As a Teams administrator, you can configure how live events work with the members of your organization. Microsoft has already created a default policy for you, and you can tweak it or create new ones. When you create a new policy, you can allow scheduling of live events, allow a transcription of the event for attendees, and set who can join scheduled events and who can record. See Chapter 9 for more information on producing Live Events in Teams.

Live events settings

In addition to creating live event policies, you can also configure settings that apply to all live events regardless of the policy they are set to use. You can configure a custom web address that people attending a live event can use in order to obtain support and also set up third-party video distribution providers.

Adjusting Settings for the Entire Organization

You can configure some settings that affect the behavior of Teams in general and across your entire organization. For example, you can allow guests to join teams and configure what they can do. (I cover this in detail in Chapter 7.)

One particularly useful setting is integrating email with Teams channels. When this setting is configured, you can send email to a special email address, and the email message will appear in a team's channel. You will find this setting in the Email integration section of the Teams Settings screen, as shown in Figure 14-5. The email address is auto-generated, and you can obtain the email address for each channel by selecting Get Email Address from the ellipsis drop-down menu that appears next to a channel name.

TIP

To avoid spam and unwanted email appearing in your Teams channels, you can filter to allow only certain domains to be able to send email to the channel. I like to set the domain of the organization I am working with so that outside members cannot send email to the channel by default.

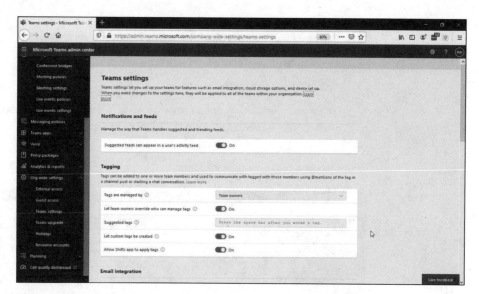

FIGURE 14-5:
Setting up email integration with Teams channels.

Identifying Locations of Offices and Buildings

The nature of the Internet is that if you are connected to it, you can be anywhere in the world and still use all the services it has to offer. Phone systems that work using the Internet, like Teams, create a conundrum. How do you keep track of an organization's physical locations like offices and other types of buildings if its members use Internet-based services like Teams? Team members could be using Teams and calling in from anywhere in the world. The Teams Admin Center has a navigational component called Locations that you can use to set physical locations for users as well as addresses for emergency services.

TIP

To provide emergency services with critical information in times of emergency, it is important to keep emergency addresses up to date and accurate. You can add physical locations such as an individual office or open workspace on a specific floor of the building so that emergency services will know exactly where to go in times of emergency.

To add a physical location to a Teams user, follow these steps:

1. **Open your web browser and log in to the Teams Admin Center at** `https://admin.teams.microsoft.com`.

2. **In the left navigation pane, expand the Locations option and select Emergency Addresses.**

3. **Select +Add to add a new emergency address, as shown in Figure 14-6.**

4. **Enter a name, a description, and the address.**

5. **Select Save to save the location.**

   The location will now appear anywhere you need to assign a location for a user. I cover working with phone numbers in Chapter 12.

Click to add a new emergency address

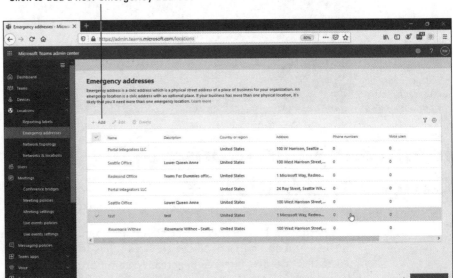

FIGURE 14-6:
Adding a new emergency address for a Teams user.

Adding Default Teams Apps

In Chapter 5, you learn how apps can be installed into Teams in order to extend Teams and add functionality. As a Teams administrator, you can control which apps are available to your organization and install apps that will appear for users automatically.

Six default apps are pinned to the left navigation pane in Teams. These include: Activity, Chat, Teams, Calendar, Calling, and Files. These apps directly relate to the apps that appear in the global default org-wide setup policy.

You can add a new default app that will appear in the navigation pane for all users in your organization by adding it to the global default org-wide policy. Trello (https://trello.com) is a popular task management system used by many organizations. Let's add it as an app to the default setup policy so it shows up for every user.

To add an app to the default setup policy for every Teams user, follow these steps:

1. **Open your web browser and log in to the Teams Admin Center at** `https://admin.teams.microsoft.com`.

2. **In the left navigation pane, expand the Teams Apps option and select Setup Policies.**

3. **Select the Global (Org-Wide Default) policy by clicking on its name.**

   The setup policy will open and you will see the default apps.

4. **Select Add Apps from the menu bar.**

   The Add Pinned Apps panel appears on the right side of your screen.

5. **Type** Trello **in the search panel, and then select Add.**

   TIP

   You can configure which apps are available in Teams using Permissions Policies. You will find the settings for this in the Teams apps area of the navigation.

6. **Select Add at the bottom of the dialog to add the Trello app to the Global (Org-Wide Default) setup policy.**

7. **Select Save to save the policy.**

   The policy now includes the Trello app in the left navigation pane, as shown in Figure 14-7.

The Trello app

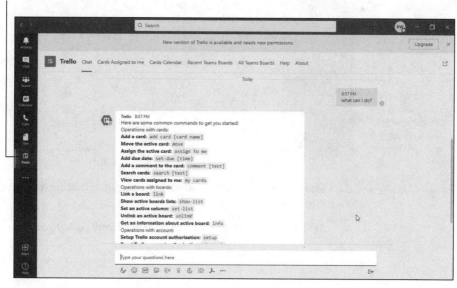

FIGURE 14-7:
The Trello app in the Teams navigation is part of the setup policy.

WARNING

It can take time for changes in policy to take effect, sometimes as long as 24 hours. I usually come back the next day after making a change and find things are working as expected. For example, after following the procedure to add the Tello app, the app did not show up in the Teams navigation right away.

In addition to making org-wide changes to the apps available to all Teams members, you can change the app setup policy for individual users, too. These changes are done on the Users settings page in the Teams Admin Center. When you change the setup policy, the navigation items the user sees in the left navigation pane in Teams will be updated to match the policy assigned.

To update the setup policy for an individual Teams user, follow these steps:

1. **From the Teams Admin Center, select the Users option in the left navigation pane.**

   A list of all Teams users appears in the main screen, as shown in Figure 14-8.

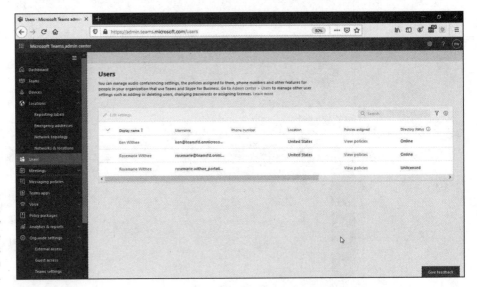

FIGURE 14-8:
Changing a user's setup policy changes the navigation items the user sees in Teams.

2. **Select a user, and then select the Policies tab to show the user's information.**

3. **Select the Edit button and then choose any policy you have created.**

TIP

You can develop your own custom apps, or have someone develop them for you, and then upload and add them to the default navigation for all Teams users. You will find the option to do this in the Teams Admin Center in Teams Apps under Setup Policies. Open the Global (Org-Wide Default) policy and upload your custom app.

Setting Policies for Chat and Channels

Teams also includes settings specifically for messages in channels and chats. (I cover chat and channels in detail in Chapter 4.) These settings are like many other settings you explore in this chapter. You configure the settings in a policy and then assign that policy to actions in Teams that relate to that policy. For meetings, the policies are called Messaging Policies, and you will find them in the left navigation pane.

Messaging policies allow you to configure how chats and channels work in Teams. You can set such options as allowing messages to be deleted, allowing previews to appear when someone pastes a URL into a message, and turning on or off receipts so others know when a message has been read.

Like most policies in Teams, every Teams user is automatically assigned the Global (Org-Wide Default) messaging policy. Selecting this default policy opens it so you can edit and adjust settings, as shown in Figure 14-9. You can also create a new messaging policy and assign it to specific users or teams by selecting Add at the top of the messaging policies list.

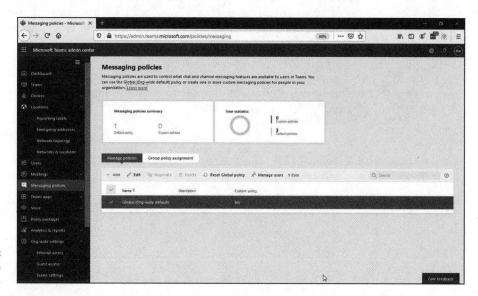

FIGURE 14-9: Configuring a messaging policy.

For large organizations, it is common to create lots of custom policies and fine-tune how people use Teams. Smaller organizations usually stick with the default policy.

TIP

Managing Devices for Your Organization

In Chapter 10, I cover Teams devices such as conference phones and desk phones. You can manage the devices that are used in your organization through the Teams Admin Center.

Using a phone designed for Teams is essentially using a computer that looks like a phone. You turn on the phone and connect it to the network and sign into it directly using your Microsoft 365 credentials. You are essentially signing into the phone and bypassing your computer. These phones are ideal for people who don't work on a computer on a day-to-day basis. They can use the large screen on the phone to attend Teams meetings and view presentations without needing another computer.

TIP

When someone plugs in a Teams-certified phone and logs in to the device for the first time, the phone will start appearing in the device management area of the Teams Admin Center. You access the list of devices associated with your Teams service in the Devices option of the left navigation pane. Select Phones, and you will see a listing of all devices. You can manage these devices here and perform several different tasks. For example, you can create custom configurations and upload them to the device and install security and other software updates. Regardless of whether you are part of a small or large organization, the device management center is a great place to keep track of all the Teams devices in use in your organization.

It is important to make sure any device you want to use with Teams is a certified Teams device. Check out Chapter 10 for more information on using devices with Teams.

TIP

6

Molding Teams to Fit Your Unique Organization

Find out how Teams works well for solo business owners and how to make the most of Teams for small and medium-sized organizations.

Learn how to scale Teams as your business grows and see why the most important aspect of success with Teams is a fast Internet connection.

Dig deeper into enterprise-specific scenarios and where to go next when using Teams in large organizations.

Look at some of the advanced features of Teams, such as Cloud Voice, compliance, and reporting.

Discover how you can leverage Teams for shift-based work and how Teams can be used in the education, healthcare, consulting, and government industries.

Chapter **15**

Using Teams in Small and Medium-Sized Organizations

S mall and medium-sized organizations have always been in a tricky situation when it comes to enterprise-grade products. Most organizations start out with just a small group of people or even a single person. The tools you use as an individual are vastly different than the tools you will need when you grow and expand to become a large enterprise. Microsoft Teams was designed to be scalable. The way you use Teams as a small or medium-sized business will be different than the way you use it as you grow.

In this chapter, you learn about using Teams in small and medium-sized organizations. You learn some of the tips and tricks that work for using Teams as a sole proprietor all the way up to a medium-sized organization with up to 250 people. You learn how to get started with Teams, how to adopt Teams, and how to scale up as your organization grows. First, though, you need to look at your Internet connection. We start this chapter there.

Focusing on the Internet

By far, the most important aspect of having a good experience with Teams no matter the size of your business is your Internet connection. Teams is a cloud-based service so all communications outside your local network travel over the Internet. The way Teams sends data over the Internet is heavily optimized; however, video and audio calls still require a lot of data to be transferred back and forth. If you have a slow Internet connection, your calls will be choppy and your video will freeze and jump. In short, a poor Internet connection will make Teams a very painful experience.

TIP

Microsoft Teams also sends data between devices on your local network in a peer-to-peer fashion. This traffic can be substantial for large enterprises (which I talk about in Chapter 16). With small and medium-sized organizations, most off-the-shelf network gear will be more than enough. If your organization is to the size where you have a network engineer who is responsible for your internal network, it is worth having this person take a look at the network section of Chapter 16.

Microsoft has tons of graphs and tables and charts to help organizations ensure their Internet connection can provide a good experience for Teams. I go into these in more detail in Chapter 16 because larger organizations have more complicated networks and Internet connections. For small and medium-sized organizations, you likely have minimal options when it comes to your Internet connection.

In general, my recommendation is to look for a connection that has at least 2 megabits per second (Mbps) of bandwidth per person in your location who will be using Teams. Microsoft states that Teams can deliver high-definition (HD) video quality over a bandwidth as low as 1.2 Mbps; however, I have noticed it is better to be on the safe side with 2 Mbps. For example, if you have five people working in your office and you will all be making calls on Teams, look for at least a 10 Mbps Internet connection.

Figure 15-1 shows the Internet options available for a company called WaveG in Seattle. Note the options call out symmetrical speeds. This means the bandwidth advertised is available in both directions (in other words, sending data from your computer to the Internet and receiving data from the Internet to your computer). Symmetric speeds are important because Teams sends data in both directions for video and audio calls. However, if both upload and download speeds are fast enough, then you don't need to worry about symmetric connection speeds. For example, you might have gigabit download speeds, which could accommodate a massive amount of traffic and only 30 Mbps upload speed. Even though you only have 30 Mbps upload speed, this would be plenty for a ten-person organization.

Be sure to check both upload and download bandwidth speeds when reviewing Internet connection offers. Some companies offer blazing fast download speeds and very slow upload speeds. This is because applications, such as video streaming services, predominately use download bandwidth and don't need a very fast upload speed. Teams data flows both up and down from your computer to the Internet, so you need to make sure your bandwidth accommodates both directions.

A gigabit is a thousand megabits. Gigabit Internet connections are becoming increasingly common in major cities. Rejoice if you have this type of bandwidth available in your area. Many rural areas struggle with even basic Internet connectivity.

Understanding How Teams Fits Your Organization

There is no hard and fast rule about the size of an organization and how you should use Teams. I have had a lot of experience with organizations of all sizes, and by observing how each uses Teams, I have discovered a general evolutionary path most organizations follow in their journey with Teams. I like to break down small and medium-sized organizations into three buckets based on the number of employees, as shown in Figure 15-2.

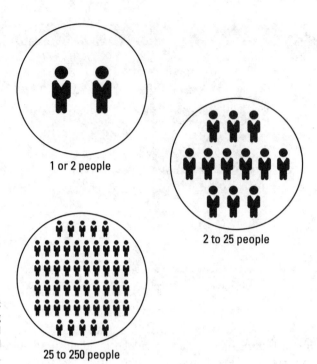

1 or 2 people

2 to 25 people

FIGURE 15-2:
Grouping
small and
medium-sized
organizations.

25 to 250 people

Many organizations start out as a single person or a person with a partner — a one- or two-person organization. The way this type of organization uses Teams is specific to that size.

The next evolution in using Teams occurs when an organization has between 2 and 25 people. It is just big enough to start thinking about having someone designated as the Teams administrator, but still small enough that everyone knows what is going on with everyone else.

The next stage in the Teams journey is when an organization grows to 25 to 250 people. I think of these as medium-sized organizations. In these organizations, there are enough people that not everyone knows what is going on with everyone else, and there are enough duties that the roles and how people use Teams need to be defined. Also, this is where governance starts to take shape.

Let's take a look at how each type of organization can use and benefit from Teams.

Keeping it simple (1 or 2 people)

Teams is valuable for even a single-person organization. You can invite guests to your teams to collaborate and communicate and use it to set up meetings and conference calls. As a solo practitioner or a two-person organization, you can keep things simple. You don't need to worry about setting permissions for yourself or your partner because you will be an administrator over the entire Microsoft 365 or Office 365 subscription and all services within the subscription.

Though you won't need to worry about permissions, you will need to become familiar with basic administration tasks. (I cover basic administration throughout the book in the relevant chapters and then go into depth on the Teams Admin Center in Chapter 13 and Chapter 14.) In addition, you will need to spend time in the Microsoft 365 or Office 365 administration centers for your subscription and be familiar with the administration of other services you can leverage through Teams such as SharePoint. These topics are significant enough to fill books on their own — check out *Office 365 For Dummies* (Wiley) and *SharePoint For Dummies* (Wiley) for more information.

As a single or two-person organization, it is important to also focus your learning on guest access, as nearly everyone you talk with through Teams (aside from your partner if you have one) will be a guest. (I cover guest access in Chapter 7.) Larger organizations often only communicate with other people within the organization. If you are a solo practitioner, you will be exclusively communicating with people outside your organization unless you tend to chat with yourself, which I have been known to do myself from time to time.

WARNING

Pay attention to the process around inviting guest users into your teams, channels, and chats. One area I have seen organizations of all sizes struggle with is in document collaboration. Teams puts a heavy emphasis on collaboration with people inside your organization. For people outside your organization, you need to pay attention to how Teams behaves, which I outline in Chapter 7.

Also pay attention to where you are sharing a file with guest users. Guest users don't have access to back-end storage locations like SharePoint by default. A good example of a "gotcha" here is when you share a file with a guest user in a chat. I have gotten caught in situations where there were three copies of the same file and nobody knew which one was the one source of truth. I had a copy of the document in my OneDrive, another copy was in the back-end SharePoint site for the team, and yet another copy was in the SharePoint site of the organization. At some point I saved a copy to my local computer, too! It took making some minor changes to the file over a conference call to get the file back to where it needed to be. In short, the way Teams displays files from various cloud locations is not always obvious, especially when dealing with guest users who have limited access to back-end storage locations like SharePoint.

Finally, I have found that conference calls and phone numbers are incredibly valuable to organizations of all sizes, and the same value applies to a one- or two-person organization as well. You can sign up for voice services and obtain a phone number, toll-free number, and conference call numbers just like the largest enterprise organization.

Taking your organization to the next level (2 to 25 people)

When an organization reaches between 2 and 25 people, you need to start thinking about scaling some of the duties in Teams as well as separating teams between internal users and guest users. Organizations of this size are still small enough that it is straightforward to keep track of your teams and channels. It is also common for this size organization to only have a handful of teams, and for everyone in the organization to be part of every team. When you reach this size, however, you might want to consider separating teams out into teams that include guest users and teams that are only for internal members of your organization, as shown in Figure 15-3. (I cover how to do this in Chapter 3.)

FIGURE 15-3:
Creating a separate team for guest users.

Guests might only be invited to this team

You also need to start thinking about who will take on the administrative roles. What I have seen with organizations of this size is that one or two people agree to take on the administrative duties for Office 365 and Teams. This includes things like adding new users, purchasing and managing licenses, and configuring admin settings that affect everyone in the organization.

TIP

Whoever signs up for the Microsoft 365 or Office 365 subscription is automatically an administrator for the entire subscription, including Teams. A common scenario is that someone is tasked with signing up the organization and then finds out he or she is the administrator by default. I like to refer to this as the "accidental administrator." The good news is that you can always assign others as an administrator, too.

I have noticed that most organizations of this size tend to spend most of their time in Teams and quickly collaborate and share files without leaving the Teams application. You will find many apps that you can install as tabs to help your organization be more productive. For example, you can add tabs for SharePoint and even Excel files. In addition, just like a one- or two-person organization, you will likely be interacting with guest users. I cover working with people outside your organization in Teams in Chapter 7.

Growing large (25 to 250 people)

In my experience, a company with 25 to 250 people is at the stage where it needs to scale its processes and start thinking about compliance and separation of duties. For example, the person responsible for the Microsoft 365 or Office 365 licensing purchases might be someone in the purchasing department, and the person responsible for the Teams Admin Center might be someone in the IT department. In addition, a power user in one team might be responsible for the administration of that team, including the apps, and a power user in another team might be the admin for that team.

With this size of organization, the number of teams and channels can quickly become overwhelming, and it is time to start thinking about compliance procedures in order to keep track of all the teams and channels. It is likely that not everyone will be in every team, and the team and channel landscape will start to become complex and overwhelming.

I am often amazed at how many teams and channels even a medium-sized organization can achieve. By default, anyone can create a new team and channel. My recommendation is to focus on having a limited number of teams and then allow channels to grow and shrink as needed.

This is the time to come up with a strategy about public and private teams and team membership. For example, you might formalize private teams for specific areas of the organization such as legal, human resources, and accounting. You might want executive-level leadership to have a private place to communicate, and you might want to formalize some "all hands" teams that you can use for announcements and to keep every member of the organization on the same page. For teams you no longer want to maintain, you can archive them. Managing teams on a large scale, including archiving them, is something I cover in Chapter 16.

When a team is no longer active, you can archive it so that you maintain the channels and messages it contains yet keep it from cluttering up the app. Figure 15-4 shows the Manage Teams screen, which also shows your archived teams. I cover the Manage Teams screen further in Chapter 16.

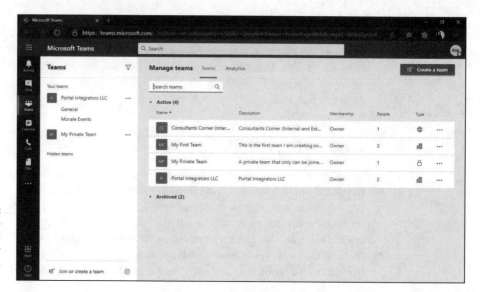

FIGURE 15-4:
The Manage
Teams screen
shows all your
teams in a
grid view.

This is also the time that individual users can start to think about tuning Teams out so that the noise they receive is relevant for them. Some of the features I find useful are notifications and hiding teams and channels. I cover this in more detail in Chapter 8.

As your organization reaches 250 people, you will be moving quickly to adopt features designed for the largest enterprise organizations that reach into the tens of thousands of members. These features include things like private clouds, hybrid scenarios, and dedicated connections to Microsoft. Chapter 16 covers some of the features designed for large enterprises.

Chapter **16**

Unleashing Features Designed for Large Enterprises

L arge enterprises have specific needs when it comes to software and communication systems. Large organizations must deal with issues such as compliance, reporting, and mass scale. Microsoft figured out how to solve these issues with its Skype for Business product and has integrated those components into Teams. So even though Teams is a new product, it was designed to pull in Skype for Business features in order to accommodate large global enterprises.

In this chapter, you learn about using Microsoft Teams in large enterprises, including how to roll out Teams across your organization and how to keep your teams and channels under control. You discover some of the advanced features of Teams, such as Cloud Voice, compliance, and reporting. You also discover some tips and tricks for using Teams in a large organization.

Managing Large Numbers of Teams

To see an overview of all your teams and manage large numbers of them quickly in a single place, you use the Manage Teams screen. To access this screen, select Teams from the left navigation pane and then select the gear icon at the bottom of the list, as shown in Figure 16-1. Note that if you are a guest user, you will see the Manage Teams link instead of a gear icon on its own, as shown in Figure 16-2.

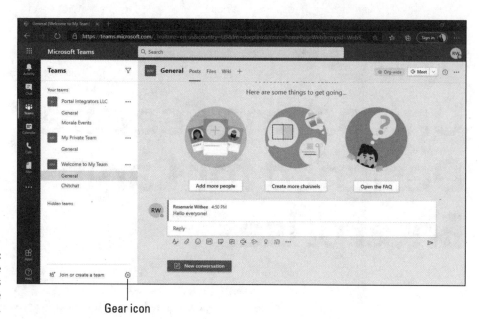

FIGURE 16-1: Opening the Manage Teams screen from the teams list.

Gear icon

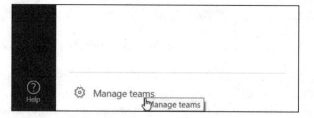

FIGURE 16-2: Opening the Manage Teams screen as a guest.

REMEMBER

If you are a guest user to the Teams account, you don't have the ability to create a new team by default, so you will not see the "Join or create a team" link next to the gear icon in Figure 16-1.

The Manage Teams screen shows an overview of all your teams in a grid view, as shown in Figure 16-3. You will see all your active teams and all the teams you have archived. The first column shows the name of the team followed by a description of the team. The third column shows whether you are a Member, Owner, or Guest to each team. The next column displays a count of the number of people in the team, and the final column displays an icon that shows you what type of team it is (Public, Org-wide, or Private). The last item in each row is an ellipsis that when clicked, displays a drop-down menu of options that will affect the entire team, as shown in Figure 16-4. These are quick options you can use to manage the team without having to go into the team and open the settings.

FIGURE 16-3:
The Manage Teams screen shows all your teams in a grid view.

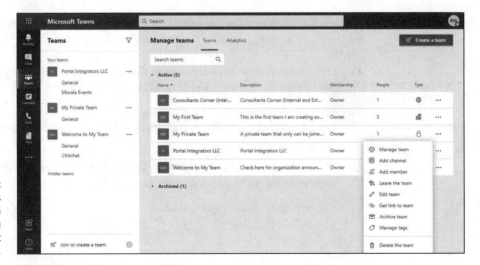

FIGURE 16-4:
The ellipsis provides a drop-down menu of options that affect the team.

With a single click you can do the following:

>> **Manage team:** This option opens the settings for the team where you can manage members, guests, and channels; set the team picture; configure member and guest permissions; view analytics; and add and configure apps. I cover these settings in Chapter 3.

>> **Add channel:** This option enables you to add a new channel to the team.

>> **Add member:** With this option you can add a new member or invite a guest to the team.

>> **Leave the team:** You can remove yourself from the team with this option.

>> **Edit team:** This option enables you to edit the name, description, or privacy information for the team. The privacy information is either Public, Org-wide, or Private as I describe in Chapter 3.

>> **Get link to team:** You can get a direct link to the team with this option. In large organizations with hundreds or thousands of teams, I find sending a link to a specific team can be a shortcut to get a group of people communicating together in the same team.

>> **Archive team:** You can archive the team with this option. This saves the information in the team.

>> **Delete the team:** This option enables you to delete the team. This destroys all information in the team.

Archiving a team

Archiving a team removes it from being active, but keeps all the information in the team. To archive a team, follow these steps:

1. **Click the gear icon that appears at the bottom of the list of teams in the left navigation pane to open the Manage Teams screen.**

   The Manage Teams screen is shown earlier in Figure 16-1. Note that if you are a guest user, you will see the Manage Teams link instead of the gear icon on its own (see Figure 16-2).

2. **Select the ellipsis next to the team you want to archive and then select Archive team, as shown in Figure 16-5.**

   The Archive Team dialog box appears.

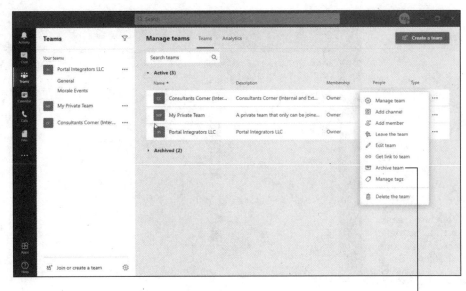

FIGURE 16-5:
Selecting the
option to Archive
team from
the drop-down
menu next
to a team.

Click to archive a team

3. **Select the check box to make the SharePoint site read-only for all team members, as shown in Figure 16-6.**

TIP

Every team has an associated SharePoint site behind the scenes. I highly recommend making this SharePoint site read-only by clicking the check box in the Archive Team dialog box. I have seen the back-end SharePoint site of an archived team cause a great deal of confusion when it is not set to read-only because people who have bookmarked it may continue to use it and have no idea the associated team is no longer active.

Want to archive "Welcome to My Team"?

This will freeze all team activity, but you'll still be able to add or remove members and update roles. Go to Manage teams to restore the team. Learn more.

☐ Make the SharePoint site read-only for team members

FIGURE 16-6:
Selecting the
option to make
the associated
SharePoint site
read-only.

Cancel   Archive

Select to make read-only

4. **Select Archive to move the team from Active to Archived status.**

The team now appears in the Archived list in the manage teams screen, as shown in Figure 16-7.

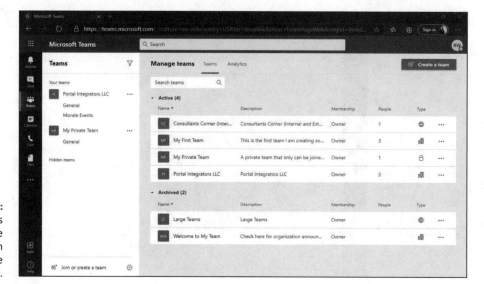

FIGURE 16-7:
Archived teams are moved to the archived section of the manage teams list.

TIP

You can restore any team that has been archived. To restore a team, select the ellipsis next to a team in the Archived list and then select Restore team, as shown in Figure 16-8.

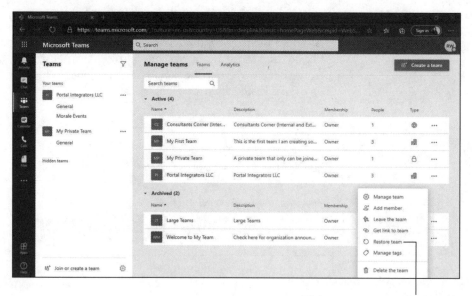

FIGURE 16-8:
Restoring a team that has been archived.

Click to restore an archived team

Deleting a team

In general, I recommend archiving teams rather than deleting them because you never know when you might need to resurrect them in the future. However, when you are confident you want to remove a team and all information the team contained, you can delete it.

To delete a team, follow these steps:

1. **Click the gear icon that appears at the bottom of the list of teams in the left navigation pane to open the Manage Teams screen.**

   The Manage Teams screen is shown earlier in Figure 16-1. Note that if you are a guest user, you will see the Manage Teams link instead of the gear icon on its own (see Figure 16-2).

2. **Select the ellipsis next to the team you want to delete and then select Delete Team.**

   The Delete Team dialog box appears.

3. **Confirm you understand that all information with this team will be lost and then click Delete Team, as shown in Figure 16-9.**

   The team will be removed from the list of teams and all information will be destroyed.

Delete "Welcome to My Team" team

Are you sure you want to delete the team "Welcome to My Team"? All channels, chats, files, and the Microsoft 365 Group for this team will be deleted.

☑ I understand that everything will be deleted.

Cancel   Delete team

FIGURE 16-9: Confirming that deleting a team destroys all information in the team and it is lost forever.

Bringing in the Network Engineers

The network and Internet connections in an enterprise organization are critical for Teams to be successful. As such, you must make sure you have network engineers in the loop. Teams sends and receives a constant stream of network traffic between your internal network and the Microsoft data centers where Teams is hosted. In addition, Teams sends traffic through your local network in a peer-to-peer fashion. In other words, if you are calling someone in the next room using

Teams, your computers can talk directly to each other instead of out over the Internet. Because Teams uses both your local network and your Internet connection so extensively, the bandwidth and requirements must be accounted for between all devices that will use Teams. Features of Teams such as video and audio calls, screen sharing, and conference calling can take up a significant amount of your network traffic, and it is important these needs are understood and met from the beginning.

Microsoft provides network guidance for engineers. The guidance is heavily technical and provides network engineers with key technical details that relate to how fast and how much data can flow through networks.

Microsoft provides Teams network guidance in two ways:

>> **Client to Microsoft Edge:** This measurement is from the Teams client device to the edge of the Microsoft network, which Microsoft confusingly calls "Microsoft Edge" — the same name as its preferred web browser. The first is from the Teams client to the edge of the Microsoft network. This means the network traffic goes from the device Teams is running on (such as your desktop or laptop computer), through your organization's internal network, out over the Internet, and into the Microsoft network.

>> **Customer Edge to Microsoft Edge:** This measurement is from the edge of your network to the edge of the Microsoft network. In other words, the traffic that is going over the Internet.

TIP

Microsoft has massive capacity built into its network, so much so that it is confident that once the traffic gets to its network, things will be fine. When you hear the term "Microsoft edge," Microsoft is not referring to its web browser product; it is referring to the edge of the Microsoft network.

TECHNICAL STUFF

The network guidance for Teams that Microsoft provides on its website is extremely technical. As mentioned earlier in this section, it is broken down into two categories: Client to Microsoft Edge and Customer Edge to Microsoft Edge. With each category Microsoft includes values for items such as one-way latency and round-trip latency. *Latency* refers to the amount of delay there is between a piece of data leaving one computer and arriving at another. Microsoft also provides details around the data loss that occurs when two computers are communicating with each other. The Internet is designed so that some data can be lost as it is transmitted over a network and the overall connection can still be fine. The technical term for this is *packet loss.* What happens is that a piece of network gear somewhere in the middle of the network might not deliver the data as expected. When this happens, the data is lost and the receiving computer has to request it to be sent again. These technical aspects are beyond the scope of this book, but they are critically important to network engineers.

Most network engineers are very particular about their networks, and rightfully so. They need to make sure legitimate network traffic passes in, out, and around their networks and that nefarious traffic is blocked. To accommodate this, nearly every large network I have seen adopts enterprise-grade firewalls. A *firewall* is a hardware or software device that filters network traffic based on seemingly infinite variables. For example, for a computer running a web server, only web traffic will be allowed to it and all other network traffic will be blocked.

The network traffic of Microsoft services uses a staggering number of different types of ports and protocols. All of these things are critical to ensure that Teams is easy to use and works as expected. Some wise person once said that making something appear simple is the hardest thing in the world to achieve.

In addition to port and protocol access, you will also find Domain Name Service (DNS) guidance. You will want to pay careful attention to DNS resolution. Microsoft Teams expects to be able to find Internet Protocol (IP) addresses for specific service names. Microsoft maintains a list of the ports and protocol DNS entries on its website and updates it frequently. The full listing can be found at `https://docs.microsoft.com/en-us/microsoft-365/enterprise/urls-and-ip-address-ranges`.

Microsoft has a great video available on YouTube that walks you through network planning in detail. You can find it by opening your web browser and navigating to `https://aka.ms/teams-networking`.

Dividing and Conquering with Fine-Tuned Admin Roles

You can use an astounding number of roles (43 at present count) to divide up administrative duties in Microsoft 365. Microsoft outlines these roles in a table in the Microsoft documentation. Included in the list is the role of Teams Admin, whose role is described as having full access to the Teams and Skype admin center, managing Microsoft 365 groups and service requests, and monitoring service health. Other roles relate to other services and features of these services and include Billing Admin, Compliance Admin, Security Admin, License Admin, and User Admin to just name a few.

Monitoring service health refers to the health of the services that make up the Microsoft 365 subscription. Teams is one of these services, and there are many more, including SharePoint for content management and Exchange for email.

I highly recommend enterprise organizations become familiar with the different types of administrators in Microsoft 365 and leverage their use to divide and focus duties. The full table of admin roles and descriptions can be found at https://docs.microsoft.com/en-us/microsoft-365/admin/add-users/about-admin-roles.

TIP

Microsoft Teams is a service that is part of the Microsoft 365 subscription. As a result, Teams administration is closely tied to the administration of all of the services offered in these subscriptions. Pay attention to the administration roles for SharePoint as well. As this book went to print, Microsoft had just reorganized and put SharePoint, OneDrive, and Teams under the leadership of Jeff Teper. Jeff is rather famous as a leader for the SharePoint product, and I see this as an evolution of the close ties between SharePoint and Teams. As a funny side note, at the 2019 Microsoft Ignite conference, one of the community leaders staged a mock wedding between Teams and SharePoint, perhaps setting the stage for the reorganization we are seeing now.

Creating a Policy to Retain or Delete Content

The Teams Admin Center provides countless options for customizing and configuring Teams for large organizations. A grouping of configuration settings is known as a *policy*, and there are many different types of policies you can set up in Teams. I cover policies in the Teams Admin Center in Chapter 13 and Chapter 14.

One policy I find useful for larger organizations is around content retention. You can set up a policy to retain content so that it is not deleted. You can also set up a policy to delete content after an expiration period. Retention policies are set in the Security and Compliance Center, which is accessed through your Microsoft 365 Admin Center.

To create a retention policy, follow these steps:

1. **Open your web browser and log in to the Microsoft Security and Compliance center at** https://protection.office.com.

TIP

   You need to be an administrator for your Microsoft 365 subscription in order to log in to the Security and Compliance Admin center.

2. **In the left navigation pane, expand Information Governance and then select Retention.**

3. **Click Create to begin creating a new retention policy, as shown in Figure 16-10.**

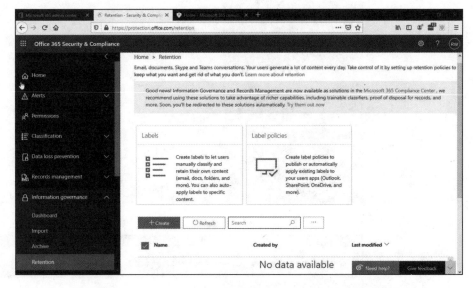

FIGURE 16-10:
Creating a retention policy in the Security and Compliance Admin Center.

4. **Provide a name and description for the policy and then click Next.**

5. **Select how long you want to retain content and then click Next.**

   You can also decide to delete content after an expiration date in this screen.

6. **Choose the services the retention policy should apply toward.**

   Make sure to scroll to the bottom and enable the Teams Channel Messages and Teams Chats to ensure the policy applies to Teams, as shown in Figure 16-11.

7. **Choose which teams and users the retention policy should apply to or exclude and then click Next.**

   By default, all teams and users are covered under the policy.

8. **Review your settings and then click Create This Policy, as shown in Figure 16-12.**

TIP

A retention policy can be used to address compliance requirements at both the corporate and regulatory level. You can also set up a retention policy to automatically delete data after an expiration time.

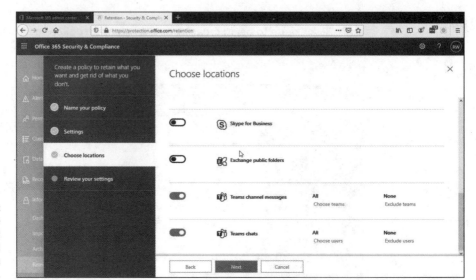

FIGURE 16-11:
Enabling the
Teams channel
messages and
chats in a
retention policy.

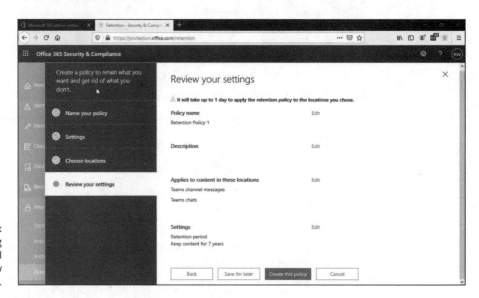

FIGURE 16-12:
Reviewing
settings and
creating a new
retention policy.

Exploring Enterprise Voice Features

Microsoft has an offering called Cloud Voice that provides enterprise features for large organizations. Cloud Voice includes options for connecting your internal phone network to the Public Switched Telephone Network (PSTN) and using your existing Private Branch eXchange (PBX) system capabilities. These topics are beyond the scope of this book, but you should be aware that they exist. Microsoft has changed the branding of some of these offerings; however, the products and capabilities have stayed largely the same. I have found that organizations that have been around for a long time already have specialized hardware, such as on-site PBX systems, and that the telecommunications engineers are happy to find that Microsoft supports this equipment.

TIP

Large organizations are happy to learn that Microsoft has several offerings that provide integration with existing telephone network equipment and network connections. Advanced scenarios are all too common with established enterprise organizations, and Microsoft has gone out of its way to make sure Teams works in almost all situations.

TECHNICAL
STUFF

When your organization has some products installed locally at your organization, and those products interface with Teams, which is hosted by Microsoft, the term often used to describe those products is *hybrid.* This means Teams uses a hybrid approach that includes some of your organization's resources and some Microsoft-hosted resources. I should also note that I have heard Microsoft use the term *hybrid* to refer to some people in your organization using the old Skype for Business and some people using the new Teams. You might read about this "hybrid" approach in Microsoft documentation, but my recommendation is to think of a hybrid environment as having some products hosted and managed by your own internal IT organization and other products hosted and managed by Microsoft in its datacenter.

Reporting and Analytics

In Chapter 13, I walk through the Teams Admin Center and touch on where to find reports. Reports and analytics are critical to larger organizations in order to obtain a view into how people are using Teams and areas that might need to be improved.

You can use the Teams Usage Report to see how active users are and where they are active in channels and chats. You can also get a view into how many guests are in a team and their privacy settings. Or, you can use the Teams User Activity Report to view how many one-to-one calls a user participated in or how active a user was in a channel or chat. You will also find reports about the devices people are using and how much they are using them. Finally, you will find reports for live events and several reports around PSTN usage.

I recommend getting familiar with all these reports and reviewing them on a frequent basis. The reports are useful for people throughout an organization including IT teams, network teams, development teams, and adoption teams.

Reports are available in the Teams Admin Center. In the left navigation pane, select Analytics and Reports and then select the report you want to view.

Earlier in the chapter I talk about how you can view and manage all your teams in a grid view. You can use a similar view to see analytic information about your teams. To view the analytics for all your teams, follow these steps:

1. **Click the gear icon that appears at the bottom of the list of teams in the left navigation pane to open the Manage Teams screen.**

   The Manage Teams screen is shown earlier in Figure 16-1. Note that if you are a guest user, you will see the Manage Teams link instead of the gear icon on its own (see Figure 16-2).

2. **Select Analytics at the top of the screen to switch to the Analytics View, as shown in Figure 16-13.**

   The Analytics View shows the name of the team, the number of active users, people, guests, and messages as well as the type of team.

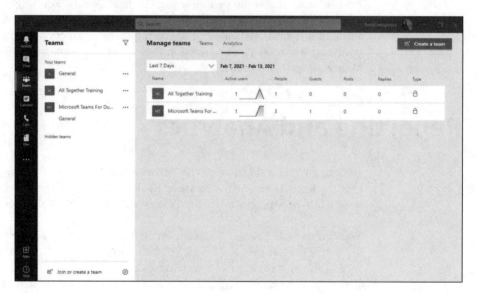

FIGURE 16-13:
View the analytics for all teams.

You can click on the name of a team to jump to the Analytics View in the settings for the team.

Upgrading from Skype for Business to Teams

The effort required to move to Teams from Skype for Business depends greatly on what version of Skype for Business your organization is currently using: the On-Premises version or the Online version. If you are using Skype for Business On-Premises (meaning your own IT department is responsible for the servers and software that run it), you will be moving from a solution managed internally to a Microsoft-managed cloud solution. I have seen this become tricky when the internal IT team is the one team that has always been responsible for the communications system and it then must pass that duty off to Microsoft.

If you are moving from Skype for Business Online to Teams, you are already using a Microsoft-managed solution and the process is straightforward. Microsoft responded to the pain that several organizations reported by providing a framework and guidance to help you migrate users to Teams in an orderly fashion. Use your favorite search engine and search for *Microsoft Teams Upgrade Framework*. The framework includes guidance on how to get a large organization from Skype for Business to Teams.

TIP

If your organization is using Skype for Business, you need to move to Teams as soon as possible. Microsoft has announced that Skype for Business Online will be retired in 2021.

Getting Help from the Experts

The most important advice I can leave you regarding large organizations is to find a Microsoft Teams expert and get advice from him or her. Microsoft maintains a high-quality bar for their Most Valuable Professional (MVP) designation, and these people know what they are doing. Microsoft MVPs are often consultants and work with many companies. They have experienced just about every problem you can imagine, and their knowledge and insight are an investment worth making.

You can find a listing of Microsoft MVPs at `https://mvp.microsoft.com`. Click on Find an MVP at the top of the page and then filter on Office Apps and Services. You can also narrow down your search to your geographic region of the world.

Chapter **17**

Learning How Teams Embraces Industry-Specific Needs

The coronavirus pandemic in 2020 forced many industries to examine their work-from-home policies. If they didn't have any when the pandemic caused many businesses to switch to a work-from-home model, the businesses quickly adapted. While there are still many jobs that cannot be done from home, what this time has shown us is that it is possible for more jobs to be done from home than perhaps we originally thought.

Different industries have different needs when it comes to software and communication systems, regardless of whether an industry's employees are able to work from home or mostly work in person in an office or other setting. The way a hospital or physician's office uses Microsoft Teams will be radically different than the way a manufacturing business or government agency uses Teams.

In this chapter, you learn how to get the most out of Teams in different industries. For example, you learn how Teams can be used in education, healthcare, and government. And you gain an understanding of how you can adapt Teams for the needs of your own industry.

Getting the Most from Teams for Education

In March 2020, the world went into lockdown. Students around the globe suddenly found themselves having to continue their learning online. It did not matter whether the schools and teachers were ready to go from all in-person classes to everything taught remotely. To paraphrase a popular saying, everyone was learning to fly the airplane as it was being built.

Although Microsoft Teams was first primarily created for companies, it did not take long before schools adopted it. Microsoft Teams allows teachers and students to keep conversations and interactions focused and work organized. The features and functionality of Microsoft Teams for Education are similar to Microsoft Teams for Work. Instead of a team, however, think about a class. Instead of managers and coworkers, think of administrators, teachers, and students.

TIP

Microsoft offers special Microsoft 365 subscriptions for education — through its Microsoft 365 Education suite of products — that are specifically designed for use in school settings. Within these subscriptions are special templates for Teams that are specifically designed for teachers and students. In Chapter 1, you learn how to sign up for a new subscription. If you are an educator, you can sign up for a subscription that is specifically designed for education. You can find out more information about Microsoft 365 Education at www.microsoft.com/en-us/education.

Creating a team from a class list

With a Microsoft 365 Education subscription, you can create a class team. (I cover creating a new team in Chapter 3.) The class team is a type of team you can select when you first create a new team, and it is only available as an option within the Microsoft 365 Education subscription. A class team is designed for a teacher to interact with students in a class. A teacher creates the team and then adds students and any co-teachers. The teachers can guide students to collaborate and work in channels, share files, and turn in assignments.

Follow these steps to create a team from a class list:

1. **Click the Teams icon in the left navigation pane.**

2. **Select Suggested classes to reveal a list of your suggested classes.**

    The Suggested classes link appears either next to the Join or create team button in the top-right corner of the Teams window, or at the bottom of the teams list.

3. **Select Join or create team and select your class from the pre-populated list.**

    You can select more than one class.

4. **Select Create and click to open the team tile when it appears.**

    Your students will be added to the team automatically.

5. **When you are ready to activate your team, select the Activate banner to make the team visible to the students.**

TIP

> You do not have to activate the team you just created right away. You can take this step after you have the time to organize, add your content, and other tasks you need to do before you have your student join. When you are ready, select the Activate banner to make the team visible to your students.

For more help, Microsoft provides an interactive video that walks teachers through how to use Teams with their classes. The video includes examples of a biology teacher managing a class of students and collaborating with the class as the students work on their assignments. You can check out the video at `https://info.microsoft.com/ww-landing-Contact-Microsoft-Education-Request-a-Demo.html`.

TIP

> Microsoft Teams is just one aspect of the Microsoft 365 Education subscriptions. You will also get the standard Office client applications such as Word, Excel, PowerPoint, OneNote, and Outlook. In my opinion, Teams is one of the most important parts of the subscription because it provides a tool for teachers and students to communicate and collaborate. However, other helpful aspects of the subscription include class and staff notebooks, digital storytelling, professional learning community groups, and using Microsoft Forms to grade quizzes.

Using Insights to assess student engagement

Teachers are often left to guess the engagement level of their students. Microsoft's Insights feature provides useful at-a-glance information on student participation in class conversations and trends in student activity. Insights provides a dashboard for teachers to see important metrics that can help in lesson planning, providing feedback, and assessing where additional help might be needed. Although Insights is not a substitute for the expertise of the teacher, it is there to give the teacher some help.

Here's how to enable Microsoft Insights for a class team:

1. **Select the Team to which you want to add Insights from the left navigation pane.**

2. **Select + to add a new tab.**

3. **Select Insights from the list.**

   Use the search function if it is not readily visible.

4. **Select Add.**

5. **Uncheck the option Post to Channel about the tab and then select Save.**

   Only teachers have access to Insights.

Using FlipGrid

FlipGrid is a social learning platform designed for classrooms spanning pre-kindergarten all the way through doctoral programs. FlipGrid can be found at `https://flipgrid.com`. FlipGrid provides a platform for educators to create online meeting places, called Grids, and then add topics to those Grids. Students then meet and discuss topics and learn with the educator. Microsoft was so impressed with FlipGrid that it purchased the company and has begun integrating it with the rest of the Microsoft services.

The FlipGrid app is integrated nicely with Teams, enabling you to use FlipGrid without leaving the Teams environment. (I cover adding apps to Teams in Chapter 5.) You can find the FlipGrid app in the Education category, as shown in Figure 17-1.

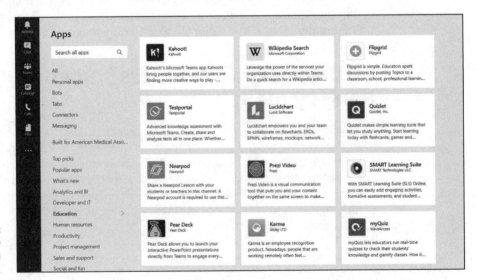

FIGURE 17-1: Adding the FlipGrid app to a team in Teams.

Note that this app is one that uses the permissions set in the Teams Permissions screen. (You access the Permissions screen by selecting Settings from your profile drop-down menu.) FlipGrid will ask for permission when the app needs to access a resource on your computer such as your microphone or video camera so you can record from within Teams. You can always go back to the settings and remove the access or limit the access at any time for your device. (See Chapter 5 for more about setting app permission for external devices.)

Using Teams in Government Agencies

The United States government has used Microsoft products for years and is embracing and adopting Teams in order to stay current. Government workers use Teams to communicate and collaborate. Governments in general have specific considerations for any software, and Microsoft has been very accommodating with the Microsoft 365 Government Cloud Computing (GCC) offering.

TIP

The Microsoft 365 GCC subscription is designed for the specific needs of federal, state, local, and tribal governments.

Teams features specific to the GCC offering include the following:

>> Customer content is stored in the country of origin. For example, the United States government cloud is stored strictly within the United States. There are also offerings for other countries that follow the same design such as China and Germany.

>> Government content is segregated from commercial customer content.

>> Only screened Microsoft employees can access government content for needs such as support and troubleshooting.

>> All features are compliant with the unique certifications and accreditations required by the relevant government.

TIP

If you are using Teams as part of a government offering, the good news is that everything I cover in this book also directly relates to you. The primary difference with Teams in government is in how you sign up for your initial Microsoft 365 subscription. Once you have Teams available to you, you can use all the features I walk you through in this book.

Microsoft made big news in 2019 when it was announced that the United States Department of Defense chose the Microsoft cloud. The contract was a Pentagon contract known as Joint Enterprise Defense Infrastructure (JEDI), and it was valued at $10,000,000,000.00. Yes, that is 10 billion dollars!

Leveraging Teams for Consulting and Service-Based Companies

I cover using Teams with small and medium-size organizations in Chapter 15, and the information in that chapter applies to consulting and service-based companies, too. I have noticed that consulting and service-based firms use the guest access and conferencing capabilities of Teams extensively. If you find yourself on a lot of conference calls, check out Chapter 9 on conducting meetings in Teams and Chapter 11 on setting up conferencing services. I also recommend checking out Chapter 7 for more information on working with guest users.

Empowering Healthcare Providers

Hospitals and healthcare providers have industry-specific needs around patient privacy and data handling in accordance with the Health Insurance Portability and Accountability Act (HIPAA). Microsoft has worked with governmental regulators in order to make sure Teams is compliant in these scenarios. Using Teams, healthcare providers can securely message patients, coordinate and collaborate procedures, provide remote health care (telehealth), and manage patient records using the electronic health record (EHR) standard format.

Microsoft is developing a Teams app that is designed specifically for the healthcare industry. The app is called Patients, and it is designed to use the standard EHR patient record format and let providers manage patient records from within a Teams channel. The app can be installed on mobile phones for mobile healthcare workers or used from the desktop and web versions of Teams.

TIP

Microsoft has put together a video that shows how Teams can be used in the healthcare industry. If you are in this industry, it is worth checking out. You can find it at `https://www.microsoft.com/en-us/microsoft-365/microsoft-teams/healthcare-solutions`.

Modernizing Retail Stores

Microsoft offers two Teams templates designed for modern retail stores: a store template and a manager collaboration template. When you create a team with one of these templates, your team will automatically include channels, apps, and the settings required that Microsoft designed for the template.

The store template automatically creates two channels for the team. The channels are named Shifts Handoff and Learning, and both are automatically set as a favorite for everyone in the team. The template also configures the team with settings designed for retail stores. For example, the team is set to public, so it is viewable by all members of the organization. In addition, permissions are locked down so that members are not allowed to create or manage channels, add or remove apps or connectors, or add or update tabs. (See Chapter 4 for more about how channels work.)

TECHNICAL STUFF

Using Teams templates is something that needs to be done by a developer. Templates are designed for organizations that need to create many teams with the same settings and configuration. Template capabilities use the underlying Microsoft Graph application programming interface (API). The interface uses a web technology known as Representational State Transfer (REST). A sample request and response is shown in Figure 17-2.

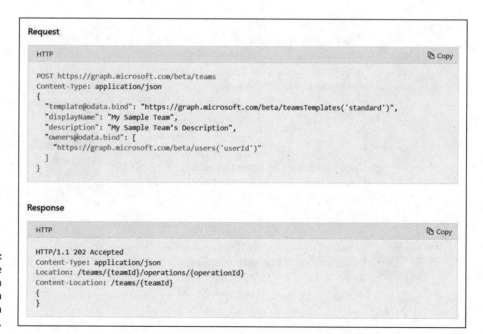

FIGURE 17-2: Using the Microsoft Graph API to create a team based on a template.

Tapping into Teams for Firstline Workers

Firstline workers are a part of almost every industry. A *firstline worker* is someone who interacts directly with the customers of the organization. For example, firstline workers include hotel agents, flight crews, hospital staff, salespeople, waiters, retail associates, and field crews. Firstline workers don't usually sit at a desk with a computer; they are generally mobile and interact face to face with customers. Teams includes several features specifically for the special needs of firstline workers.

The Shifts app in Teams is designed for shift workers such as firstline workers. Shift workers have unique needs such as signing up for shifts, clocking in and out, reviewing schedules, requesting time off, and swapping shifts with others.

You can find the Shifts app in the left navigation pane of Teams. If you don't see it, you can click More Apps and find it in the apps store. I cover Teams apps in detail in Chapter 5.

When you first open the Shifts app, you are provided with the option to create a schedule for each team, as shown in Figure 17-3. Teams first needs to know the time zone of the closest city, as shown in Figure 17-4. Once you confirm the time zone, Teams will set up the Shifts app and provide you with a tour.

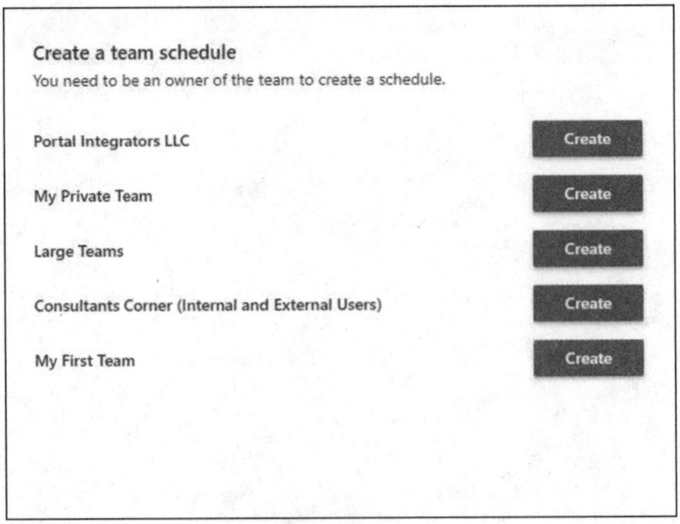

Create a team schedule
You need to be an owner of the team to create a schedule.

Portal Integrators LLC — Create

My Private Team — Create

Large Teams — Create

Consultants Corner (Internal and External Users) — Create

My First Team — Create

FIGURE 17-3: The Shifts app in Teams.

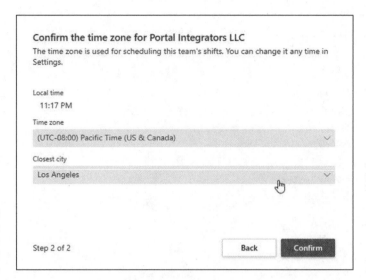

You will see a list of schedules and shifts, as shown in Figure 17-5. You can add new groups and shifts much like you would in your calendar. You can manage requests by clicking the Requests tab at the top of the screen. You can then make a new request for time off, for a schedule swap, or to offer a shift you have already signed up for to someone else, as shown in Figure 17-6.

FIGURE 17-6:
Making a shift request in the Shifts app in Teams.

TIP

The Shifts app includes several settings you can configure. Select the Settings tab from the main Shifts screen to open the settings screen. There you will find settings for schedules, shifts, requests, and the time clock, as shown in Figure 17-7.

The Shifts app was created after a stand-alone service called StaffHub was pulled into Teams. Microsoft is on a path to make Teams a central app for most of its other services, and the Shifts app showcases the direction other scenarios will take as well.

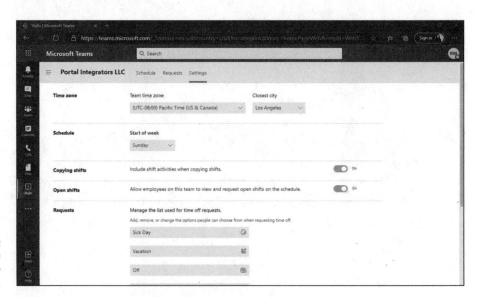

FIGURE 17-7:
Configuring the settings of the Shifts app.

7

The Part of Tens

IN THIS PART . . .

Find out how to be as efficient as possible in organizing, scheduling, and conducting a meeting.

Learn how to keep meeting noise under control, use a whiteboard, and share your screen during a meeting.

Learn how to capture and retain notes from a Teams meeting.

Discover apps available for Teams to help with design, development, productivity, and customer service.

Figure out the best places to get more information about Teams.

Chapter **18**

Ten Tips for Better Teams Meetings

We all have our fair share of meetings. And now, in the time of COVID-19, it may seem that meetings have taken over our life, from work meetings to school to friendly get-togethers to socialize. Meeting online has become such a part of our culture that even my 6- and 4-year-old nephews are used to jumping onto video calls to attend class.

Meetings come in all shapes and sizes with the only constant being that they fill up our schedule. With so many meetings on our plates, it is important to be as efficient as possible in organizing, scheduling, and conducting a meeting. Fortunately, Microsoft Teams includes several features that are particularly useful for meeting efficiency. In this chapter, I share my top ten tips for conducting better meetings in Teams.

Chatting During a Meeting

The most common activity I do in Microsoft Teams is chat with other people. And I find it especially helpful to be able to chat with colleagues during a Teams meeting. A group chat is created automatically at the start of every Teams meeting that includes all the meeting participants. The chat window appears on the right side of the screen. While a meeting is going on and people are presenting and talking with audio, other people can be chatting in the chat window. This simple mechanism proves to be incredibly powerful. For example, suppose you missed something the presenter said. Rather than interrupt the entire meeting and ask the presenter to repeat him or herself, you can just type in the chat and ask someone in the chat for clarification or to fill in a gap. I find I do this all the time in large meetings.

After a meeting has ended, the chat continues to be active and anyone can continue posting messages. For recurring meetings, the chat will carry over from meeting to meeting, so there is always a record of past meetings and anyone on the meeting invite can jump into the chat for upcoming meetings. I have seen larger companies use this to keep track of agenda items for upcoming meetings. People will post in the recurring meeting's chat through the week and then during the meeting, the team will review the chat and discuss the items.

TIP

You may want to turn off message notifications during a meeting if a lot of people are chatting while someone is speaking on audio. A notification will chime with each new message, which can be distracting. Here's how to turn off the sound for incoming messages:

1. **Click your profile picture that appears in the top-right corner of the Teams screen and select Settings.**

2. **In the drop-down menu that appears, select Notifications.**

3. **Under Appearance and Sound, toggle "Play sound for notifications" to off.**

Capturing a Meeting with a Recording

I cannot tell you how many times a recording of a meeting has saved my team a lot of headache. A recording captures everything that happened in the meeting. A recording can be shared with others who were not part of the meeting, and reviewed by those who were part of the meeting. If everyone understands and agrees that meetings will be recorded, I highly recommend recording meetings.

TIP

Teams won't let you record a call between two people due to privacy considerations. Once a call has more than two people, it becomes a meeting and you can record it.

Teams notifies the meeting attendees when a recording begins. However, a best practice is to make sure everyone is completely clear and comfortable with recording the meeting beforehand so that there aren't any issues down the road. A mention at the start that you intend to record the meeting is always a good idea.

Recording a meeting is easy to do in Teams. To begin the recording:

1. **Join an existing meeting or start a new one.**

2. **Open the meeting controls by selecting the ellipsis from the toolbar.**

3. **Select Start Recording from the pop-up menu that appears, as shown in Figure 18-1.**

   Once the recording starts, everyone in the meeting will be informed.

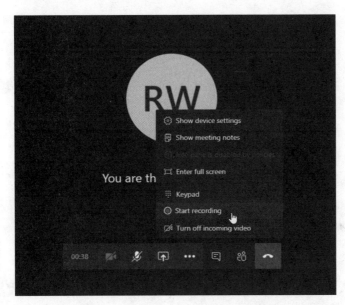

FIGURE 18-1:
Starting a
recording of a
Teams meeting.

4. **To end the recording, click the ellipsis again and select Stop Recording.**

   You can also end the recording by ending the meeting.

   The recording will be made available to the meeting channel, as shown in Figure 18-2. Anyone in the channel can click the recording to view the meeting.

A recording of a meeting is an incredibly powerful tool. You can share it with others who weren't able to attend the meeting, or use it down the road as a reminder of what was discussed and/or decided upon. The recording itself is in a service called Microsoft Stream. You can get a direct link to the meeting by selecting the ellipsis from the recording in the channel and then selecting Get Link, as shown in Figure 18-3. In addition, you can open the recording directly in Stream or even make the recording its own tab in the channel.

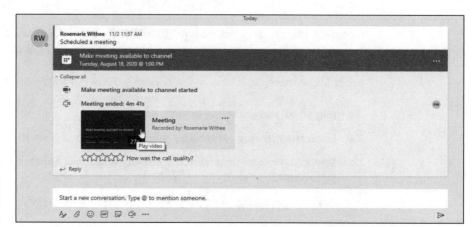

FIGURE 18-2:
Viewing a
meeting
recording in a
channel.

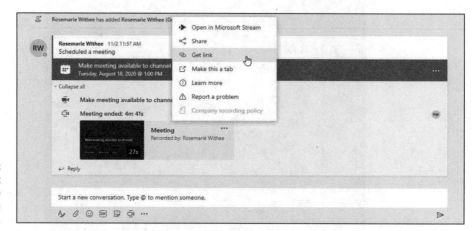

FIGURE 18-3:
Getting the direct
link to the
recording of a
meeting.

Keeping Noise Under Control with Mute

When I am in a meeting, I like to keep my microphone muted unless I am speaking. That way the other participants don't hear any background noise that might be happening around me. Most people follow this same meeting etiquette, but everyone forgets from time to time. Someone might ask if everyone could please mute their microphone, but this can be disruptive to the meeting.

If you are the organizer of the Teams meeting, you can mute the microphones of other participants. I have used this many times when someone's microphone is picking up background noise, such as a barking dog, but I don't want to disrupt the meeting by asking the person to mute his or her microphone.

To mute one of the participants of the meeting, go to the meeting roster that appears along the right side of the meeting window, select the person's name, and choose Mute Participant. To mute everyone, select Mute All from the roster. Both options are shown in Figure 18-4. The participants you mute will be notified that you muted them, and they can unmute themselves at any time.

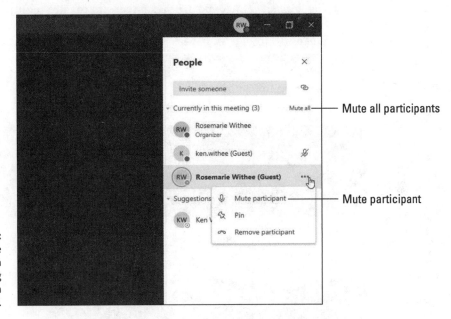

Mute all participants

Mute participant

FIGURE 18-4:
Muting the microphone of a meeting participant in Teams.

TIP

After you mute someone, it is a good idea to send that person a private chat message to let him or her know you did it. Almost every time I have done this, the person thanks me and lets me know that he or she just ran to grab a coffee or use the bathroom and forgot to mute the microphone.

Blurring Your Background

One of the benefits of online collaboration software like Teams is the flexibility of being able to hold a meeting with team members anywhere you have an Internet connection. And using video adds tremendous value to the meeting; however, it also introduces a challenge. What if you find yourself working somewhere you don't want everyone to see? For example, I often take a meeting from home instead of walking into my office. When I am sitting at my kitchen table, you can see our makeshift open pantry in the background. It would be a great background if I was in a meeting with chefs, but it can be distracting for any other type of meeting.

Teams has a cool feature that lets you blur your background but keep your face in focus when on a video call. Everyone in the meeting can see you clearly, even when you move your head around while you are talking, but whatever is behind you and in the background is blurred. No more worrying about any dirty laundry, literally, that might be making an appearance without your knowledge!

Before you join a meeting, you are presented with toggles to turn on your camera and microphone. In between those toggles is a blur toggle, as shown in Figure 18-5, that you can use to blur your background. When you toggle on the blur option, your background will be become blurry, but your face will stay in focus. If you have already joined the meeting, you can find the blur option in the More Options menu, as shown in Figure 18-6.

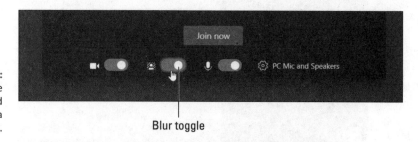

FIGURE 18-5: Blurring the background before joining a Teams meeting.

Blur toggle

FIGURE 18-6: Blurring the background after joining a Teams meeting.

Taking Notes

Recording a meeting is ideal for capturing the meeting in its entirety, but as a practical matter, what you usually need at the completion of a meeting are meeting notes. You can use the notes, also called *meeting minutes,* to capture a record of key decisions and action items.

Teams has a feature designed for capturing meeting notes. The notes are shared so that everyone in the meeting can contribute and view notes as they are added. I can't tell you how many times I have been in a meeting and someone took down notes incorrectly. A simple miscommunication can have ripple effects down the road. When everyone is reviewing and adding to the meeting notes in real time during the meeting, the possibility of miscommunication is greatly reduced.

You can add notes about a meeting before the meeting starts or during the meeting. If a meeting was set up and tied to a Teams channel (which I cover how to do in Chapter 9), you can go into the channel and discuss the meeting there. If the meeting did not have a channel, you can still add notes.

To add pre-meeting notes, follow these steps:

1. **Open your calendar and select the meeting you want to add notes to.**

2. **Choose to chat with participants, as shown in Figure 18-7.**

   Teams will create a chat for the meeting, and all meeting participants are automatically added to it. When the meeting takes place, the chat will be part of the meeting.

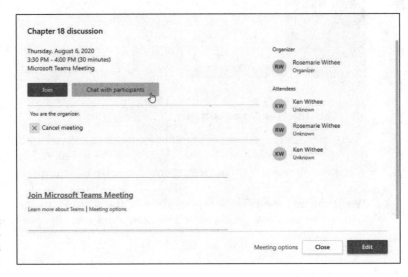

FIGURE 18-7:
Adding pre-meeting notes to a meeting.

Once a meeting starts, you can add official notes to the meeting beyond chat. To open the meeting notes or to start taking notes, follow these steps:

1. **From the meeting options menu, select the Show Meeting Notes option (refer to Figure 18-1).**

   If you have already created notes for the meeting, the meeting notes will open on the right side of the screen. Or, if notes haven't been added to the meeting yet, you will have the option to create notes for the meeting once the meeting has started, as shown in Figure 18-8. To create new meeting notes, continue to Step 2.

FIGURE 18-8:
Adding meeting notes during a meeting.

2. **Click the Take Notes button.**

   Teams will create meeting notes for the meeting, and you will be able to see the new notes section along the right side of the screen. You can now add notes or review any pre-meeting notes added before the meeting started.

When you add meeting notes, members of the channel, or meeting chat, will be notified so that everyone can follow along and add their own notes or review existing notes.

TIP

You can even add the meeting notes as a tab to the meeting (see Figure 18-9). You find the option to add the meeting notes as a tab by clicking the ellipsis toward the top of the notes screen and choosing to add the notes as a tab.

Meeting Notes tab

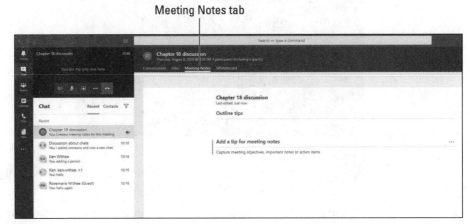

Using a Whiteboard

Some of the most productive meetings I have had over my career are with a group of people standing in front of a whiteboard sketching out ideas. It is an aspect of communication that is hard to beat. Microsoft has recognized this and added a feature to Teams called Whiteboard.

Microsoft Whiteboard is a shared screen that allows you to sketch diagrams. The way you draw on your screen depends on your device. If you are using a standard desktop computer, you use your mouse or a graphics tablet that connects a digital pen to your computer. If you are using a device that has a touch screen, you can use your finger to draw on the screen. My favorite way to sketch on the Teams Whiteboard is with the stylus pen on my Surface laptop. I find it very natural and easy to use.

To use the Whiteboard feature in Teams, follow these steps:

1. **Join an existing Teams meeting or start a new one.**

2. **From the meeting controls, expand the Share dialog box by selecting the icon that looks like a computer monitor with an arrow going through it.**

   The bottom of the screen will expand, and you will see options for sharing your screen, a window on your screen, or a PowerPoint file. On the right side of your screen you will see the option for Whiteboard, as shown in Figure 18-10.

FIGURE 18-10:
Opening the
whiteboard from
the sharing box in
a Teams meeting.

3. **Select Whiteboard and the screen will update, displaying a digital whiteboard, as shown in Figure 18-11.**

You can select the pen color and pen width and begin drawing on the screen. Everyone in the meeting will see what you are drawing, and they can jump in and add their own drawings or edit an existing drawing.

The whiteboard persists even after the meeting so that you can always go back to it and add new sketches or modify existing sketches. Once you activate the whiteboard, it will be displayed as a tab on the channel or chat. You can export the state of the whiteboard at any time by clicking the settings icon in the top-right of the screen and choosing Export Image. I like to do this in order to lock the whiteboard and capture the state at any given time. This is much the same as taking a picture of a physical whiteboard to make sure you have the drawing on hand in case anyone comes along and erases it.

FIGURE 18-11:
Sketching on a
shared digital
whiteboard in
Teams.

TIP

Every team in Teams has a digital whiteboard that can be used for meetings.

Sharing Your Screen

It is much easier to look at your own computer screen than to look over the shoulder of someone else. Using Teams, you can share your screen with others, and they can share their screen with you.

During a Teams meeting, you can share your entire screen, a specific window, a PowerPoint presentation, or a whiteboard (covered in the previous section). Personally, I like to share just the window or PowerPoint slide I am talking about in the meeting. For example, if I am showing a website, I just share the web browser window instead of my entire desktop. If I am walking through a PowerPoint presentation, I just share the PowerPoint window.

There are many reasons you might not want to show your entire desktop. For example, your digital desktop might be messy with various files that you are in the middle of organizing. Or, you might have sensitive material that should not be seen or recorded by everyone in the meeting. Regardless of the reason, you can share just what you want the team to focus on and leave the rest of your desktop hidden.

To share your desktop, a window, or a PowerPoint presentation, follow these steps:

1. **Join an existing Teams meeting or start a new one.**

2. **From the meeting controls, expand the Share dialog box by selecting the icon that looks like a computer monitor with an arrow going through it.**

   The bottom of the screen will expand, and you will see options for sharing your screen, a window on your screen, or a PowerPoint file.

3. **Select the option you want to share with the meeting.**

   A red box will outline what is being shared with others so that you know exactly what they can see, as shown in Figure 18-12.

4. **To stop presenting, select the Stop Presenting button at the top of the display window.**

FIGURE 18-12:
Sharing a
PowerPoint
presentation
during a Teams
meeting.

Taking Control of Someone Else's Screen

In the previous section, you discover how to share your screen with others. You can also have someone else take control of your screen or ask to take control of someone else's screen. When you take control of another person's screen through Teams, you can move that person's mouse around and type on his or her screen using your own mouse and keyboard. I use this frequently when I want to show someone how to do something on his or her computer.

TIP

Someone cannot take control of your screen without your permission. If someone requests to take control of your screen, you will see a message appear asking if you want to allow the person to take control of your screen or not. If you approve the request, that person will be able to control your mouse on your screen; however, if you deny the request, that person won't be able to take control.

To give control of a shared screen, select the Give Control button that appears at the top of the sharing area. When you select this button, a drop-down menu appears that lists everyone in the meeting. You can choose who to give control of your screen to. You can take back control using the same method.

Organizing Teams to Fit Your Meeting Needs

I tend to like the defaults of how Teams is laid out for most meetings. Teams will often make smart decisions and switch between showing people on the main screen and showing a presentation on the main screen. Teams will also detect who is speaking and enlarge that person's video so that you can focus on the person speaking.

However, you might want to take control and shift how you view things. You can switch between people and presentations by clicking on the videos of the participants or the presentations. You can also take the video of a participant and pin it so that it is always displayed. Sometimes I like to pop a video out of Teams and drag it over to another monitor. All this flexibility ensures you can adjust a meeting to fit your needs.

Using Teams While a Meeting Is in Progress

During a meeting, most of the Teams screens are dedicated to the meeting. This is valuable when you want to focus on the meeting. However, you can still use other parts of Teams when a meeting is in progress. For example, if there is a large meeting that I need to listen in on but not focus all of my attention, I will minimize the meeting and use other portions of Teams. Minimizing the meeting is as simple as clicking on another portion of Teams, such as another channel or chat. When you click outside of the meeting, Teams automatically minimizes the meeting into a small window at the top of the left navigation pane, as shown in Figure 18-13. To go back to the meeting and maximize the window on your screen, simply click inside the meeting window.

The minimized meeting window

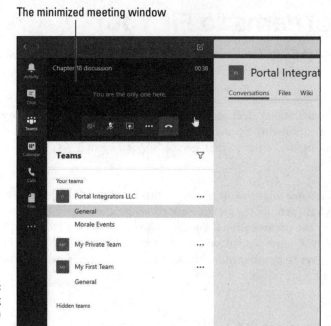

FIGURE 18-13:
A Teams meeting
that has been
minimized.

Chapter **19**

Ten Teams Apps Worth Discovering

I use many different Microsoft Teams apps on a daily basis. I use apps for everything from design, development, productivity, and customer service to social media, surveys, and marketing. There are even apps specifically designed for industry-specific needs such as education.

In this chapter, I highlight ten useful apps for Teams that you may want to check out, too. There are many, many apps in specific categories that could be listed here; however, I spread my picks across different areas to provide you with a good understanding of what Teams can do when you extend it with apps.

REMEMBER

Once you find apps you like, check out Chapter 5 for information about how to install and use apps in Teams.

Microsoft Office

It makes sense that Microsoft Teams works well with the other Microsoft Office products. You will find tight integration with apps for Word, Excel, PowerPoint, and OneNote (https://products.office.com/en-us/microsoft-teams). These apps often come preconfigured, and you can add them to teams and channels and customize how you use them within Teams in general. Figure 19-1 shows the Excel app rendering a spreadsheet within Teams.

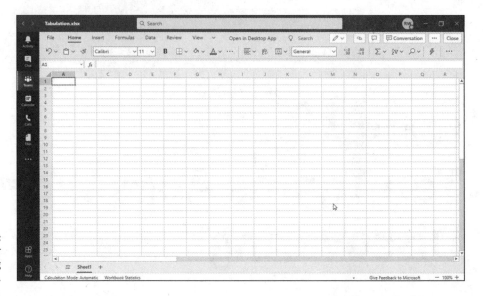

FIGURE 19-1:
The Excel app for
Teams rendering
a spreadsheet.

Another set of useful Microsoft Office apps for Teams are Flow and SharePoint. Microsoft Flow is used to build workflows between the different Office products. Microsoft SharePoint is a content management platform. Both are available with Microsoft 365 depending on your license.

I find it incredibly useful to build flows that interact with Teams. For example, I like to use Microsoft Flow to add notifications to my Teams channels when something happens in SharePoint that needs my team's attention (such as an approval).

To learn more about Microsoft Flow, take a look at *Microsoft Office 365 For Dummies* (Wiley), where it is covered in more detail. And to learn more about Microsoft SharePoint, check out *Microsoft SharePoint For Dummies* (Wiley), which tells you everything you need to know about getting up and running with SharePoint.

Task Management

If you work with a team, you most likely use some type of task management product. All the top products have apps available for Teams. You will find apps for Asana, Azure DevOps, Jira, Microsoft Project, Trello, and many others.

Most of these apps introduce notifications in the form of a bot. Using the bot app, you can interact with tasks in the relevant task management system. I find these apps really improve productivity because I don't have to jump out of Teams in order to mark a task as complete or create a new task. Figure 19-2 shows the Trello app (`https://trello.com`) being used in a channel in Teams.

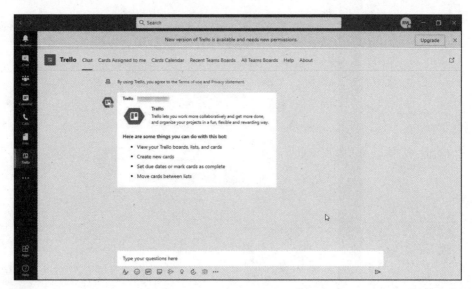

FIGURE 19-2:
The Trello app for Teams.

TIP

A new Microsoft product called Planner (`https://products.office.com/en-us/business/task-management-software`) seems to be making a big splash in the task management field. Think of Planner as a simpler version of Microsoft Project. The big difference with Planner is that it was born as a Microsoft 365 service, whereas Project started out as a downloadable client. If you are looking for a simple, yet powerful, task management system that you already have licensing for as part of Microsoft 365, then check out Microsoft Planner.

Design

Microsoft Teams embraces digital designers with several apps that integrate with the most popular digital design services. You will find apps for such popular collaborative design services such as Marvel App (`https://marvelapp.com`) and Freehand by InVision (`www.invisionapp.com/feature/freehand`).

One of my personal favorites is the Adobe Creative Cloud (CC) app for Teams (www.adobe.com/creativecloud.html). The app lets you access your Adobe Creative Cloud assets from within Microsoft Teams. It supports all the main file types, such as PSD, AI, INDD, and the new XD type from Adobe XD CC. Figure 19-3 shows using the Adobe Creative Cloud app in a Teams chat.

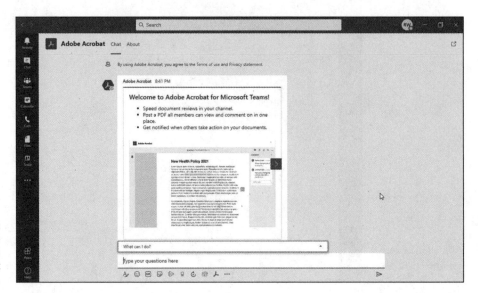

FIGURE 19-3:
The Adobe Creative Cloud app in a Microsoft Teams chat.

Customer Service

Keeping customers happy is critical for any organization, and Microsoft Teams has apps that integrate with many customer service products. A few of my favorites include Intercom, Zendesk, and zoom.ai.

Using these apps, you can add tickets from within a Teams channel, view existing tickets, and update tickets based on customer interactions. Figure 19-4 shows the Zendesk (https://www.zendesk.com/microsoft-teams) page that walks through setting up the Microsoft Teams app. The page is entitled "Microsoft: Setting up the Microsoft Teams — Zendesk Support Integration." You can find it using your favorite search engine.

The process of installing an app is generally easy and straightforward. You install the app and then authenticate it to work with the relevant service. If the app needs permissions in Teams, it will ask for them when you install it.

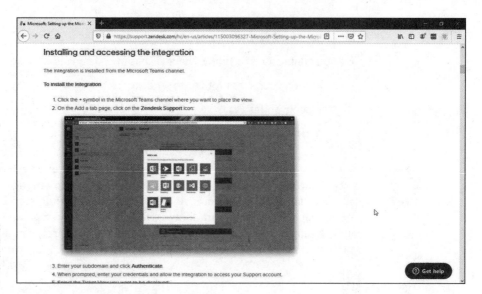

FIGURE 19-4:
The setup page
for the Zendesk
app for Teams
integration.

TIP

Most third-party software companies that have an app for Teams also have a web page explaining how to set up the app and use it in Teams. Many of these companies also have forums where people discuss the best ways to use the service in Teams.

Development

Software development has taken on an entirely new meaning in the modern era. Developing software solutions isn't just about writing code anymore. Being a developer means building something using tools, and often those tools can be integrated with apps in Teams. For example, the development platform GitHub (https://github.com) is used for developing content as well as websites. I am not a developer, but I find myself working extensively with GitHub these days. Other clients I work with use Azure DevOps (https://azure.microsoft.com) and yet others use PowerApps (https://powerapps.microsoft.com) to build mobile solutions.

Using the GitHub app in Teams you can:

>> View information about pull requests

>> Write comments in issues and pull requests

- » Create, read, update, close, and re-open Issues

- » Add notifications to Teams channels based on changes made in GitHub

- » Work with your subscriptions to repositories

- » View repositories available

- » Search through issues and pull requests and view results in channels

TIP

I use the search functionality of the Teams app store extensively. For example, when I search for the term *github,* I see the GitHub app among the results, but I also see other apps that reference the word *github.* GitHub is used extensively for code management, so if I am looking for development-type apps, I will explore the other apps that are pulled off the github keyword. You can do the same with other key words in your searches.

Education

Education is a unique industry that spans teaching tiny tots how to use silverware all the way to world-renowned researchers collaborating about the latest break-throughs in artificial intelligence. One critical aspect to ensure success in any level of study is communication. Parents need to communicate with teachers; students need to communicate with each other and with their teachers; and researchers need to collaborate and communicate with the broader community. Several Teams apps are designed specifically for education. EdCast, FlipGrid, and Haldor Ed are some services that I have used and recommend.

TIP

A common theme throughout the various education apps for Teams is that they provide a way to stay within Teams and still use the value these services and products provide. The Teams apps for these services provide multiple levels of integration with the idea that people in and around education should be able to use the service without leaving the central communications hub of Teams. For example, the FlipGrid app (https://info.flipgrid.com) lets educators ask questions in Teams using video and then students can respond. Students can also communicate with each other, which creates a network of student learning that is facilitated by Teams. Figure 19-5 shows the FlipGrid Help page that describes the Teams integration their app provides.

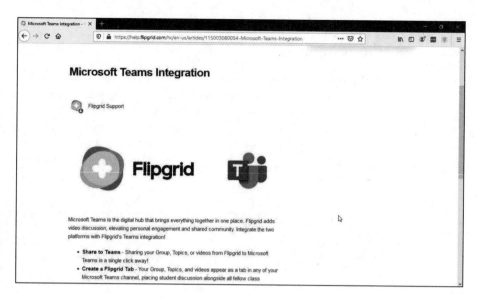

FIGURE 19-5:
The FlipGrid
Help page
explaining its
app integration
with Teams.

Social Media

Social media provides a mechanism for organizations to connect directly with its customers. Today, it is common for customers to use social media to interact with each other and discuss organizations and products.

You will find two types of social media apps for Teams. There are apps for the social media platforms themselves, such as Facebook, Twitter, and LinkedIn. And there are tools used to help organizations manage their presence on these platforms, such as Sociabble (www.sociabble.com/microsoft-office-365).

One app I find particularly useful is the Twitter app. Using this app, you can keep track of tweets and hashtags you are following and have them delivered directly into the Teams channel for the appropriate teams.

Survey

It is always a good idea to get a feel for what people are thinking. Several apps for Teams enable you to use and send surveys to people within and outside of your organization. One of my favorites is built right into Microsoft 365 and is known as Forms. Another popular survey service is called Survey Monkey. There are Teams apps available for both.

Marketing

Most organizations need to think about marketing, and there are many marketing-related services and products to choose from. Most of the top marketing products provide a Teams app for integration. A few of my favorites include Constant Contact, Google Analytics Insights, and MailChimp. Figure 19-6 shows adding the Google Analytics Insights app (https://marketingplatform.google.com) to a team. Once added, you can have Google send reports and metrics directly to your Teams channel.

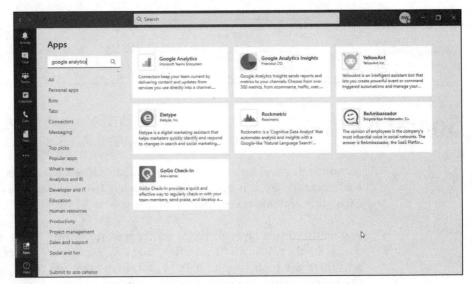

FIGURE 19-6:
The Google Analytics Insights app in Teams.

Miscellaneous

Two additional apps for Teams that I find incredibly useful are Power BI and Stream. Both are Microsoft services that integrate well with Teams. Microsoft Power BI (https://powerbi.microsoft.com) is a data analytics service (see Figure 19-7). Using Power BI, you can pull in data from just about any source you can imagine (databases, Excel spreadsheets, web services, and so on) and then build reports with the data using the Power BI tool. You can also set the data that Power BI pulls into the service to refresh on a set schedule. For example, you could set Power BI to run every hour and pull sales data from one database, marketing data from another database, and customer service data from some other web service. All of these separate sources of data could be combined into a single report that is refreshed hourly. Power BI is a powerful tool, and it integrates closely with SharePoint.

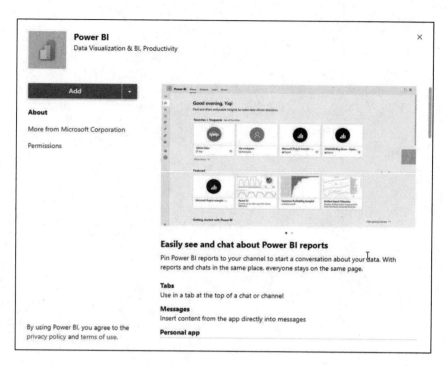

FIGURE 19-7:
The product page
for Microsoft
Power BI.

Microsoft Stream (`https://products.office.com`) is a video-streaming service that you can use to upload, share, and view videos. It is built into Teams and you can use it to embed videos. You will find it as an option when you add a tab to a channel, as shown in Figure 19-8.

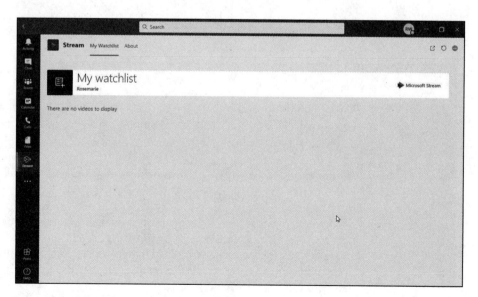

FIGURE 19-8:
Adding Stream
as a tab on a
channel in Teams.

Chapter **20**

Ten Ways to Learn More About Teams

I f there is anything the year 2020 taught us, it is that things change quickly and sometimes suddenly. Microsoft Teams continues to evolve and change on a seemingly hourly basis. The user interface changes, new features are added, existing features are tweaked, and the details change. In short, Microsoft is continually improving Teams to make it a better product and to make you more productive. This book serves as a good introduction to get you started. The concepts in this book won't change, but the specifics will.

In this final chapter, I list ten ways where you can get more information and continue your learning journey with Teams. I have found that the places I list here have the best content on how to maximize what Teams has to offer. The list contains both free and paid resources in online and in-person formats. Working with a modern cloud-based service like Teams is a constant learning journey, and I continue to learn new things every single day.

Get Information Directly from Microsoft

Microsoft Teams has grown faster than any other Microsoft product in history. This isn't an accident, and Microsoft has devoted a massive amount of resources to ensuring the product succeeds. Microsoft maintains a couple of websites that include documentation for Teams. These sites contain a treasure trove of learning resources and cover everything from end-user guidance to hard core administration procedures. Be sure to bookmark these sites so you can pull them up frequently.

» `https://docs.microsoft.com` is focused on how to do more administrative tasks, but also includes content for regular users and power users. You will find Teams in the Office section. Figure 20-1 shows the Teams landing page for administrators.

» `https://support.microsoft.com` is a relatively new site that replaces `support.office.com`. This change reflects the fact that Microsoft has integrated its products and services and Microsoft Office is no longer such a stand-alone product. Microsoft's internal mantra is that it is now "One Microsoft." This is opposed to the past culture at Microsoft where each product team was nearly its own company, and integration between products was hard to find. When you land on the `support.microsoft.com` page, you can scroll down and select Microsoft Teams to view the Help center. Here you will find online classes, training, and more tips about using Teams.

FIGURE 20-1:
The Welcome to Microsoft Teams page on Microsoft Docs.

Enroll in an Online Class

Learning through one of the online class platforms is a popular way to learn new things. Online classes offer how-to videos that walk you through a specific task or scenario. I have used the following platforms to learn about Teams, and I recommend them.

TIP

Check with your local library to find out if it has a subscription to an online learning platform. Many libraries make this available with the only caveat that you need to go into the library to log in to the platform.

» **Lynda.com/LinkedIn Learning:** The Lynda.com site has become one of my favorite sources for learning Microsoft technologies. Lynda.com (www.lynda.com) used to be its own training site until LinkedIn acquired it and it became LinkedIn Learning (www.linkedin.com/learning). Microsoft has since acquired LinkedIn, so it makes sense that the platform will continue to include great Microsoft training content. A quick search for Microsoft Teams training yields 162 courses, as shown in Figure 20-2.

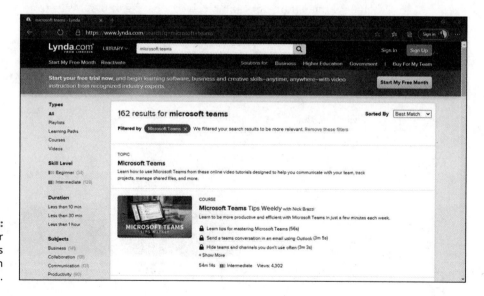

FIGURE 20-2:
Searching for Microsoft Teams courses on Lynda.com.

» **Udemy.com:** This site (www.udemy.com) provides another wealth of online learning courses. I did a search for Microsoft Teams and the site provided 7,809 results. With such a wealth of content I tend to filter the results based on ratings of the instructors. This is one of my favorite sources for all types of learning online, and it includes a vast amount of Microsoft Teams content.

>> **Edx.org:** This site provides university level courses online in all manner of subjects. When I searched for Microsoft Teams, I received 42 courses. Each of the courses is self-paced, and the interface is easy to use. I have enjoyed taking courses here.

Keep Up with Experts

Microsoft continues to nurture a program for experts. The program provides a designation for key community contributors and experts in various Microsoft technologies and products. The designation is known as a Most Valuable Professional (MVP), and it is considered a top honor. Most MVPs maintain blogs, and you can stay up to date with the latest features by reading their current posts.

TIP

Most MVPs maintain a blog where they cover the latest happenings in their areas of expertise.

You can search for MVPs at `https://mvp.microsoft.com`. I entered **Teams** into the search parameters and received a listing of 824 MVPs from all over the world, as shown in Figure 20-3.

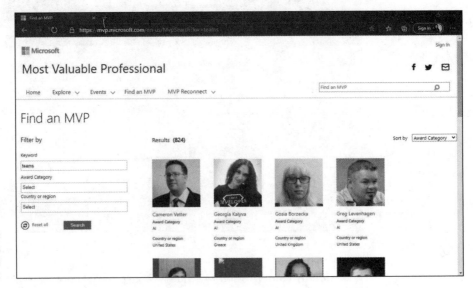

FIGURE 20-3: Viewing Teams MVPs from all over the world.

Attend User Groups and Meetups

Getting together with others around a common cause is a great way to dig deeper into any subject. Name just about any subject and you will likely find a group of people that gets together once a month to discuss the topic. And Microsoft Teams is no exception! You can use your favorite search engine to look for groups near you.

TIP

I recommend starting a group within your organization for others that are interested in getting the most out of Teams. It is a great way to have a big impact in your organization. You can learn and share with others how Teams can be used to improve productivity.

The Microsoft Teams Users Group defines themselves as "The definitive meetup for Microsoft Teams professionals." Their website is at `https://teamsug.com`, shown in Figure 20-4, and you can search the site for groups in your area. Another great place to find meetups of all sorts is Meetup (`www.meetup.com`). The site has a topic specifically for Microsoft Teams, and you can search the site to find meetups in your area.

FIGURE 20-4: The Microsoft Teams Users Group website.

Get Certified

Microsoft certifications have always carried significant weight. They are not easy to obtain and are considered a gold standard. Microsoft has a certification designed for Teams called Microsoft 365 Certified: Teamwork Administrator Associate. This certification covers several aspects of teamwork using Teams, SharePoint, and OneDrive. You can find information about this certification and others at `www.microsoft.com/learning`.

TIP

Earlier in this chapter I talked about the `docs.microsoft.com` site. You can find information about training and certification there as well. Use your favorite search engine and search for *Microsoft Teams Training.* The first listing that appears (that isn't an ad) should be the page dedicated to Teams training, as shown in Figure 20-5.

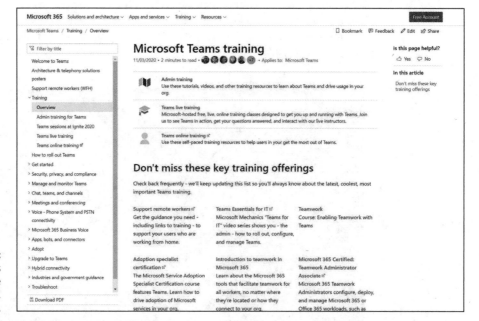

FIGURE 20-5:
Microsoft Teams training on the docs.microsoft.com site.

Subscribe to the Microsoft Teams Podcast

I love to wake up in the morning and listen to a podcast while I am getting ready for my day. To learn more about Microsoft Teams, you can add the Teams On Air podcast to your listening rotation. Teams On Air is a podcast dedicated to everything Microsoft Teams. It is created and presented by the Microsoft Teams product group, which releases a new episode every two weeks. The podcast features product updates, how-to tutorials, and the latest feature releases. Teams On Air is an audio podcast but also includes a visual component.

You can subscribe to the Teams On Air podcast in all the common places. The official site is located at `https://aka.ms/TeamsOnAirPodcast`, as shown in Figure 20-6. I listen on Apple Podcast, and I have also seen it on Player FM, YouTube, Libsyn Pro, and even Spotify.

FIGURE 20-6: The Teams On Air podcast site.

Attend the Microsoft Ignite Conference

I talked about local meetups and user groups earlier in this chapter, and conferences are similar. The difference is in the scale. Whereas a local meetup or user group might include 25 people, the Microsoft Ignite conference (`https://myignite.microsoft.com`) might include as many as 25,000 people.

TIP

Other conferences focus on Teams, but the biggest one is Ignite (see Figure 20-7). Ignite is the mother of all Microsoft conferences, and I would recommend attending if you can find the budget.

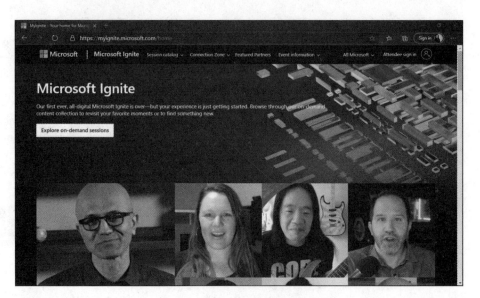

FIGURE 20-7:
The Microsoft
Ignite conference
home page.

Ignite takes place toward the end of the year. Lately it has been taking place in Orlando, Florida, but it has also taken place in Las Vegas, Nevada. Ignite covers all Microsoft products including Teams. You can find more information about Ignite using your favorite search engine.

Get Updates in Your Inbox

Microsoft maintains a blog for Teams, and you can subscribe to it so that any new posts appear in your inbox. To subscribe, use your favorite search engine and search for *Microsoft Teams Blog.* On the blog page you will find an RSS feed button, as shown in Figure 20-8. You can use this link to set up the RSS feed in your Outlook client.

You can find details on setting up an RSS feed in Microsoft Outlook in *Microsoft Outlook 2019 For Dummies* by Faithe Wempen and Bill Dyszel (Wiley), and a detailed procedure on the For Dummies website (www.dummies.com/software/ microsoft-office/outlook/how-to-set-up-an-rss-feed-in-microsoft- outlook-2019).

TIP

The Microsoft Teams group also maintains a Twitter account where you can get instant updates on Teams. The Teams Twitter handle is @microsoftteams.

RSS feed

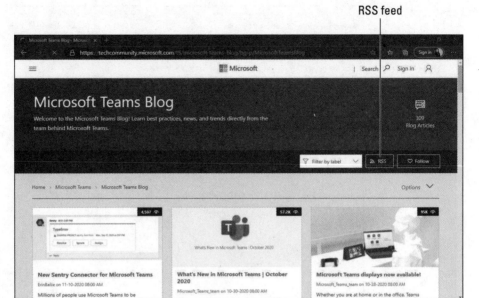

FIGURE 20-8:
Subscribing to the Microsoft Teams blog.

Discover the Microsoft Teams Roadmap

It used to be that Microsoft would release new features and software every three years like clockwork. That all changed with new services like Teams. Microsoft adds new features to Teams at a breakneck pace. It seems like every week I wake up to a new feature showing up in Teams. To keep up on the upcoming features, I follow the roadmap Microsoft has outlined for Teams. You can find the roadmap by searching for *Microsoft Teams Roadmap* in your favorite search engine. A snapshot of the roadmap is shown in Figure 20-9. You can see what features Microsoft is currently developing and when they are scheduled to ship.

TIP

If there is a feature you want added to Teams but you don't see it in the roadmap, you can add your voice to suggested features on the Teams User Voice. You will find this site at `https://microsoftteams.uservoice.com`. It is a site where the community can add new ideas for features and vote on existing ideas. Microsoft keeps a close eye on the site and implements the most popular feature requests.

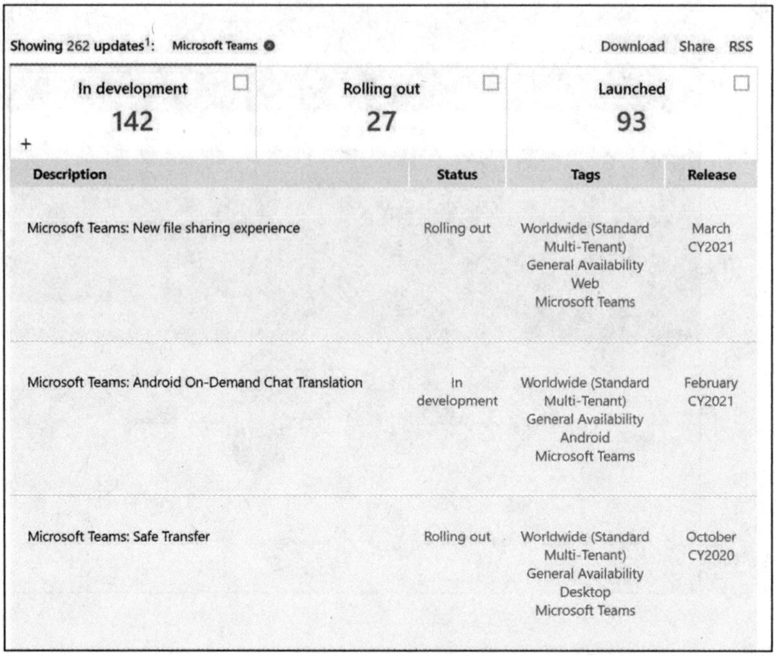

Showing 262 updates[1]:	Microsoft Teams ●		Download Share RSS

In development	Rolling out	Launched
142	27	93

Description	Status	Tags	Release
Microsoft Teams: New file sharing experience	Rolling out	Worldwide (Standard Multi-Tenant) General Availability Web Microsoft Teams	March CY2021
Microsoft Teams: Android On-Demand Chat Translation	In development	Worldwide (Standard Multi-Tenant) General Availability Android Microsoft Teams	February CY2021
Microsoft Teams: Safe Transfer	Rolling out	Worldwide (Standard Multi-Tenant) General Availability Desktop Microsoft Teams	October CY2020

FIGURE 20-9:
The Microsoft Teams roadmap.

Continue Learning with Rosemarie (Your Author)

Last — but hopefully not least! — I have embarked on a journey to share my hard-earned knowledge with others. I compiled an incredible stash of tips and tricks I've learned working with hundreds of clients over the years. Working with organizations around Microsoft 365, Office 365, SharePoint, and Teams, I have figured out what works and what doesn't.

You can find me on my Learning with Rosemarie page at `https://www.m365.tech`, as shown in Figure 20-10.

FIGURE 20-10:
My Learning with
Rosemarie site.

Index

apps *(continued)*
  from third-party companies, 78
  third-party company, 78
  Trello
    adding to default setup
      policy, 214
    description of, 79
    example of, 272
  Zendesk, 78, 274–275
Apps screen, 38
Apps tab, 72
Archive team option, 232
artificial intelligence (AI)
  software application, 82
Asana, 79
Audio Conferencing feature,
  137–138
audio devices, 178–180
auto attendants
  description of, 188
  numbers for, 188
  routing callers with, 190–191
Auto Attendants screen, 191
auto-start application, 42
Azure Active Directory
  business-to-business users.
  See external users
Azure DevOps app, 275

B

backgrounds, blurring, 261–262
Blocked Contacts option, 43
blog, learning about Microsoft
  Teams from, 288–289
blur toggle, 262
blurring backgrounds, 261–262
Bot Framework, 82
bots
  apps with, 273
  description of, 84
  differentiating humans
    from, 82
  for Trello, 73

Box app, 79
breakout rooms, 141–146
Bridge Settings, 210

C

Calendar area, 24
Calendar default app, 214
calendars, viewing to see
  scheduled meetings,
  viewing scheduled
  meetings, 130–131
call answering rules, for
  voicemail, 187
call history, 206
call queues, 187–190
Call Queues screen, 189
callers, routing with auto
  attendants, 190–191
Calling default app, 214
calling plans, 167–168, 174
Calling settings, 107–111
calls
  incoming
    adding delegates for,
      183–185
    audio devices for, 178–180
    call queues for, 188–190
    customizing, 181–182
    overview, 177
    phone number types for,
      187–188
    restricting with Do Not
      Disturb, 182–183
    routing with auto attendants,
      190–191
    setting up voicemail, 185–187
  phone
    adding phone numbers for,
      166–171
    dialing phone numbers from
      Teams app, 165–166
    making, 161–165
    private, 107
    receiving, 163–165

  on Teams, 44
  on Teams mobile app, 97–98
  testing, 180
  private, 107
  routing with auto attendants,
    190–191
  test, 178
  video, connecting to Chats,
    139–140
  voicemail answering rules
    for, 187
Calls area, 24–25
Calls dashboard, 163–165
cameras, 154–155
CC (Adobe Creative Cloud)
  app, 274
certifications, learning about
  Microsoft Teams by
  obtaining, 286
Channel mentions setting, 124
channels
  allowing guests to create or
    update, 113–114
  allowing guests to delete, 114
  breakout rooms for, 142
  connecting to people through
    adding moderators to, 57–58
    configuring, 54–57
    creating new, 51–54
    instant messaging, 48–49
    moving to Chats, 58–61
    overview, 47
    reacting to messages, 66
    sending messages through,
      49–51
    sending messages with no
      text, 62–65
  defined, 10, 38
  description of, 44, 48
  filtering by, 121–122
  hiding, 119–121
  installing connectors for,
    72–74
  meeting invites for, 143

E

EagleEye Director 2, 155
Edit sent messages setting, 107
Edit team option, 232
Edit this channel option, 57
education
  apps for, 276–277
  industry-specific needs on
      Teams for
    assessing student
        engagement with Insights,
        247–248
    creating teams from class
        lists, 246–247
    FlipGrid, 248–249
    overview, 246
electronic health record
    (EHR), 250
email
  adding users with, 110–111
  avoiding spam, 212
  integrating with Teams
      channels, 213
emojis, adding in Chats, 63–64
enterprises, large
  managing with Manage Teams
      screen
    admin roles for, 237–238
    archiving teams, 232–234
    creating retention policy,
        238–240
    deleting teams, 235
    getting expert help, 243
    importance of reports and
        analytics, 241–242
    network guidance for,
        235–237
    overview, 230–232
    upgrading from Skype for
        Business to Teams, 243
    voice features for, 240–241
  overview, 229
events
  invites, 99
  live events

Live events settings, 212
    organizers, 149
    policies, 211–212
    Teams Live Events
        feature, 136
  planning on Teams mobile
      app, 99–100
  private, 148
  producers, 149
  public, 148
Excel app, for Teams, 271
expert help, managing large
    enterprises with, 243
external users
  defined, 104
  description of, 10
  guest user access vs., 115
  interacting with, 114–116

F

FAQ (Frequently Asked
    Questions), 50
features
  Audio Conferencing, 137–138
  Get email address, 55
  Get link to channel, 55
  Logging for meeting
      diagnostics, 43
  New meeting experience, 43
  Teams Live Events, 136
  voice, managing large
      enterprises with, 240–241
  Whiteboard, 265–267
files
  adding in Chats, 64–65
  default app for, 214
  sharing on Teams mobile app,
      98–99
Files area, 26
Files default app, 214
Files tab, 68–69
firewall, defined, 237
firstline worker, industry-specific
    needs on Teams for,
    252–254

FlipGrid app, 248–249, 276
Flow app, 271. *See also* Power
    Automate
Freehand by InVision, 273
Frequently Asked Questions
    (FAQ), 50
Freshdesk, 78

G

GCC (Government Cloud
    Computing), 249
General section,
    42–43
General settings, viewing, 209
Get email address feature, 55
Get link to channel feature, 55
gifs, 63–64. *See also* Giphy
gigabit internet connections, 223
Giphy
  content rating, 108
  using in conversations, 108
GitHub app, 275, 276
Give Control button, 268
Global (Org-Wide Default)
    messaging policy, 217
Google Analytics Insights app,
    277, 278
Google Drive, 79
Google Workspace, 9
GoToMeeting, 211
government agencies, using
    Teams in, 249–250
Government Cloud Computing
    (GCC), 249
Graph app, 251
graphics processing unit
    (GPU), 42
grouping, 223–228
grunt work, 82
Guest settings, configuring, 106,
    113–114
guest users
  access
    external user access vs., 115
    overview, 103

About the Author

Rosemarie Withee is president of Portal Integrators (www.portalintegrators.com) and founder of Scrum Now in Seattle, Washington. Portal Integrators is a Scrum-based software and services firm. She is the lead author of *Office 365 For Dummies* and *Microsoft SharePoint For Dummies*.

Rosemarie earned a Master of Science degree in Economics at San Francisco State University and an Executive Master of Business Administration degree at Quantic School of Business and Technology. In addition, Rosemarie also studied Marketing at UC Berkeley-Extension and holds a Bachelor of Arts degree in Economics and a Bachelor of Science degree in Marketing from De La Salle University, Philippines.

Dedication

I would like to dedicate this book to my husband, Ken. Having to be in a bubble for the last year has not been easy, but we both managed because of his patience. I also dedicate this book to my families both in the Philippines and here in the United States, and to my nephews and niece, Lucas, Miguel, and Victoria, who never fail to provide so much joy especially during these uncertain times.

Author's Acknowledgments

I would like to acknowledge my husband Ken and our families in both the United States and Philippines. An extraordinary amount of special thanks to Kelsey Baird, Katharine Dvorak, Guy Hart-Davis, and the rest of the *For Dummies* team for providing more support than we ever thought possible. It is truly amazing how much work goes into creating a single book.

Publisher's Acknowledgments

Acquisitions Editor: Kelsey Baird

Managing Editor: Michelle Hacker

Project Editor: Katharine Dvorak

Technical Editor: Guy Hart-Davis

Production Editor: Mohammed Zafar Ali

Cover Image: © ronstik/Shutterstock